Exile in Erin

Other books by William Barnaby Faherty, S.J.

A Wall for San Sebastian

Henry Shaw: His Life and Legacies

Jesuit Roots and Pioneer Heroes in the Middle West

American Catholic Heritage

The Call of Pope Octavian: A Novel of the 21st Century

A Gift to Glory In: The First Hundred Years of the Missouri Botanical Garden

St. Louis: A Concise History

Gateway to the Moon: Building the Kennedy Space Center Launch Complex (with Charles Benson)

Moon Launch (with Charles Benson)

The St. Louis Irish: An Unmatched Celtic Community

Exile in Erin

A Confederate Chaplain's Story
The Life of Father John B. Bannon

by William Barnaby Faherty, S.J.

Missouri Historical Society Press • Saint Louis
distributed by University of Missouri Press

Published in the United States of America by the
Missouri Historical Society Press
P.O. Box 11940, St. Louis, Missouri 63112-0040

Library of Congress Cataloging-in-Publication Data

Faherty, William Barnaby, 1914–
    Exile in Erin : a Confederate chaplain's story : the life of Father John B. Bannon / by
William B. Faherty
        p. cm.
    Includes bibliographical references and index.
    ISBN 1-883982-46-4 (alk. paper) – ISBN 1-883982-47-2 (pbk. : alk. paper)

    1. Bannon, John B., 1829–1913. 2. Chaplains, Military — Confederate States of
America — Biography 3. Confederate States of America — Army Chaplains —
Biography 4. Confederate States of America. Army. Missouri Brigade, 1st. 5. United
States — History — Civil War, 1861-1865 — Chaplains. 6. United States — History —
Civil War, 1861-1865 — Religious aspects. 7. Catholic Church — United States —
Clergy — Biography. 8. Catholic Church — Ireland — Clergy — Biography. 9. Exiles
— Ireland — Biography. 10. Saint Louis (Mo.) — Biography. I. Title.

    E635.B36F34 2002
973.7'78'092—dc21
[B]   2002013184

Distributed by University of Missouri Press
Design by Nicholas J. Hoeing
Printed and bound in Canada by Friesens Printing

∞ the paper used in this publication meets minimum requirements of the ANSI/NISO
Z39.48-1992 (R 1997) (Permanence of Paper).

Cover photographs: stained glass windows, St. John the Apostle and Evangelist Church,
St. Louis. Photographs by Cary Horton and Melinda Muirhead © 2002. Missouri
Historical Society Photograph and Print Collection.

    02   03   04   05   06   5   4   3   2   1

To my nephew and grandnephews
Tony and Sean, Matthew, Joseph, and Gregory

Contents

Foreword

The American Civil War seems to hold an unending fascination for many of us. Devotees visit battle sites and monuments. Families treasure a sword, a medal, or perhaps a uniform from a Union or a Confederate ancestor. Civil War re-enactors explore and relive the intriguing minutiae of life in camp, in battle, and on the home front. Genealogists search extensively for their predecessors' involvement in this tragic period of the American past. Scholars publish an annual barrage of volumes on any and all aspects of this war between brethren, while playwrights, screenwriters, and novelists have added their interpretations of issues that divided not only our country but also close kin, lifelong friends, whole congregations, and especially St. Louis neighborhoods and city structure.

Letters, diaries, and journals of those who lived, in the North or in the South, through the war and its aftermath are ever-popular sources of research. Each story is different, but each story that has come down to us becomes a part of our own story. What has survived from these times is all we have left to construct the story of the past, and William Barnaby Faherty, S.J., is in this sense a master builder.

Father Faherty has told a wealth of stories in his long career as a priest, teacher, and writer, in novels, in studies with a Catholic subject, in St. Louis histories and books on such diverse topics as the Apollo space program and dissenting priests in America, and in conversations that display the true art of the Irish (and American Irish). Now it is the life of another Irishman that has captured Father Faherty's attention, the story of a priest from the Emerald Isle who sought his lifework in St. Louis in the decade before the Civil War. The Civil War vastly changed the life and the work of Father John B. Bannon, as that war changed so many and so much.

The Civil War is not my area of expertise, but its issues and circumstances are part of my family story. My father's family moved from New England to Kansas as part of the movement to keep Kansas a free state. Staunch abolitionists, they were associated with John Brown at some point. So, I have a personal Civil War heritage and historically should not be in sympathy with this Confederate chaplain born across the sea. Yet I now share some space on this planet where Father Bannon formed his own opinions and resolves, and as I pass within view of the spire of St. John the Apostle and Evangelist Church near City Hall, I know that part of his story is incontrovertibly part of mine.

St. Louis was not ravaged by the war, at least not with the same kind of devastation as, say, Atlanta or Vicksburg. But we in this divided city in a slave-holding, pro-Union state had our own wastes and ruins to rebuild in the decades after the near-rupture of the Union. How strong, how effective, even how complete our rebuilding was, is still under scrutiny, as is all of the past we can know. Father Faherty's biography of his fellow Jesuit of long ago is a tale well told and worth the telling, but *Exile in Erin* can also prompt us to ask ourselves the questions that we as humans in history always need to ask: What have we done well, and what should we have done differently? What can we take from this story, this era, to plan a better, more stable future for those who come after us?

—ROBERT R. ARCHIBALD, PH.D.
PRESIDENT, MISSOURI HISTORICAL SOCIETY

Preface

When I first saw the Stars and Bars of the Confederate flag in an art-glass window at St. John the Apostle and Evangelist Church in St. Louis, I became intrigued with the life of the pastor Father John B. Bannon, chaplain of a unit of the state militia, who built the Romanesque edifice in 1858 but gave it up in late 1861 to serve the spiritual needs of the militiamen who had, in the meantime, gone South to join the First Missouri Confederate Infantry.

After several years of dedicated service at the Battles of Pea Ridge, Corinth, and Vicksburg, Father Bannon accepted the commission from Confederate president Jefferson Davis to go to his native Ireland and explain the cause of the Confederacy. This he did so well that vindictive anti-Lincoln "Radical Republican" lawmakers in Missouri prevented his return to his chosen city and state.

Instead, after the war he remained in his native land, joined the Jesuit order, and won acclaim as Ireland's greatest pulpit orator of the 1880s. The only other prominent Confederate who remained in exile was Secretary of State Judah Benjamin, who won success in the practice of law in London.

At the time, forty years ago, that I discovered the Confederate flag and the matching Stars and Stripes in the windows at St. John's Church, an elderly lady of the parish, Daisy Le Grave, asked me to rate her book-length manuscript on the life of the famous chaplain. This I gladly did. While not a trained historian, Miss Le Grave had gathered much data on the activities of Father Bannon and on local attitudes during the period of the Civil War. She wrote well but unfortunately surpassed Scarlett O'Hara in her disdain for all things Yankee. The manuscript lacked balance. Perhaps for that reason, she had never found a publisher. I wanted to learn more about Father Bannon.

I looked into the material already published about him in the history of the Archdiocese of St. Louis and in journals of Catholic history that told of his diplomatic service for the Confederacy. The more I read, the more I stood in awe of this unusual man who gave up a flourishing metropolitan parish to serve his men in the field. I later found that he was the only chaplain in either army to do so. By this decision, he also departed from the path of his advancement in the Catholic Church. Several of his successors at St. John's became bishops.

Further, he was cutting himself off from his Missouri base. By the time he went South, Missouri had voted to stay in the Union. The governor and the rump legislature had withdrawn from Jefferson City and lacked resources to win back the state. Federal forces had cut off from the Confederacy the strong, Southern-oriented section, the "Little Dixie" area of central Missouri. In the end, economic realities tied Missouri to the Union.

During my years as a professor of history at Saint Louis University, an opportunity came to learn more about the versatile Father Bannon. Philip Tucker, a graduate student with a great interest in the Civil War in Missouri, was researching the story of the First Missouri Confederate Brigade. Father Bannon was "unofficial chaplain" of that unit. I asked Tucker to provide me with copies of any material on the chaplain. He gave me a surprising amount of data, including Father Bannon's wartime diary, preserved, remarkably, not in Missouri but at the Caroliniana Library in Columbia, South Carolina.

Tucker and I had talked of co-authoring a book on the total career of the great chaplain, but those hopes withered over the years. On finishing his doctorate, Tucker took a position with the Air Force History Team, and I accepted contracts to work on other books. As a result, we lacked an opportunity to carry out our original plan. He decided to write chiefly on Father Bannon's war years. In 1992, his book, *The Confederacy's Fighting Chaplain*, published by the University of Alabama Press, won the Douglas Southall Freeman Award.

I saw the need to tell the story of Father Bannon's fourth career as a pulpit orator in Ireland. A grant from the Galway–St. Louis Sister Cities Committee provided time for research in Ireland. There, I had the help of Father Kevin Laheen, who followed in Father Bannon's footsteps as a home missionary. Father Laheen had edited the diary of Father Robert Haly, the head of the mission band when Father Bannon had joined it. Father Laheen highlighted Bannon's activities as the veteran missionary had recorded them.

Father Laheen took me to the prep school at Castleknock, where young John Bannon had received his early formal education, and to the seminary of Maynooth, where he had studied theology and was ordained to the priesthood. Next, we visited every parish in Ireland where Father Bannon had preached.

In 1994, Father Laheen and I co-authored a small book on Father Bannon's fourth career that received fine reviews. Since then I uncovered more material about Father Bannon's family, his time in St. Louis, and his late years in Dublin. A complete biography of Father Bannon required comparative studies of experiences and pastoral techniques with those of other chaplains, Union and Confederate. I perused the few books available on chaplains in general. Books on two other Confederate chaplains had appeared over the years. I also researched the careers of chaplains at the archives of religious orders such as the Holy Cross Fathers at the library of the University of Notre Dame and the Jesuits at the Midwest Jesuit Archives in St. Louis. In-house publications of these religious orders carried letters and autobiographical sketches of members who served as chaplains. At the same time, histories of religious sisterhoods in the South threw light on the experiences of nun-nurses who had worked with Father Bannon during the conflicts at Corinth and Vicksburg. Father Bannon deserved a full-length study.

What confirmed this judgment was an undated clipping from the *Missouri Republican*, presumably from the early 1880s, that I found at the Missouri Historical Society. The feature article named the fifty most influential St. Louisans. The two Catholic bishops made the list, as did one pastor. Father Bannon was that man, still important in the eyes of the writer, even though he had left the city twenty years before.

Acknowledgements

Professor Emmet Larkin's studies of the Irish in the nineteenth-century Catholic Church and Father Todd Morrissey's biographies of its great Irish clergymen of the period added authoritative contributions to an understanding of Father Bannon's Irish years. Nancy Merz, Associate Archivist of the Midwest Jesuit Archives, and John Waide, Archivist of Saint Louis University, offered valuable advice. Mary Struckel expertly typed the numerous drafts of this manuscript. John P. and Ann Flanigan and Edward C. Cody and his associates in the Galway–St. Louis Sister-Cities Committee were supportive throughout the time of research and writing.

Exile in Erin

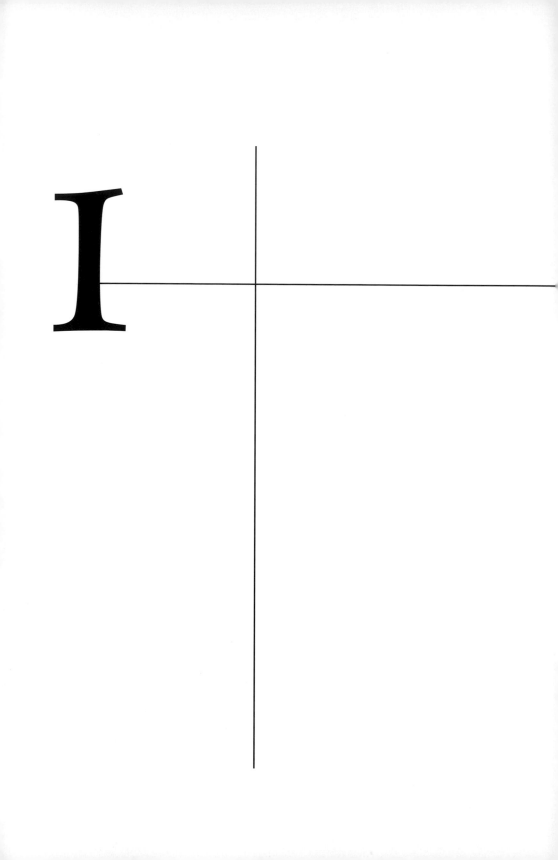

I

Early Years

John B. Bannon was the son of James Bannon, a grain dealer in Rooskey, Ireland, a town on the Shannon River in Roscommon County, and Fanny O'Farrell, the daughter of Michael O'Farrell of Lansbrough, in County Longford. O'Farrell owned extensive properties in his own county and neighboring Roscommon. Five months before John's birth on December 29, 1829, Michael O'Farrell had assisted his son-in-law in developing a partnership with James Corcoran, a corn broker on James Street in Dublin.[1] The James Street address eventually became the Bannon residence.

The year of John's birth brought new hope to Ireland. Over the centuries, British laws had excluded Catholics from teaching school, practicing law, manufacturing products, acquiring free-hold lands, and participating in government on any level, from town councils to Parliament. Laws deprived Irish Catholics of land and reduced them to dependence. By the mid-eighteenth century only 5 percent of Ireland's acreage remained in Catholic hands.

On April 13, 1829, Parliament passed the Catholic Emancipation Act, which allowed Daniel O'Connell to take his seat in that renowned assembly. It removed many restrictions on Catholics but still required them to support the Anglican "Church of Ireland." Two hundred and eighty Anglican parishes had no pew holders. The road to justice proved to be as long as the way to Tipperary, but Irish Catholics were moving on that road. This was the situation in Ireland during John Bannon's early years.

When he reached prep-school age, Bannon's parents considered St. Vincent's College in Castleknock, just beyond the three-mile pleasant drive through Phoenix Park at the west end of Dublin. This first-rate school stemmed from the zeal of four recently ordained priests of the Diocese of Dublin. They had banded together in 1833 under leadership of Peter Richard Kenrick. But a short time later Kenrick felt a call to assist his brother Francis Patrick Kenrick, bishop of Philadelphia, and left for America. The other young men then sought the instruction of the dean of Maynooth Seminary, Father Phillip Dowley. He joined them to open a school in the heart of Dublin and guided their efforts according to the spirit of the French saint Vincent de Paul.

Two years later they moved to Castleknock. The school prospered and became the fountainhead of the Vincentian Irish Province. The lovely white buildings standing amid rolling hills were less than ten years old when young Bannon arrived in 1845. The ruined castle crowning an adjoining hill had looked down on invading Danes a thousand years before. Eight priests taught the ninety boys in the school.

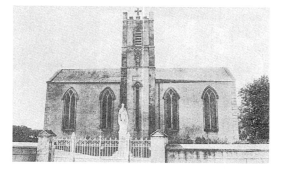

Right: Rooskey Church as it looked originally.
Below: The church at Rooskey on the Shannon in west central Ireland, where John B. Bannon was baptized in 1829.

Young Bannon and his first-year classmates learned fractions, English composition, geography, history, arithmetic, and bookkeeping. In the second year, they studied the geography of Africa and America, rhetoric, the history of Rome, and Latin and Greek. It was a traditional European plan concentrating on the humanities. Young Bannon gained distinctions in all of his classes.

From 1846 to 1850, the years of the Great Famine that wiped out a million people and sent another million to America, young Bannon attended the preparatory department of the Royal Seminary at Maynooth near Dublin. He studied rhetoric, logic, algebra, plane and solid geometry, trigonometry, metaphysics, and natural philosophy. He failed to garner as many distinctions as he had at Castleknock. After finishing his course at the minor seminary, he began his three-year theology course in 1850.

The seminary at Maynooth had an intriguing history. From the rise of Protestantism in the sixteenth century until the French Revolution of 1789, young Irishmen who wanted to be priests had to leave their homeland and study in either France or Spain. When the French Revolution broke out, aristocratic England did not want young Irishmen studying to be priests in a country that welcomed ideas of "liberty, equality, and fraternity." So England, the oppressor,

Above: The bridge over the River Shannon at Rooskey.

became the sponsor of priestly education. An act of Parliament set up the Royal College of Maynooth in 1795. It originally included a lay academy during the early years of the century, but by the time of John Bannon's arrival it welcomed only clerical students.

The routines at Maynooth in the early 1850s matched those of seminaries throughout the world: early rising, meditation, Mass, a light breakfast, and classes in moral and dogmatic theology taught in Latin. Silence prevailed during much of the day. During these years John Bannon felt a call to work in the New World. He heard the plea of Archbishop Peter Richard Kenrick for assistance in his distant midwestern American archdiocese of St. Louis. This was the same Kenrick who, slightly more than twenty years before, had been the original leader of the founders of Castleknock College but had gone off to help his brother in Philadelphia. No doubt Bannon's teachers at Castleknock had spoken often of their erstwhile colleague.

Back in 1844, the St. Louis prelate had written to the president of the Leopoldine Society of Vienna, "No city in the United States enjoys greater opportunities for the practice of the Catholic religion, so there is none that expresses Catholic life and character better than St. Louis."[2] The combination of faces and factors that brought this about will surface in the next chapter.

When Bannon finished his theology course in the spring of 1853, Archbishop Paul Cullen of Dublin ordained him. Shortly thereafter, the new priest told the archbishop that he hoped to work in the United States, and particularly in St. Louis, where more than ten thousand Irish immigrants dwelled in a more friendly atmosphere than anywhere else in America. In August, Archbishop Cullen granted this request. He attested to Bannon's good character and recommended him to all Catholic bishops, especially the archbishop of St. Louis. [3]

St. Louis: Church and Community

Father Bannon left no record in diary or letter of his first impression of St. Louis, as his steamboat moved under the bluffs north of Carondelet and he saw the bustling waterfront and the impressive stone cathedral that dominated the area. The Catholic Church in St. Louis stood on a plateau of prominence unmatched throughout the country. The only archdiocese in the Midwest, it set the tone for Catholicism in the Mississippi Valley. St. Louis priests and laymen began the first university west of the great river. Ten religious institutes of men and women brought the Christian message to the people of the St. Louis Archdiocese, more than in New York or Boston. Archbishop Peter Richard Kenrick, a towering personality, had few theological peers anywhere in the world. Catholic business and professional men had long held prominent places in the city; French Catholics had founded St. Louis.

St. Louis dominated religious activities in mid-America. St. Paul, Minnesota, was an infant city, Chicago eleven years old. Dubuque, Iowa, a solid but small Catholic center, gave little promise of growth. Priests from St. Louis had already become bishops of eight cities, among them old Detroit and young Chicago. During the lifetime of Kenrick, ten other priests from St. Louis would lead dioceses from Philadelphia to Los Angeles.

The entire archdiocese, by then coterminous with the state of Missouri, numbered 145 churches and 125 mission stations, with sixty-nine clergymen on mission and twenty-nine otherwise employed in schools and hospitals. It developed a theological seminary in Carondelet. Vincentian Fathers ran a preparatory seminary in Perryville, Missouri, and a college at Cape Girardeau, staffed parishes and missions in southeast Missouri and at St. Vincent's Parish in St. Louis, and sent missionaries to Texas. Eighteen Jesuits taught at Saint Louis University. Other Jesuit priests and brothers conducted their own seminary at Florissant,

Missouri, and served at five parishes, two in St. Louis and three in outlying areas. From St. Louis, Jesuit missionaries, such as Peter Jan De Smet, Christian Hoecken, and John Schoenmakers, went west to teach Christianity to the Osage, Potawatomi, and Salish.

The French, Irish, Anglo-American, and German Catholics had built thirteen churches in the city. Newcomers from Bohemia organized St. John Nepomuk's parish, the first Bohemian church in the New World. In welcoming immigrants from the continent of Europe and seeking for them pastors who knew their native languages, Archbishop Kenrick gained a reputation as the "Father of the Immigrant."

Leading citizens of all denominations sent their daughters to the Catholic academies—the Convent of the Sacred Heart or the Visitation Academy, which had moved to St. Louis from Kaskaskia, Illinois, in 1844. Sisters of St. Joseph came from France to teach hearing-impaired girls and opened an academy in Carondelet. Sisters of Charity staffed the City Hospital, an orphanage, and a parish school. Ursuline Sisters from Germany and Austria planned to start an academy. Sisters of the Good Shepherd began their ministry among disturbed young women. Mercy Sisters were to reach St. Louis a year later.

Five parishes conducted schools for boys. Two units opened at St. Francis Xavier Parish: one for the 250 who spoke English and one for the 130 who spoke only German. The Brothers of the Christian Schools opened a college on the near-south side the year of Father Bannon's arrival.

Convert Robert Bakewell edited a Catholic paper, the *Shepherd of the Valley*, and took part in the religious controversies of the time. Prominent lay Catholics, led by Dr. Moses Linton and Judge Bryan Mullanphy, started the first American unit of a new charitable organization, the St. Vincent de Paul Society, founded a short time before in France.

St. Louis faced a short-lived surge of anti-immigrant bigotry stirred by nativists who called themselves "Know-Nothings." They vandalized homes and stores of Irish merchants during election time in 1852 and would do so again in 1854. The agitation split the Protestant and Catholic Irish, who had previously worked together in the interests of their fellow Irish in America and Ireland, and brought about the separation of the St. Louis College of Medicine from Saint Louis University. These disturbances, however, affected only slightly the wider St. Louis community. The Catholic archdiocese continued to thrive. On arrival in 1853, Father Bannon found that he had agreed to work in a flourishing religious and economic center.

Situated on a terrace above the west bank of the Mississippi, St. Louis controlled the trade of the midcontinent. The Mississippi River provided access from Minnesota Territory to New Orleans. The Ohio River, which flowed into the

Mississippi slightly more than two hundred miles to the south, gave the city access to the East. The Missouri River, which joined the Mississippi twelve miles north of St. Louis, allowed the venturesome to reach the High Plains and the Rocky Mountains beyond.

Local merchants supplied the townsfolk, the farmers on the rich acres of the Mississippi Valley, the fur traders in the Rockies, the army on its frontier posts, and travelers going west. These last included homesteaders heading for Oregon, goldrushers going to California, Mormons on the way to Utah, and Native Americans looking for a permanent home in Indian Territory. Trade through Santa Fe brought gold and silver from the mines of Mexico in return for the goods that St. Louis merchants could provide.

Earlier, the city had spread north and south along the river, with slight movement west. By 1855, houses were going up increasingly west of Eighteenth Street, the former city limits. St. John the Apostle and Evangelist Parish, where Father Bannon would serve a few years later, would see tremendous growth. It was the first parish west of Eleventh Street.

French pioneers, mostly from French Canadian villages in Illinois, had founded St. Louis. After the Louisiana Purchase, few French came. Individual Anglo-Americans, chiefly from the Middle Atlantic states, settled in St. Louis. Many Irishmen came, among them John Mullanphy, John O'Fallon, and others who prospered in business and contributed generously to schools and hospitals. A few German Catholics and Evangelicals arrived in the early days of Missouri's statehood. In 1838, a group of Saxon Lutherans opened a church and school in the Soulard district on the near-south side.

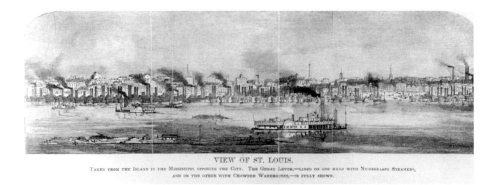

VIEW OF ST. LOUIS,

TAKEN FROM THE ISLAND IN THE MISSISSIPPI OPPOSITE THE CITY. THE GREAT LEVEE,—LINED ON ONE HAND WITH NUMBERLESS STEAMERS, AND ON THE OTHER WITH CROWDED WAREHOUSES,—IS FULLY SHOWN.

Above: The St. Louis waterfront at Father Bannon's arrival.

Above: Young Father Bannon in 1861.

In the late 1840s and early 1850s, Irish and Germans came in great numbers so that, by the time of Father Bannon's arrival, immigrants outnumbered the native born. The Irish had fled the famine. The politically liberal Germans escaped the tyranny of Prussia after the failure of the Revolution of 1848. They were strong Unionists and opposed slave labor.

During the years 1830–50, St. Louis had grown from a small river town into an important city. With 5,852 inhabitants in 1830, the population had jumped to 16,469 in 1840 and 77,860 ten years later. The 1850 census ranked St. Louis eighth among the important cities of the nation, second only to Cincinnati in the Midwest. Except for New Orleans, all other cities were on the Atlantic Coast. Like so many frontier places, St. Louis numbered 11,000 more men than women. One third of the city's 4,054 African Americans were free. During the 1850s, the city would double its population to reach 160,773 in 1860.

3

First Years in St. Louis

John Bannon left no written record of his impressions of his ocean voyage to America or of his steamboat trip up the Mississippi, the usual route to St. Louis in those pre–Civil War years. The Ohio and Mississippi Railroad (later the Baltimore and Ohio) did not reach East St. Louis until 1857. He served as the assistant pastor at the cathedral on Walnut Street near the waterfront for a few months. In the fall of 1855, the archbishop named him assistant pastor of the Immaculate Conception Church at Eighth and Chestnut Streets. The pastor, Father James Duggan, held the post of vicar general of the archdiocese. Two years later, on January 9, 1857, when Pope Pius IX named Father Duggan auxiliary bishop of St. Louis, Father Bannon became pastor.

On September 5, 1858, Archbishop Kenrick called the Second Provincial Council of St. Louis and appointed Father Bannon secretary of the meeting. The council centered on technical aspects of church law. Interestingly, it said nothing on the issue convulsing the country at the time, the question of slavery. Archbishop Kenrick believed in absolute separation of church and state. Most American people looked on slavery primarily as a political issue.

This meeting gave Father Bannon an opportunity to meet the bishops of the Midwest. Only one, the Dominican, Bishop Richard P. Miles of Nashville, Tennessee, had been born in America. A native of Maryland, he had studied under the Dominicans in Kentucky, joined the order as a young man, served as prior in Kentucky, and became Dominican provincial superior before accepting his call to the episcopate. John Baptist Lamy, a Frenchman, came over the Santa Fe Trail from the distant territory of New Mexico, a part of the Union for only ten years at the time. A colorful figure, he would gain wide fame as the prototype of author Willa Cather's hero in her novel *Death Comes for the Archbishop*. Bishop John Martin Henni of Milwaukee first saw light of day in the forest canton of Chur in Switzerland. Jesuit John Baptist Miege, a native of Savoy, then a province of Italy, guided the Kansas Territory as vicar apostolic. Father Henry D. Juncker had come from Lorraine, a province in the eastern section of France, to do pastoral and missionary work in Ohio before becoming bishop of Alton, Illinois. Timothy Smith, a native of County Clare in Ireland, joined the Trappists at age twenty-eight in October 1838, founded New Mellary Abbey in Iowa, and then, early in February of the year of the provincial council (1858), became bishop of Dubuque.

In meeting these churchmen from varied backgrounds, different countries, and unique dioceses, young Father Bannon gained a vivid view of the diversity of the United States. He saw, too, the problems facing the Catholic Church in caring for the colonial Maryland Catholics, the French of the Mississippi Valley, the old families of New Mexico who had lived along the Rio Grande for seven generations, the Native Americans of various tribes who had lived here for countless generations, and the newly arriving immigrants from fifteen countries in Europe.

Father Bannon took part in interparochial activities. He joined the St. Louis Catholic Literary Institute at Saint Louis University five blocks north and five blocks east of St. John's. He became chaplain of a militia company, the Washington Blues, under the leadership of Captain Joseph Kelly, and the unofficial chaplain of the Emmet and Montgomery Guards, Irish companies in the Missouri Volunteer Militia Brigade. General Daniel Morgan Frost, a native of New York State and a member of St. Francis Xavier Parish, who had served in the Mexican War, headed the brigade. The Washington Blues met on the last Sunday of each month. Many of its members also belonged to the Temperance Society, of which Father Bannon served as spiritual director.

Another Irish-born priest, Father Patrick O'Brien, had organized a new congregation ten years before and built a small church in the west end of St. Louis called St. John the Apostle and Evangelist. In 1857, Father O'Brien took a leave of absence for a holiday trip to Ireland. When he returned in May 1858, the archbishop named O'Brien pastor of St. Michael's Parish on the north side.

In November of that year (1858), Archbishop Kenrick appointed Father Bannon pastor of St. John's Parish and commissioned him to erect a church large enough for pontifical functions and a rectory suitable for a residence for auxiliary bishop James Duggan. Since at the time warehouses had begun to clutter up the area of the cathedral on Walnut Street, Archbishop Kenrick may well have looked forward to moving to the tree-filled neighborhood of St. John's—as he would do shortly after the Civil War.

Archbishop Kenrick failed to specify the boundaries of the parish at the time he commissioned it. A few years later he would define them clearly. From

Gratiot Street on the south of the Mill Creek Valley, the boundary stretched along Eleventh Street to Franklin Avenue; west, with a dogleg, to Twenty-first Street; and then back to Gratiot. This area boasted the finest residences in the newer part of the city, and included the Lucases, the Hunts, the Von Puhls, the Prattes, the Nidelets, and other established families. By 1860, two new parishes had opened beyond to the west—St. Malachy's at Ewing and Clark Streets, ten blocks west and four blocks south of St. John's, and St. Bridget's, ten blocks north and eight blocks west at Jefferson and Carr.

Father Bannon left a diary or journal of activities twice during his life. One of these was during the construction of his church. He had had debts at his earlier parish, and now he was obligated to contract still other responsibilities. Only one of the parishioners, lawyer Alexander J. P. Garesche, son of a prominent St. Louis family of West Indian background, offered enthusiastic assistance. Garesche's brother, Frederick, incidentally, was a Jesuit with strong Southern leanings, and another brother, Julius, was a colonel in the United States Army.

Bannon recognized the difficulties of his position: first, to take the place of a popular priest, Father Patrick O'Brien; and second, to ask for money for a larger church. But he courageously set his mind and hand to the task. Like many other immigrant pastors from Ireland, he had seen the ruins of countless churches and monastic chapels in his native land. During several centuries the invading Danes,

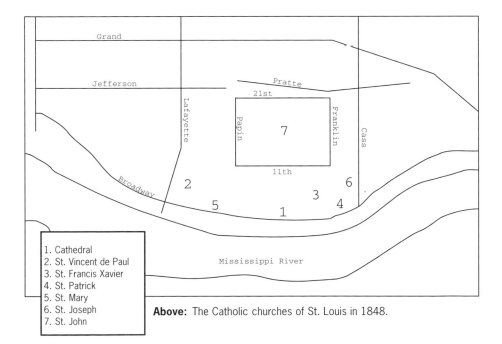

1. Cathedral
2. St. Vincent de Paul
3. St. Francis Xavier
4. St. Patrick
5. St. Mary
6. St. Joseph
7. St. John

Above: The Catholic churches of St. Louis in 1848.

Normans, and Anglo-Saxons had taken over the best churches and destroyed the other churches and monasteries. In the "land of the free" his parishioners, mostly moderately well-off people of French and Irish background, had the resources to build a worthy temple for the worship of God. Initially, Father Bannon dreamed too expansively. Perhaps he had forgotten that a panic had hit the country the year before. Nonetheless he went ahead.

On Sunday afternoon, November 14, 1858, Father Bannon called a meeting of the parishioners. Chauvin V. Lebeau chaired the assembly. Alexander J. P. Garesche served as secretary. The men thanked Archbishop Kenrick for choosing their parish as the residence of Bishop James Duggan, his coadjutor, and for sending them Father John B. Bannon as their pastor. Father Bannon relayed the archbishop's wish that they build a new church and a rectory of appropriate size as the residence of a bishop. The men chose a planning committee made up of Thomas Ryan, Thomas Slevin, and Patrick Gregory.[1] The pastor asked the assembled men to pledge what they could. The amount reached $4,070 on that day. Two weeks later the pledges rose to $5,287.[2]

Architect Patrick Walsh presented to the archbishop a blueprint for an impressive brick building of Italian Romanesque style and won the prelate's approval. On February 2, 1859, after the celebration of a Solemn Mass for the feast of Candlemas, the McMurray Company began digging the foundations for

Left: Father Bannon was a pastor during the building of St. John the Apostle and Evangelist Church at Sixteenth and Chestnut.

the new church. Timothy Cavanagh signed a contract for the masonry, James George for the brickwork, and T. Dowd and Company for the iron casting. Irish immigrants obviously had moved into the building trades.

Father Bannon scheduled the laying of the cornerstone for 5 P.M. on the first Sunday in May. He decided to place in the stone coins from the year 1859 and the May 1, 1859, issue of *The Western Banner*, the local Catholic paper. The Jesuit orator Cornelius Smarius gave the oration. Prominent priests of the region, such as Fathers Patrick Feehan, John O'Reilly, C.M., Francis Ziegler, and Michael Tobin, gave support by their presence, along with Archbishop Peter Richard Kenrick. Workers erected a platform against the old church and covered it with carpets and tapestries. These temporary stands could seat two thousand ticket holders. Outside, the members of the Catholic Total Abstinence and Benevolent Society were to keep order and collect fees for the seats. Unfortunately at 4:30 a sudden drenching rain caused confusion, prevented the use of the rich vestments, detracted from the solemnity of the ceremony, and reduced the hoped-for collection to a trifle.

Other problems arose shortly afterward. A workman, John Edward Garland, fell from a scaffold and died some days later at the Sisters' Hospital. Then the walls began to bulge. The archbishop felt that architect Walsh might profit by consultation and sought Jay Johnson, a prominent architect, as consultant. Walsh had spoken highly of Johnson, as if they were personal friends, but resigned when he found that Johnson had been asked to look over his work. The archbishop then suggested Robert Mitchell,★ who had designed the beautiful rock building at St. Stanislaus Seminary in Florissant ten years before and had previously worked on the Old Courthouse.

★

Mitchell died at sea when a storm wrecked the ship that was bringing him back from further architecture studies in Europe a few years later.

In his diary Father Bannon wrote:

> Mr. Mitchell suggested that we either construct abutments on the outside or bind the roof and side wall by a tie-beam crossing from the level of the walls. Neither of these suggestions was practical in my consideration. A tie-beam would have flattened the ceiling of the church and spoiled the design, besides involving the loss of the ceiling joists, which, having been cut circular, could not have been available for a flat ceiling. The construction of the buttresses was equally objectionable as being built within a few feet of property limit. We would have to apply to the City Council for permission to appropriate the sidewalk.[3]

Father Bannon suggested that Mitchell rest the base of the circular roof on pillars secured to the walls. The new architect approved, and work resumed.

Building a church is not the only task of a pastor nor is it the total concern of the parishioners. A church is a boon to the goals of both: worshiping God and leading a Christian life. From the beginnings of the parish several men chose to serve God in the newly formed St. Vincent de Paul Society, a benevolent society founded in France several years before by a layman, Frederick Ozanam. The members helped the poor by personal effort and involvement, not by remote philanthropy.

Father John Timon, the provincial superior of Congregation of the Mission, brought the notion of the society to St. Louis in 1845. A group of laymen, including the two architects of St. John's Church, organized the first unit of the society in America. During the first thirteen years of its existence, the cathedral unit served all parishes. Then in 1858, a second parish unit started, and in the spring of 1859 four other parishes followed.

In November 1859, the men of St. John's voted to form a unit. They chose as president Patrick Gregory, head of the firm that had contracted to plaster the church. Father Bannon was the spiritual director. The members were soon helping the poor, especially near the river on the near-north side, where many destitute refugees of the famine had "squatted." The St. John's segment soon became the second largest unit of the society, next to that of the cathedral parish. All the while Father Bannon had to perform his routine parish duties: baptisms, confessions, sick calls, sermons, special devotions, and parish Masses. He witnessed the marriage of Daniel A. Taylor and Emile de Bau on January 23, 1860. Distinguished citizens attended the wedding, among them Sylvester Chouteau and Théophile and Sylvester Papin, descendants of Pierre Laclède, founder of St. Louis. Taylor became mayor of the city the following year.[4]

In the meantime work continued on the church. In late April, Patrick Gregory commenced the plastering. On Monday evening, May 21, Father Bannon reported to his parishioners on the condition and finances of the new church. He asked their opinion whether the church should be opened on the finishing of plastering or whether subscriptions should be renewed to defray expenses for painting and frescoing to complete the church.

At a meeting the following Monday, about half the subscribers who had attended the first meeting arrived at the appointed time. They showed no inclination to renew the subscription list. Of those who gave in their names, only nine persons renewed it to the full amount. Thomas Bourke and Alexander J. P. Garesche alone spoke positively about the frescoes and the interior painting. All the others were willing to have the church completed but suggested no means of paying the bills. All but these two seemed anxious to escape from any further expense beyond that already incurred by the first subscription.

---

4   THE WESTERN BANNER.

THE WESTERN BANNER.

ST. LOUIS. NOVEMBER 3, 1860.

THE MULLANPHY BEQUEST.

Judge Bryan Mullanphy, son of an Irish immigrant, and Mayor of St. Louis for a term, bequeathed, at his decease, in 1850, as the Courts have decided, property valued at over half a million dollars, to be used in aid of the immigrant class, supposed by some to be limited, in his intention, to the class for which, as a member of the Irish Emigrant Society, he might be expected to have entertained the strongest feelings, and by others presumed to include every poor and needy visitor from every quarter of the globe.

The loose wording of the bequest has entailed no little difficulty on the Mayor and Common Council, authorized to supervise its disposition—so much, indeed, that, aware as we are of the determination of the Judge's relatives to apply the bequest, if decided favorably to their claims, to equally charitable purposes, we could almost wish the ambiguity of the will, and the trouble of administering on it equitably, had been obviated by the more direct agency of the testator's public-spirited heirs.

However, the decision of the Courts, and the action already taken by the Common Council have rendered wishes of this sort, if entertained, inoperative; and nothing remains to be done except to determine the manner in which the bequest shall be fulfilled, in letter and spirit, so far as may be.

ST. JOHN'S NEW CHURCH.

The following article appeared in our St. Louis Saturday Edition:

Of the many visitors to the new church during the week of the Fair, we did not meet one who was not surprised and pleased that the descriptions and details, florid and enthusiastic as they were, fell far behind the real merit of the artistic decorations of the interior. Few there were, either of those who visited the church and were so agreeably surprised beyond their expectations, who did not liberally recompense the zealous and laudable exertions of the ladies who had furnished the tables for the Fair. For evidence of our statement, we have but to allude to the report of the Fair, printed on the next page, from which it appears that 1495 visitors contributed the amount of $3,627 50, the gross proceeds, a sum which, under the auspices of a more prosperous business season, would have been more than doubled, but which, in view of the present stagnant condition of trade, may be considered a very liberal and generous response to the appeal of the pastor; not more, however, than we expected to be realized, considering the popularity he enjoys and the high apreciation in which his persevering labors in behalf of the new church, are held by his parishioners. From a card in another column it appears the new church will be dedicated to the service of God on Sunday week, Nov. 4th. The ceremony will be performed by his Grace the Archbishop, after which Solemn High Mass will be celebrated by the Very Rev. J. Melcher, V. G., pastor of St. Mary's. The Rev. Father Garesche, S. J., will preach the dedication sermon.

The choir of thirty voices will be under the direction of Mr. Vogel, whose orchestra of twenty-five instruments has been engaged for the occasion, the old organ being of too small a compass to support the chorus or give effect to the varied beauties of Haydn's Third Mass which has been in practice for the past month, and will be so rendered on Sunday week as to give the citizens of St. Louis a true idea of the power, sweetness and variety of the compositions of this great master.

At 3 P. M., as usual, Vespers will take place.

Rev. Mr. Feehan, of the Immaculate Conception, will preach at 7 1-2, P. M.

Handel's *Hallelujah* chorus, and other choice pieces of church music, will be rendered by the choir.

On Tuesday and Wednesday evening, the 30th and 31st inst., the pews in the new church will be offered for rent, so that the parishioners may have the security of a seat on the day of dedication.

We understand that the pastor intends to fix a moderate rent on each pew, and only in case where two or more persons may desire to secure the same pew, to decide the ownership by auction.

The anxious desire of many, not of the parish, to secure a pew in the West End church of St. Louis, will, we expect, push the result up, in some cases, to a high figure. So may it be, as the pastor feels the pressing responsibility of reducing the debt on the edifice as speedily as possible, that he may be at liberty to apply the overplus to the erection of a school house and residence—two buildings sadly needed in that locality.

Above: *The Western Banner* featured the building of St. John's and the start of the

Left: *The Western Banner* told that Judge Bryan Mullanphy gave his inherited fortune of $500,000 to help immigrants to St. Louis on the same page as its article on the opening of St. John the Apostle and Evangelist Church.

At that point Father Bannon set limits. Unless the parishioners could promise the $5,000 in cash or notes payable within two or three years, he would suspend work on the church at whatever position it was at the time and leave the church unfinished. This seemed to stir action, and the parishioners promised the needed amount.★★

On August 15, the parish held a benefit picnic at Concordia Park on Seventh Street opposite the Arsenal Gate. The members of the Roman Catholic Total Abstinence and Benevolent Society kept guard and policed the grounds. The Hibernian Benevolent and Shamrock Benevolent Societies and the Washington Blues under Captain Kelly attended. The Montgomery Guards under Captain Naughton arrived late in the evening. Ladies of the parish were active on this occasion: Mesdames Conrad, West, Madden, Scott, P. Gregory, Dougherty, Burroughs, Bourke, J. Mullholland, Durkan, Lynch, Carly, Logsdon, Long, Riley, and Geraghty. The festival exceeded expectations with a total gain of $1,275.25.

On October 8, the carpenters removed the scaffolding from the interior of the church. On the following Monday, October 15, the ladies of the parish opened a weeklong bazaar, called "Fancy Fare," in the church. The list of ladies taking part included most of the picnic-planners and the Mesdames Papin,

★★

A century and a half later the building still serves its people.

Thatcher, Chaissang, Bonn, Jones, Rozier, Ivory, Templeton, Spaulding, Gore, Rosenfeld, Shields, Burroughs, Burie, Bouvier, Long, Slevin, Higgins, Powell, and Tomlinson, and Miss Bessie Eldon. The men, led by George W. West, captain of the Missouri Guards, and Messrs. Conran, Madden, and Louis Charleville, Jr., offered refreshments for sale in the organ gallery.

The gifts that the ladies offered at the prize booths stretched from a Charter Oak cooking stove and gilt bedstead to a boy's saddle and a family Bible. Dr. Florentius Cornyn, head of the City Hospital and reserve surgeon of the state militia, won the silver tea service.[5]

Father Bannon sent a letter to *The Western Banner* thanking the ladies and men who worked on the booths and the guests for their support. With gross receipts of $3,627.50 and only $351.60 for expenses, the net was $3,275.90. Above all Father Bannon felt gratified that the people were pleased with their new church.[6]

A choir of thirty voices under the direction of Professor Vogel and an orchestra of thirty instruments had been practicing Haydn's "Third Mass" for a full month.

On Sunday, within the octave of All Saints, November 4, 1860, Archbishop Kenrick dedicated St. John's Church, assisted by the Very Reverend Joseph Melcher, V.G., soon to become bishop of Green Bay; the Very Reverend Father Ferdinand Coosemans, S.J., the rector of Saint Louis University; and Fathers Patrick Ryan and D. Lillis. Father Ferdinand Garesche, S.J., preached after the gospel. At Vespers Father Patrick Feehan spoke, and the choir rendered Handel's "Hallelujah Chorus." Father Bannon sadly mentioned in his diary that the collection received during the day and in the evening amounted to the munificent sum of $15. The expenses went slightly over $100.[7] On the day of the dedication, pew holders were privileged to welcome as many into the church as their pews would contain. The expanding West End, just north of the area where Chouteau Pond had once been, now had a temple to rival the cathedral and the churches of St. Francis Xavier and St. Vincent de Paul. Square twin towers faced west on the northeast corner of Fifteenth and Chestnut Streets. A circular window graced the facade and long, narrow, round-topped windows marched down the sides of the church.

Collections must have picked up shortly after the dedication if one judges from internal improvements that followed shortly thereafter. Adolphus J. Oloff, an artist from St. Petersburg, Russia, undertook a large painting of the Transfiguration, modeled after Raphael's masterpiece. It covered the wall behind and above the high altar.

Early in 1861, Father Bannon signed a contract with Henry Pilcher and Sons Company to build an organ for the new church. High in the rear balcony he built the handsome organ case that housed the two manual, thirty-four-stop (1,529 pipes) Pilcher organ. Shortly after its installation, a huge crowd assembled at the invitation of the Pilchers on Monday, March 11.

Many outstanding organists of the area, among them Joseph Gratin and William Robyn, vied for the opportunity to offer some selections and display the powers of the instrument to the manifest delight of all. The *St. Louis Republican* for March 14, 1861, stated:

> The organ is a magnificent affair, probably the most powerful in the city, and one that for richness and purity of tone, we venture to assert, is not excelled by any. The deep rolling pedal bass was a striking feature and elicited unbounded admiration. Indeed we do not remember ever to have listened to deeper and at the same time, more sonorous and melodious tones.[8]

The twenty-two-foot-wide organ case stood thirty-three feet high. The main group of front pipes stood out in a semicircle of nine feet in diameter finished at the top with a bold cornice surmounted with a dome and cross. The depth of the organ from front to back was fifteen feet. The case was finished in glossy white with gilded ornamental parts and gilded front pipes.

By that time Father Bannon must have relaxed after all the worries and problems that faced him during the two years the church was under construction. One of the main reasons that Father Bannon could relax a little was the Thornton bequest. A wealthy Catholic from St. Louis County by the name of John Thornton, who had extensive investments in the area of Dubuque, Iowa, left $461,488.41 to the St. Louis Archdiocese for charitable and religious purposes.[9] The first settlement was made in 1858, the third and final settlement in March 1861. Among those listed in Archbishop Kenrick's account book as enjoying the advantages of this benefaction of John Thornton was St. John's Church for $14,394.67.[10] This interest-free allotment gave many parishes an opportunity to build their church and to pay back the archdiocese gradually over the years. Eventually, St. John's paid its obligation to the archbishop. By that time Father Bannon had gone elsewhere.

4

The Nation Walks to the Brink

During the years when young Father Bannon was finding his place in a new country, a new city, and a new archdiocese, as well as building St. John's Church, momentous events threatened the nation. In 1854, Senator Stephen Douglas of Illinois had sponsored the Kansas-Nebraska Bill, which opened up those territories for settlement. Whether Kansas and Nebraska entered as slave or free states depended on the decision of the settlers. A bloody struggle ended with a free-soil victory, but gangs of Kansas "Jayhawkers" and Missouri "border ruffians" harassed each other.

Abraham Lincoln, an Illinois lawyer who had served in the Thirtieth Congress (1847–49) as a member of the Whig Party, challenged Democratic senator Douglas in the off-year election of 1858. The ensuing debate in seven congressional districts of Illinois gave Lincoln public prominence and allowed the candidates a chance to state their positions before the nation. Lincoln won many popular votes, but the state legislature chose Douglas. They would face each other again in the presidential race two years later. That election would hit Missouri hard.

Father Bannon left no record of his attitude toward these national issues at the time. Perhaps he followed his archbishop in leaving political matters to the politicians. Eventually, however, they would touch him directly. He was a resident of Missouri and chaplain of a unit in its State Guard. His people were involved, and he would be soon as well.

Missouri differed from the agricultural slave states of the Gulf South in the variety of its people, multiformity of its land, and diversity of its economy. Mining and manufacturing matched agriculture. Commerce held a far greater place than in most slave states. Tennessee and Arkansas had nothing in their economies to match the Santa Fe trade that had moved west from St. Louis for the previous forty years.

Missouri's few plantations hid in the "Bootheel," the delta-flat southeast section that wielded no political power. The pro-South power lay in "Little Dixie," a band of counties that stretched from Hannibal on the Mississippi River to St. Charles immediately northwest of St. Louis, thence along the north bank of the Missouri to Boonville, and then on both banks to the western boundary of the state. "Little Dixie" split the state. Eight of the eleven Missouri governors had come from this area. But the city of St. Louis sat astride its line of river communications with the South. Missouri had no railroad connection with other slave states.

Farmers from the northern states had moved into the fertile lands along the Iowa border, an area that boasted the only railroad that crossed the state and tied it to the free states whence those farmers or their ancestors had come. Some northern farmers had settled in southwest Missouri, along with other Unionists from the hills of Tennessee and North Carolina. In the Ozark hill country of south central Missouri, politics was a local matter and, as with other hill peoples, usually anti-planter in orientation.

German farmers, strongly free-soil and Unionist, Catholic or Evangelical in religion, settled along the south bank of the lower Missouri River, below the state capital, Jefferson City. Many Germans, too, had settled in St. Louis. In the

Above: First Missouri State Guard at Camp Lewis in 1861.
Facing: Slavery in Missouri in 1860. Slanted lines indicate presence of slaves.

late 1840s, a large body of Germans—"Free Thinkers" and "Free Soilers"—had come to St. Louis after failing in an attempt to unite their native land. They would fight to keep America united, as would earlier German immigrants.

About the same time, a large group of immigrant Irish, driven from their native land by the potato blight, sought homes in St. Louis, where many Irish had already established themselves in business, education, and government. Most of the Irish joined the Democratic Party in politics and practiced their Catholic religion. Many joined units of the State Guard. They gave little heed, however, to any secessionist oratory.

The Know-Nothings, an anti-immigrant secret society, harassed the newly arrived Irish during the elections of 1852 and 1854 and then joined the newly forming Republican Party. New England abolitionists turned their oratory as fiercely against Catholics as against slaveholders. The leaders of the Republican Party hesitated to condemn unlawful acts of individuals as long as they were aimed at slave owners. The spirit of Oliver Cromwell seemed alive in parts of the North. The Irish clung more strongly to the Democratic Party.

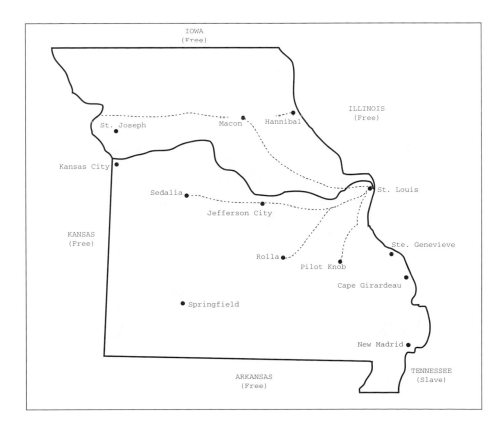

Visitors to St. Louis, such as Englishman Francis Grierson in his book *The Valley of Shadows* (1858), saw the Southern atmosphere of the city of St. Louis. Grierson and the other observers also recognized that slavery was becoming a minor part of the state's economy. Businessmen were tying themselves to the industrial and commercial interests of the Northeast. The prospects of railroads from the eastern seaboard weakened the traditional river ties with the South.

Alone of all the states of the Union, Missouri gave all its votes to the candidate of the Democratic Party, Senator Stephen Douglas of Illinois. The traditionally Southern-oriented section of the state, the "Little Dixie" areas of west-central Missouri, voted for the Constitutional Unionist, Senator John Bell of Tennessee. A few here and there voted for Vice President John C. Breckenridge, the choice of the Deep South. Not many Missouri voters, except the German Americans in St. Louis and counties to the west along the lower Missouri River, voted for Lincoln.

Slavery existed in Missouri, but only 9 percent of Missouri's wealth was in slaves. No concentration of slaves brought fear of bloody revolts as swept through the Deep South after John Brown's raid on Harpers Ferry. In St. Louis itself, only 3,000 out of 160,000 residents were African Americans, half of whom were free. A number were rich—they did not cross the river to free soil but stayed in the city.

Some powerful Missourians, like their counterparts in Kentucky, looked upon their state as a possible buffer between the extremists of Massachusetts and those of South Carolina. A few, like Lieutenant Governor Thomas Reynolds, worked for secession. Many, like Governor Claiborne Jackson, who had muted his secessionist feelings to win the election, wanted to secede once the Deep South began to separate from the Union. The recently arrived German immigrants were willing to fight to save the Union.

But no matter where sympathies lay or where emotion might have urged one, Missouri—an industrial and commercial as well as an agricultural state—had no future in a planter-ruled, rural commonwealth. The state would have been a peninsula of the Confederacy, stretching three hundred miles above the Mason-Dixon Line. Kansas stood on the western border, Iowa to the north, and Illinois to the east.

Cotton may have reigned in delta lands, but Missouri had many kings, queens, and a few princes. Missourians grew cotton, it is true, but also tobacco, hemp, corn, wheat, and fruits and vegetables for the local market. They also made boats, barrels, furniture, and tools. They mined lead and other products of the rich soil. They made bricks, quarried stone, and hewed lumber. They bought and sold and shipped.

Soldiers such as General Daniel Morgan Frost and ex-governor General Sterling Price, and lawyers such as ex-governor Trusten Polk and William Slack, might go South, but not the bankers, the brewers, the lead and brick producers, the coopers, and the boat builders. But when war did come, the division of the state made this struggle more poignant than it was for Minnesota or Mississippi, where the people united in their views.

Shortly after the election of Lincoln, and while Father Bannon prepared for the dedication of St. John's Church, trouble flared on the state border 250 miles to the west. Two years before, the notorious John Brown had raided Vernon County on the western boundary of Missouri, south of Kansas City, to free a number of slaves before heading east to plan his slave revolt. Now in the fall of 1860, Jayhawker James Montgomery threatened to raid Vernon County and its southern neighbor, Bates County.

The citizens of those areas appealed for help to Governor Robert Marcellus Stewart, a foe of secession and a supporter of railroads. Governor Stewart decided to put the railroad from St. Louis west to Sedalia to good use. Previously, those who took part in the border struggles came from the western counties. By calling militia units from St. Louis under General Frost, Governor Stewart lessened the border aspects of the campaign.

The Western Banner listed the officers and men of the Irish American companies that had been called up: the Sarsfield Guards, under Captain Charles Rogers; the Washington Guards, under Captain Patrick Gorman; the Washington Blues, under Captain Joseph Kelly; and the Montgomery Guards, under Captain Patrick Naughton. Twenty-five to forty men made up each unit. Only one had an old

Left: In the 1850s state senator Daniel Frost fostered the creation of a state militia to cooperate with those of Kentucky and Maryland to form a safety belt between extremists in the North and the South.
Right: Father Bannon took the train to Sedalia with the Missouri militia in the fall of 1860.

St. Louis French name; the rest were Irish.[1] They took the Pacific train for
Sedalia. Father Bannon went with them to that point.

Two weeks later, *The Western Banner* reported that the expedition was going
well. In the meantime federal troops, under General William Harney, had arrested
several of Montgomery's Kansans. General Frost planned to act in concert with
General Harney when the situation warranted.[2]

The Jayhawkers retreated in the face of the formidable force that Governor
Stewart was sending. After a short time, the counties in west-central Missouri
had calmed down. Frost left a small token force under General John Bowen, and
the rest returned to St. Louis.

Militarily the action proved insignificant, but psychologically it had a great
impact. Troops from eastern Missouri had mobilized to defend their western bor-
ders against raiders from Kansas. The raiders were abolitionists. The St. Louisans
defended their state and, unwittingly in many cases, the right of their fellow citizens to hold slaves. This added an entirely new dimension to the outlook of the
recently arriving Irish immigrants in the State Guard.

The campaign brought Father Bannon into personal touch with many men
with whom he would serve in the months and years ahead. He had many
opportunities to meet with General Frost, a convert to Catholicism, and General
John Bowen, a St. Louis architect of Georgian background who married a
Catholic. Father Bannon would serve with Frost at Camp Jackson several months
later. Bowen's path would cross the priest's two years later in the Mississippi
towns of Grand Gulf and Vicksburg.

The states of the Deep South were seceding from the Union, but Missouri
still held a majority of Union supporters. All the while, secessionists in St. Louis,
who called themselves "Minute Men," presumably had their eyes on the arsenal
that held sixty thousand muskets, more than half the number in the entire South.

On January 11, 1861, forty regulars arrived from Newport Barracks, North
Carolina, under the leadership of Lieutenant Thomas W. Sweeny, who had lost an
arm in the Mexican War. Sweeny marched his men to the courthouse on Third
and Olive Streets, where the government held $400,000 in gold. Many local citi-
zens looked upon this military venture as an unwarranted federal intrusion in a
sovereign state. Tempers flared. General William Harney, commander of military
forces in the area, wisely advised Sweeny to move his forty soldiers to the arsenal
thirty-three blocks to the south. This he did.

On the day after Sweeny arrived, Archbishop Kenrick advised the Catholics of
St. Louis to avoid situations where a spark could set off an explosion. He stated:

> Beloved Brethren: In the present disturbed state of the public mind,
> we feel it is our duty to recommend to you to avoid all occasions of pub-

lic excitement, to obey the laws, to respect the rights of all citizens, to keep away as much as possible from all assemblages where the indiscretion of a word, or the impetuosity of the momentary passion might endanger the public tranquility. Obey the injunction of the Apostle Peter: "Follow peace with all men."[3]

A pro-Confederate officer, Lieutenant St. George Croghan, confronted Lieutenant Sweeny with the warning that the Minute Men would try to take the arsenal. Sweeny said to Croghan: "I'll blow it to hell first, and you know I'm the man to do it."[4]

General Harney, who sent Sweeny and his unit to the arsenal, had gained a reputation as a peacemaker between whites and Indians in the West. He was well known in the St. Louis area. His wife was a daughter of the late local merchant and philanthropist John Mullanphy and sister of a one-time mayor. Harney was related by marriage to General Daniel Morgan Frost, the head of the state militia in the area. He chose to pursue a conciliatory policy during those trying days.

Above: Camp Jackson as federal training ground in 1862.

ENTRANCE TO THE ARSENAL AT ST. LOUIS. (See page 151.)

Top: The federal authorities fortified St. Louis against possible Confederate raids.
Bottom: Wood engraving of the entrance to the arsenal at St. Louis, 1861.

The influential congressman Francis Blair thought otherwise. He prevailed on the War Department to call Harney for temporary duty in Washington, D.C., and bring from "Bleeding Kansas" a gruff, die-hard New Englander, Captain Nathaniel Lyon, and put him in control of the St. Louis Arsenal in early February 1861. On February 18, the Missouri State Convention voted for the Union. A day later, Jefferson Davis took his oath as president of the newly formed Confederacy. Lyon's company of regulars responded by moving the supply of arms from the arsenal to a secure place across the river in Alton, Illinois.

In March, Abraham Lincoln took the oath of office as president. A month later, Confederate president Davis approved orders for the Southern artillerymen to fire on Fort Sumter. Lincoln called for four thousand Missourians to defend the Union. Lyon soon had them.

Governor Jackson, who had muted his secessionist inclinations to win the governorship, reminded the state legislators of Missouri's ties with the South. He asked the Confederate president for supplies and instructed the State Guard to meet in camps throughout the state in May.

Above: A lithograph of Camp Jackson, c. 1862, shows the neighborhood much the same as the year before.

General Frost mustered in the St. Louis units of the state militia at Camp Jackson at Lindell Grove. Named for Claiborne Jackson, the reigning governor, not for Andrew Jackson, the seventh president of the United States, the grounds lay between Olive on the north, Laclede on the south, Compton on the east, and Grand on the west. Several hundred pro-secession Minute Men joined them.

How much time Father Bannon spent at the encampment is not clear. He could easily drive the twenty blocks from his rectory to Lindell Grove. Presumably, he stayed at the residence overnight, had morning mass at St. John's, took care of parish business, and then visited the encampment during the day.

Captain Kelly's secession-minded Washington Guards left for Jefferson City to drill outstate units. A daughter of one of the Camp Jackson officers gave the opinion years later that General Frost should have closed the camp after Kelly's men left. She recalled: "None of the others wanted to go South."[5] In support of this view, a volunteer stated that he believed the First Infantry Regiment of the Missouri Volunteers would have joined the Union army "had it not been for the Camp Jackson affair."[6]

Nearly a century and a half later, Lyon's reaction to Camp Jackson still gathers mixed reviews. He mustered into federal service four thousand men, mostly German immigrants, surrounded the encampment, and forced Frost to surrender. The name J. Bannon appears on this list of prisoners.[7] Instead of marching the surrendering militiamen south through open country and east to the arsenal, Lyon moved them through large crowds of relatives and friends. A civilian fired a shot and killed a Polish officer. His foreign-born troops returned fire and killed a number of people. Neither Father Bannon nor any witnesses mentioned the priest's presence.

Tension gripped the city as when ominous clouds gather in the southwest and rumors of tornadoes spread abroad. A mob threatened the office of the *Missouri Democrat*, the Republican paper. Others rushed against the gun store of H. E. Dimick on Main Street. Police Chief McDonough marched twenty policemen to protect the store and keep the mob unarmed.

General Harney returned from Washington and met with General Sterling Price, former governor and head of the state militia. The two old soldiers signed a compromise, the Price-Harney Agreement. Harney agreed not to move federal troops about the state. Price, in turn, pledged to keep order throughout Missouri and to protect the interests of all. What Father Bannon thought of the Price-Harney Agreement, no record avers. The agreement certainly reflected the peaceful wishes of Archbishop Kenrick.

Congressman Francis Blair and Captain Lyon, however, looked on Harney's promise as appeasement. Lincoln removed Harney and named Captain Lyon a brigadier general and commander of federal forces in the Missouri area. Governor

Right: Congressman Francis Blair thought General William Harney too conciliatory and urged President Lincoln to put Captain Nathaniel Lyon in charge at the arsenal in the spring of 1861. Blair later rose to the rank of major general and served on Sherman's staff.

Jackson and General Price conferred with Lyon in St. Louis on June 12. Jackson offered to demobilize his newly formed militia, halt further movement of armament into the state, and put down any insurrection, if Lyon would keep his troops in St. Louis and demobilize the home guard that Congressman Blair had encouraged in various locations in the state.[8]

Lyon did more than refuse the compromise. He allegedly stated that he would have preferred to see every Missourian dead and buried rather than to agree to restrict movement of federal troops in the state. Lyon gave Governor Jackson and General Price one hour to get out of St. Louis.

On July 3, Lincoln named John C. Frémont as commander of the Western Department. A pathfinder in the west in the 1840s and Republican candidate for president in 1856, Frémont was known in St. Louis as a son-in-law of the popular Democratic senator Thomas Hart Benton. Frémont had much going for him but squandered his opportunities. He delayed in arriving in St. Louis, and when he did come, he placed St. Louis under martial law and freed the slaves in Missouri without Lincoln's consent. The president countermanded the order.

When General Lyon faced the Confederate forces of Price and McCulloch at Wilson's Creek near Springfield in southwestern Missouri, Frémont sent no help. A sniper's bullet cut down Lyon. Franz Sigel, leader of the St. Louis Germans, mistook gray-clad Louisianans for hoary-garbed Iowans and barely escaped disaster. The Union troops drifted back to the railroad at Rolla. In the city the Federals set up seven forts along Jefferson Avenue. Someone suggested that the stone wall that Henry Shaw had built along the east side of his garden might be one place to halt the victorious Confederates as they approached St. Louis. But McCulloch refused to push farther and withdrew his Texans and Arkansans back across the southern boundary of Missouri.

Price moved his ten thousand victorious Missouri troops against Colonel James Mulligan's three thousand Chicago Irish volunteers defending Lexington, a Missouri River town near Kansas City. Frémont hesitated to send reinforcements, and Mulligan had to surrender. Lincoln dismissed Frémont after a hundred days of failure. The federal authorities agreed to exchange General Frost and his command for Colonel Mulligan and his Chicago troops. His parole over, General Frost, with many of his Camp Jackson men, joined Price at his headquarters in Springfield, Missouri.

All that long summer and fall, Father Bannon had continued with his work at the parish under parole. But now more and more, his militiamen were following Frost and slipping through Union lines to join Price. They had no chaplain. On the other hand, many priests could serve at St. John's. In the meantime, the Confederacy had driven back the Union army at Bull Run and seemed to have established itself as a going nation, now with eleven states. Later on, Father Bannon spoke of the Confederacy as an agricultural nation threatened by an overpowering industrial country, as Ireland chafed under British rule. Whether or not he held that view in the fall of 1861 is not known, but clearly his militiamen had need of his services. Should he confer with Archbishop Kenrick? He knew what the answer would be. The archbishop had refused the request of the Jesuit missionary Peter De Smet to serve as Union chaplain, lest the federal authorities use his presence as a recruiting device. Kenrick wanted only the papal flag waving over the cathedral. He neither approved nor advocated either cause, while holding to his seminary promise of refraining from political activity. Lincoln had said the issue was union or division, a political matter.

While this seems strange from the vantage of a century and a half, it should be remembered that two years later Pope Pius IX himself urged both Archbishop John M. Odin of New Orleans and Archbishop John J. Hughes of New York to work for peace, but never mentioned the moral or ethical issues involved.

Archbishop Kenrick had allowed Father Bannon to wear two hats: the biretta of the pastor, and the forage cap of the chaplain. The archbishop never called the priest back from the field. He left no record of his views on Father Bannon's choice of ministries.

When Father Bannon made up his mind to follow his men, he called together some of his parishioners, among them the man who had strongly supported the building of the church, Alexander J. P. Garesche.[9] Their pastor told them of his determination. They respected his concern for the men in the field. He was giving up an excellent pastorate and prospects for advancement. A man of his gifts could well hope for high positions in the Church. His friend Captain Joseph Boyce certainly thought so. He wrote, "He sacrificed himself as he was to be made bishop, but his love of duty to his state and devotion to his many parishioners and friends caused him to abandon his future advancement in the Church."[10]

If one may judge from the fact that three of Bannon's successors at St. John's—Fathers John Hennessey, Patrick Ryan, and John Joseph Hennessey—became bishops and that Archbishop Kenrick resided at the parish in his late years, one could readily conclude that Captain Boyce had made a fair assumption.

After Mass on December 15, 1861, Father Bannon visited the Lucas family at 1513 Locust Avenue. By that time martial law was in full effect in St. Louis. At the conclusion of his visit, he had to slip inconspicuously out the back door in disguise. It was fortunate that he did. Another guest, Union general Enoch Stein, arrived at the front door at the same time.[11] Bannon left St. Louis heading for southwest Missouri, accompanied by two young men of prominent St. Louis families, Robert A. Bakewell and P. B. Garesche.

The priest left a letter for Archbishop Kenrick with the latter's secretary, P. S. Langston. Approaching the prelate, the secretary said, "Father Bannon has gone south, your Grace."

"I have heard so," was the response.

"And he left this letter to be delivered to you."

"Keep it," the archbishop said. "The message was never delivered."

People might wonder why Father Bannon did not go personally to take leave of the archbishop. Father Bannon knew without a touch of doubt that he had no chance of gaining permission. Archbishop Kenrick had already taken a stance of Olympian neutrality. He separated church and state more absolutely than Jefferson did in his writings. Kenrick spoke out for neither the North nor the South. He refused to allow the national flag to fly over the cathedral, saying, "It does not belong there." Archbishop Kenrick would never have granted Father Bannon nor anyone else permission to go South. Likewise, he never took sides publicly.

The archbishop would send Father Patrick Feehan as a civilian chaplain to give spiritual help to Union soldiers in local encampments and, after the battles of Wilson's Creek and Shiloh, at the expanding hospitals. Kenrick directed Father Patrick Ryan to offer Mass and hear confessions for Confederate prisoners who

Left: Holding his posture of non-interference in political affairs, Archbishop Kenrick never opened Father Bannon's farewell letter and turned down Father De Smet's wish to serve as a federal chaplain.
Below: The captured battle flag of the Missouri Guard.

would soon crowd the old McDowell Medical College, newly dubbed the Gratiot Street Prison. At the conclusion of the war, the archbishop would recommend Father Feehan, who had assisted Northern soldiers, for a Southern diocese; and Father Ryan, who had helped the Southerners, to a Northern archdiocese. No one was more neutral than Kenrick.

Since the only other group of Catholics, besides the St. Louisans, in the Confederate armies of the Trans-Mississippi were the Louisiana French, whose chaplains spoke presumably only French, there would have been no priest to take care of the spiritual welfare of the many men from St. Louis who were serving under Price.

In one sense, the militiamen decided the issue for Father Bannon. They went South. They needed him. He heard their call.

5

Father Bannon Goes "South"

The three would-be Confederates dodged Union patrols, crossed swollen icy streams, traversed hilly wilderness, and spent Christmas God-knows-where in their risky journey to southwest Missouri. Bannon, Bakewell, and Garesche hid by day and rode by night, no doubt stopping occasionally at what they knew to be a friendly farmhouse. Union troops guarded the two rail lines out of St. Louis: one southwest to Rolla, the other south to Pilot Knob in the mining country one hundred miles away. The fugitives stayed clear of these paths.

After hiding in the woods and getting lost on January 16,[1] the trio reached the area of Springfield, southwest Missouri's largest city, with two thousand inhabitants, on January 22. Price's army encamped several miles south of the town at Fulbright Spring, a small watercourse trickling toward clear Sac River. The newly arriving St. Louisans reached the encampment a day later.[2]

Father Bannon met many old friends and some men he had long admired, such as general and former governor Sterling Price and his staff. The group included Colonel Benjamin Allen Rives, a former state legislator from Ray County, near Kansas City.[3] He also met Colonels Frank Von Puhl, Emmet McDonald, and Colton Green, Captain Wright Schaumburg,[4] and Lewis and William Clark Kennerly, nephews of the great explorer General William Clark.

Father Bannon's arrival boosted the spirits of the beleaguered Confederates in the far corner of their state, which had, against their hopes, decided to stay with the Union. In the records of service, North or South, there is no other example of a pastor who gave up a fine church he had built to serve the men in the field. Father Bannon had deep sympathy for the Southern cause and came to look on the South's fight for independence in the same way he saw Ireland's centuries-old struggle for freedom from the exploiting English.[5]

On a blustery Sunday, January 25, Bannon finally met some of the young men to whom he had already risked his life to minister, the St. Louis Irishmen of

Captain William Wade's Light Artillery Unit. Captain Wade, a popular man, forty-two years of age, was described by an associate as "fearless under fire, unmoved in danger, devoted to his duty and his command—on the field the beau ideal of the gallant soldier, and in the parlor a refined and elegant gentleman . . . known to every private and the personal friend of every officer, and respected and loved by all. . . ."[6] After expiration of the guard enlistments, Wade and his cannoneers were by then members of the Missouri Light Artillery.

Besides the personal leadership of their captain, the men of the unit had the good fortune to serve under one of three Irish-born lieutenants, whom they had known in St. Louis: Richard C. Walsh, John Kearny, and Samuel Farrington.

Father Bannon went to work immediately, hearing thirty confessions from the unit from 11 A.M. to 2 P.M. Several of them were natives of Ireland. Then the priest went to Henry Guibor's battery, which would carry on throughout the war and merit a stone memorial next to the Missouri memorial at Vicksburg. Guibor, a Saint Louis University graduate of Alsatian ancestry, would survive the war and become the focal person of the Confederate veterans in the years after the conflict. Guibor had organized his battery, officially the St. Louis Light Artillery, at

Above: Captain Emmet McDonald, a lawyer, refused parole, claiming that Captain Lyon had no legal grounds for keeping him in custody.

Above: Revered general and former governor Sterling Price led the Missouri Confederates at Wilson's Creek, Lexington, Pilot Knob, and Corinth. He lived in St. Louis for a short time after the Civil War and was buried in Bellefontaine Cemetery. Father Bannon met with General Price and became "unofficial chaplain" for the Catholics in the First Missouri Confederate Brigade.

Memphis in November 1861, with sixty-eight members. William Corkery was lieutenant, and William Mooney, E. Woods, and T. Malone were the sergeants.

From the beginning, Bannon became part of the high command's activities, regularly dining with Captain Wade and other high-ranking officers among the State Guard and Confederate ranks, mingling with Price and the general's staff. Little did the priest realize that his unit, Wade's Battery, had become part of a brigade destined to earn distinction as one of the most elite combat units during the Civil War. The First Missouri Confederate Brigade consisted of Captain William Wade's Light Artillery, Colonel Elijah Gates's First Missouri Cavalry, Colonel John Q. Burbridge's First Infantry, Colonel Benjamin Allen Rives's Second Infantry, and Captain Samuel Churchill Clark's Battery. Commanding the brigade was Colonel Henry Little, the son of a Maryland congressman and a Mexican War hero who had only grudgingly cast his lot with the South after much personal anguish. Colonel Burbridge, incidentally, had graduated from Saint Louis University.

Above: Memorial for Henry Guibor's battery.

Father Bannon enjoyed good luck on January 27, when the priest traded his drafty tent for a comfortable boarding house in Springfield.[7] Here, the St. Louisan began to deal with urgent personal concerns, washing clothes and writing letters to the many friends who believed he had met a dismal fate at the enemy's hands.

Shortly before reaching the Confederate outposts, Father Bannon had begun to keep daily notes. His first entry, on January 16, proved typical of others. He simply wrote: "Hid in a woods . . . got lost. . . ."[8] The priest's daily notations were to the point. He often abbreviated, and he left out verbs when they were not necessary. It might seem that he intended the words to remind him what happened. It could in no way serve as a journal for others to read. Nonetheless, the mere annotations, names, statistics, and distances suggested much. Entries from his first few days with the Missouri Confederates were typical: ". . . changed clothes . . . visited General Price . . . hail and wind. . . . Said Mass at General Frost's tent. . . ."[9]

Later in Mississippi, he wrote: "Showers all day. . . . Mass at 8 o'clock . . . captured blankets . . . enemy entrenching at Farmington. . . . First Brigade five miles from Corinth. . . ."[10] Sometimes he would write a mere name such as "Bp. [for Bishop] Elder,"[11] and "Govr. [Governor] Polk."[12] He spelled French names as he heard them sound: Father Dicharry became "Fr. Decker," Guibor he spelled "Guibgoe," and Garesche, his traveling companion from St. Louis, he listed as "Garashe."[13]

No doubt the mere name would call to his mind events and circumstances. He occasionally would include rumors that came from other theaters of the war. But he never commented on the attitudes, capacities, strategies, failures, or successes of the officers who led the armies he served. A perusal of the diary, however, would suggest that the priest had great regard for Generals Sterling Price and Henry Little.[14]

Strangely, the only times he wrote at length were the busiest times, namely the days of battle. The longest and most complete accounts dealt with such conflicts as those of Pea Ridge and Elkhorn Tavern.[15] With other evidence to corroborate the priest's remarks, the diary remains a valuable bit of history. Fortunately, early in the twentieth century, he gave the document to a young Southern scholar, Yates Snowden, destined to become South Carolina's best historian of his time. While Snowden never used it in any major publication, he did preserve it and leave it for future historians in the South Caroliniana Library at the University of South Carolina–Columbia.

Bannon's duties soon stretched far beyond Wade's Battery, making the priest travel from camp to camp to hear confessions of Catholics in various units—especially that of Captain Patrick Canniff, a twenty-four-year-old Irish-born saddler from St. Louis, and his largely Irish, independent Confederate company.[16] Bannon also preached at Little's headquarters at the Fulbright Springs, south of

Springfield,[17] and ministered to virtually every unit in Price's army. He heard confessions of the men of Captain Emmet McDonald's company in Colonel Rawling's regiment.[18] The men of General Steen's division asked him to hear their confessions, but through a breakdown of communications, no one showed up when he arrived at their campsite.[19] On February 9, he celebrated Mass at Confederate headquarters;[20] on March 1 at McDonald's Company,[21] and on the next day in the tent of his old friend, General Daniel Frost.[22]

The priest made his presence felt throughout the entire First Missouri Brigade. More St. Louis Irish belonged to this unit than to any other command in the army, among them many former Washington Blues and members of the Catholic Total Abstinence and Benevolent Society. These soldiers soon became men without a state.[23] Only a rump section of the state legislature supported secession and had to withdraw from Jefferson City when the troops did. Price's army soon had to retreat, too, with a mighty Union army moving southwest from Rolla toward Springfield. The Missouri volunteers had no uniforms. The rump government had no resources at its command and could promise nothing to its soldiers.

During the early months in camp, Father Bannon dined with a number of old and new friends: with Captain Wade and General Harding on January 31,[24] with Captain McLean of General Rains's headquarters on February 2, and on February 11 with Colonel John Q. Burbridge, who would eventually command the Fourth Missouri Cavalry in Marmaduke's division. Later on Father Bannon would be a regular guest at the mess of Colonel Henry Little.[25] While Father Bannon often enjoyed officer's fare, most chaplains enjoyed only a private's rations. But, unlike Father Bannon, they also received $50 a month salary, according to historian Charles F. Pitts in his book *Chaplains in Gray*.[26]

A look at the circumstances of the average Confederate chaplain will provide a background for a clearer understanding of Father Bannon's role with the First Missouri. Chaplains enjoyed no rank, insignia, or command. They had to provide their own transportation to camp and bring their own horses—as Father Bannon had done. There was no chief of chaplains or supervisory body to coordinate efforts.

If a chaplain wanted to carry a gun, he could do so. In short, he could preach on Sunday and target Yankees during the week. Father Bannon carried no weapons. The Ninth Arkansas, on the other hand, organized at Pine Bluff the day before the Battle of Bull Run in 1861, numbered forty-two preachers in its ranks. A Methodist minister, Colonel Bradley, commanded this "Preachers Regiment," as it came to be called.[27]

On the subject of preaching, historian Pitts has these interesting words in *Chaplains in Gray*: "The main burden of the chaplain's message dealt with sin and retribution, pardon and salvation." The favorite hymns were "Amazing Grace," "Nearer My God to Thee," "Rock of Ages," and "Jesus, Lover of My Soul."[28]

Father Bannon had arrived at Price's winter encampment at the time when the terms of enlistment of the Missouri Guard were expiring and Missouri units were forming. Each regiment had already chosen its chaplain. The Catholic soldiers were so widely distributed throughout the regiments of the First Brigade that they could not form a bloc to vote for Father Bannon. As a result, he became "unofficial chaplain" of the First Missouri Brigade. The Confederate command pattern had no such official position as "brigade chaplain," as Colonel Albert Blanchard of the Army of Northern Virginia found out. He wanted the First Louisiana Regimental chaplain, Father Darius Hubert, S.J., to move up with him and serve the entire brigade when he took charge of it.[29] Since Father Bannon lacked regimental status, he received no salary. He had brought along $300 with him from St. Louis, and an assistant took up a collection at Sunday Mass.

Father Bannon came to Price's camp with unsurpassed credentials. He had graduated from one of the most prestigious seminaries in the English-speaking world. The great archbishop of the American West, Peter Richard Kenrick, had called him to shepherd a growing congregation of devout people. He had built an impressive church for the service of God. He had a command of the English language and a fluency of expression that would bring him wide acclaim as a preacher in years to come. His sermons showed a mastery of Scripture and of ancient Christian traditions. His voice resonated with an Irish lilt. His men knew him from the days of peace and during the southwestern campaign of late 1860. He had shared their distressing surrender at Camp Jackson. While most of the other chaplains had been rural pastors, he came from the metropolis of the Trans-Mississippi. He had to slip through hostile lines to reach his men.

In the rough-and-tumble of camp, with more than its share of cursing, wenching, drunkenness, and neglect of religion, he set an example of patience, self-control, sobriety, and dedication to God. He never preached "Demon Rum," but he must have thought it was a demon, because he never touched a drop of it. He had been head of the Temperance Society in St. Louis, the outstaters had heard, and all his Irish from St. Louis belonged to it.[30] He taught by example as well as by word. In the puritanical religious atmosphere of his time that saw the greatest sins in gambling and drinking, he advocated a balanced code of morality. Declining to call drink an evil in itself, or to rail against card playing, he taught moderation in all things.

Above all, he had at his disposal a sacramental system that dated back to the early Christians: the Eucharist, Penance, and the Last Annointing. He could forgive sin in God's name. He could offer Mass regularly, whether in camp or on the march, at a known place in the line, or at the battery of Captain William

Wade. As time went on, he developed a procedure before each battle that will become clear as the story progresses.

At first, the Confederate soldiers from "Little Dixie" in outstate Missouri did not really know what to think of the Catholic chaplain—"Father" Bannon, the St. Louisans, even the officers, called him. Many outstaters had met few Catholics in their lives. Yet many of the St. Louis soldiers were Catholic, and Father Bannon was finding Catholics all over Price's army from rural Missouri.

Bannon was not lean and gaunt, as rural Missourians expected a "preacher man" to be. He was more than six feet tall, erect, broad shouldered, and sturdy

Above: Absalom Grimes, a mail carrier to General Sterling Price.

looking, with steel-rimmed glasses and deep black hair. He had the appearance of a senator from Scott County or a banker from Boonville. He would soon grow a vigorous dark beard.

During his worship service he would amaze curious members of other denominations by wearing a colorful robe of a type they had never seen before, and begin in a foreign tongue equally strange to their ears. Someone thought it was Latin, and he was proven right. But when the time came for Father Bannon to give a sermon he spoke clear English that sounded through the whole valley where the troops bivouacked. Most of the soldiers stopped whatever they were doing and listened. Many members of other denominations walked toward Wade's battery and sat down to listen to the Word.

Father Bannon gave the Word with power. His eloquence amazed them. The chaplain could put it where they were before God and where they should be. He talked mostly about the Lord Jesus forgiving the thief who was sorry for his evil deeds, and about the prodigal son and the Heavenly Father's mercy.

At this time, Father Bannon met one of the most colorful personalities in American history, Mississippi River captain Absalom "Ab" Grimes, the Confederate mail runner. As flamboyant as Jeb Stuart and as resourceful as "Stonewall" Jackson, the handsome bearded Grimes slipped repeatedly through Union lines to bring mail from relatives in Missouri to men in Price's army and take back their messages in turn. Imprisoned several times in the Gratiot Street Prison in St. Louis, he escaped regularly. Finally, wounded and captured, he endured more than one hundred lashes from a vindictive jailer.

When one reads his story, as edited by historian M. M. Quaife and published by Yale University Press, one wonders why his name has not become a byword in American lore such as Kit Carson or "Wild Bill" Hickok. Be that as it may, he tells of meeting with his fellow members of the First Missouri Brigade when General Price appointed him official mail carrier for the Confederate Army with the rank of major. The officers gave him a friendly handshake and a few words of encouragement.

"Father Bannon, our Chaplain," Grimes recalled, "then congratulated me on my appointment, but he added that he did not deem it an appointment in which congratulations could be appreciated because I would be in constant danger of being arrested and hanged as a spy or of being shot in trying to escape capture."[31] Shortly after this conversation, Father Bannon would call on Ab Grimes to take a letter to a friend in St. Louis.

No one provided as much moral inspiration to the highly touted First Missouri Confederate Brigade during its first two years than Chaplain John Bannon. Destined to become one of the South's elite fighting machines, the brigade would regularly take greater risks and higher losses than comparable units in Confederate armies of the West, usually fighting at the most critical sectors of each hard-contested field. Nevertheless, after each bloody engagement, the men of Missouri had the uncanny ability to rebound successfully after frightful casualties and each bitter reversal to arise and face the next challenge. Perhaps more than any other brigade member's, Father Bannon's influence and guidance were decisive factors. He instilled hope when there was none and courage to confront impossible odds.

Curtis Moves into Arkansas

On Christmas Day in 1861, shortly after Father Bannon had left St. Louis, Major General Henry W. Halleck, Union commander of the Department of the Missouri, appointed Brigadier General Samuel R. Curtis—a West Point graduate of 1831, a veteran of the Mexican War, and a U.S. congressman from Iowa—to be the new federal commander of the Southwestern District of Missouri. On the next day, Curtis left St. Louis by way of the Pacific Railroad for Rolla, Missouri, to take command of troops bivouacked there. He set out to drive the Confederates from Missouri. He pushed his men southwest along Telegraph Road to Springfield.

When Curtis and his men approached that city on February 12, 1862, the Confederates moved out. Confederates retreated down Telegraph Road. They camped at the site of their first great victory, Wilson's Creek, where rebels from Missouri, Arkansas, and Texas had defeated the Federals under Generals Nathaniel Lyon and Franz Sigel the previous August. Here, on February 14, Colonel B. A. Rives gave the priest a maneuver-by-maneuver account of that Confederate victory, whose success, like that at Bull Run, amounted to little when the Texan, General Benjamin McCulloch, would not join Price in pursuing the defeated Federals. That night Father Bannon wrote in his diary: "Slept well in the open air first time."[1] On the next night the priest camped south of Cassville, a town sixteen miles from the Arkansas border. The Federal forces pressed the Rebels and drove in pickets on February 15 but refused battle. The retreating Confederates neared the border of Arkansas.

Years later, a printed copy of a letter of Father Bannon turned up in the *Billon Scrapbook* at the Missouri Historical Society in St. Louis. The date given was July 16, 1862, and the place of origin Priceville, Missouri. By July 16, 1862, Father Bannon was serving in northern Mississippi, not in Missouri. Further, the

Above: General Samuel Ryan Curtis left his office in St. Louis to lead the Federals against Price in southwest Missouri in early 1862.

context of the letter suggests that the date was actually February 16, just before the Confederates moved across the state line into Arkansas. Perhaps the priest named the last Missouri camp Priceville. Father Bannon no doubt asked his new friend, Captain Absalom Grimes, to carry his message to his friend in St. Louis.

Father Bannon began:

> My position here is a volunteer chaplain. Some regiments have Catholic chaplains, the number of Catholics being so many as to give them the majority.... In Price's Army we have about 1500 Catholics.... Trusting as I do on the voluntary gifts of the Catholics whom I serve, I think I fare much better than as a commissioned chaplain. ...
>
> Since my arrival . . . I have messed with Colonel Little, for 22 years an officer in the Federal Army, and a relative of Colonel Morrison of Carondelet.... The only privation we have yet suffered is separation from our friends.[2]

The Confederates moved down along Telegraph Road running southwest from Springfield, Missouri. As they were leaving the Sugar Creek Valley, the Federals attacked their rear near Elkhorn Tavern, a place where the two armies would have a showdown less than a month later. There, a few miles inside the Arkansas border, twenty-six hundred Confederates under Colonels McRae and Cabel joined the Missourians.[3]

On the following day, February 17, the Federals moved forward and, with a battery of howitzers and three thousand cavalry, harassed Price's rear guard. But Colonel Little's First Missouri Brigade twice drove them off. The attackers fell back and harassed the retreating Missourians no more. In the afternoon, three thousand Arkansas and Texas troops came in support. Many of these Arkansans were farm boys from the area whose units had only lately been called up. The combined Southern forces camped in Cross Hollow one hundred miles from Springfield.[4]

The reinforced Missouri Confederates expected an attack by Curtis's men all the next day. Batteries stood in position. But the Federals fell back. General McCulloch took charge of the Confederate forces. Just as after Wilson's Creek the previous August, he refused to move forward. Unhappy, the Missourians retreated with the other Southerners toward Fayettefille, Arkansas.[5]

Two days later the Confederates passed through that town. By that time Louisiana troops had arrived and Father Bannon had an opportunity to confer with Father P. F. Dicharry, chaplain of the Third Regiment Louisiana Volunteers,[6] on leave from his position as chancellor of the Diocese of Nachitoches, Louisiana.[7] Father Bannon wrote little in his diary during the following seven days. But on February 28 he lectured to the first regiment of Colonel Burbridge on the establishment of the Christian Church.[8] On March 1, the priest offered Mass at Captain Emmet McDonald's Company in Colton Green's command.

With the arrival of troops from Louisiana, Arkansas, and Texas, Price's Missourians outnumbered Curtis's forces. But they were now in Arkansas, a seceded state strong on states' rights, not overly concerned about Missouri, and led for the moment by General McCulloch. The total picture had changed. Only reluctantly had the Arkansans crossed the state border the previous August to help Price's Missouri Confederates in the Battle of Oak Hill, or, as the Federal forces termed it, Wilson's Creek. Had McCulloch been willing to go deeper into Missouri at that time, it is conceivable that Price could have threatened St. Louis.[9] But such was the strength of the states' rights view that the Arkansas commander refused to pursue the defeated Federals. McCulloch had retreated, and now the Missouri troops had withdrawn from their own state and joined him in Arkansas.

The northwestern section of Arkansas resembled the hill country of western Virginia and North Carolina, eastern Tennessee, and south-central Missouri. These last three contained many Unionists and few planters, and the mountainous counties seceded from seceding Virginia. One might have expected the hilly section of Arkansas to stay in the Union. It did, until the firing on Fort Sumter. Then only an old mountaineer, Isaac Murphy, voted against secession.

In 1860, 325,000 white men and 111,151 slaves lived in Arkansas. Most of these bondsmen worked for masters who had, at most, 2 slaves. Only 10 planters had from 50 to 100 slaves. The "natural state"—as it came to call itself—was not a planter's paradise.

When the governor called for volunteers, close to 50,000 seemed willing to take their squirrel guns off the rack and march out to defend the state. They had little inkling of the bloody, relentless conflict that the North's industrial might and huge reservoir of manpower would eventually win. They looked to a defensive struggle, bigger in scope but on the lines of a large-scale feud between the Hatfields and the McCoys. The state had no lead mine, no iron foundry to bring out guns, and one small shop to sew uniforms.

An outstanding Arkansas historian, John Gould Fletcher, wrote of the arrival of Price and his Missourians: "The ablest man on the near horizon was Sterling Price . . . fifty one years old with a distinguished career behind him. He was a Welsh Celt, with an unusual fund of expansive good nature, immense personal courage and an irresistible charm."[10] By way of contrast, Fletcher wrote lukewarmly about the flamboyant McCulloch.[11]

The fifty-three-year-old, Virginia-born Price had served with distinction at Santa Fe during the Mexican-American War, and as governor of Missouri in the middle 1850s. Not a graduate of West Point, he owed his success, in the words of a friendly correspondent, "to practical good sense and hard fighting."[12] Tall and well over two hundred pounds in weight, he had a grandfatherly look that earned him the nickname "Pap" Price.

Price had ten thousand Missourians at his back, but the legalistic Confederate president seemed to ignore them since the state had never officially joined the Confederacy. "Davis," Fletcher wrote, "never troubled to give him a chance."[13] No doubt the fact that Price had not attended the United States Military Academy colored Davis's attitude. To alumni of West Point, a "last in his class" Pickett rated higher than a "firstest with the mostest" Forrest. Davis also passed over Arkansas's great divisional commander, another non–West Pointer, Patrick Cleburne.

It is interesting to note that Kentucky-born Jefferson Davis had represented Mississippi in the Twenty-ninth U.S. Congress at the same time as Sterling Price, a native of Virginia, had represented his chosen state, Missouri. Both resigned their seats in 1846 to take part in the war with Mexico. Now Davis graced with his imperial presence the newly set up White House in Richmond, and Price camped in a tent in northern Arkansas, hoping to drive Curtis back and return to Missouri.

The Missourians wanted to push back toward their own state, but McCulloch refused to follow the enemy. That left the Missourians no alternative but to continue the gradual retreat. Price and McCulloch simply could not work things out.

Brigadier General McCulloch, a regular officer in the Confederate army and commander of the Southern forces in Arkansas, considered his rank superior to that of Major General Price, commander of the Missouri State Guard. To settle this states' rights dispute, Jefferson Davis violated his own states' rights theories and set up a new military department, the Trans-Mississippi District. The Confederate president placed Major General Earl Van Dorn, a native Mississippian and a grandnephew of President Andrew Jackson, in charge. Van Dorn had gone to Little Rock in late January and in early February had written Price, then still in Missouri. After a short stay in the Arkansas capital, the Mississippian made his headquarters in Pocahontas in the northeastern part of the state, far from the Missouri Confederates. He had his headquarters closer to St. Louis than Price did by at least one hundred miles. But if he wanted to get to the River City, he needed an army.

The flamboyant Van Dorn stood only two inches taller than Napoleon, but he outdistanced the brilliant Corsican in grandiose schemes. An excellent rider, he had charged gallantly through the Mexican War. But the Comanches he slaughtered in 1858 turned out to be at peace with the whites. And in north-western Arkansas, he would find no peaceful Yankees. Most of his conquests would come in boudoirs rather than on battlefields. In the end, an irate husband,

Right: General Van Dorn divided his forces in the face of an entrenched enemy and sent the First Missourians on an uncleared road around Pea Ridge.

not a Federal sharpshooter, would cut him down. Unfortunately, before that day Van Dorn led many Missourians to their graves, some in Arkansas and some, later on, in Mississippi, with no apparent gain from their sacrifices.

With Union general Ulysses S. Grant moving on Albert Sidney Johnston's Rebel forces protecting the Memphis to Chattanooga Railroad near the Tennessee-Mississippi border, Van Dorn planned to push his available forces toward St. Louis, the base for Federal operations in the West, and cut Grant's supply lines. Finally, in late February, Van Dorn left his post at Pocahontas in northeastern Arkansas and reached Price's men south of Fayetteville in the northwestern corner of the state in early March.

On Sunday, March 2, Father Bannon noted two events in his diary: "Said Mass in General Frost's tent. General Van Dorn arrived at 4 'clock."[14] As one reads on through Father Bannon's jottings, incidentally, one will find no close association with the Mississippian, such as the priest had with Generals Price, Frost, Little, and, later on, Bowen.[15] The normally hard-riding Van Dorn had come in a carriage with his mount tied behind. Even though he was an expert rider, he had jumped one time too many and fallen. It was not a good omen.

Van Dorn gave orders to march at sunrise on March 3 without baggage and with three days' rations.[16] Price's men marched eighteen miles to Fayetteville and camped without tents.[17] They moved at daylight on the following day beyond the mountains and camped in the woods.[18] Snow fell all that night.[19] On March 6, Confederate colonel Gates overtook men under Sigel's command. The Confederates captured one cannon and one ammunition wagon and took several prisoners. Curtis's men had scattered widely on a fifty-mile-wide line from the Oklahoma border to Huntsville, thirty miles east of Fayetteville. Now the Union general ordered all to unite near the Missouri border.

Sigel's rear guard delayed the Confederates while he moved his men, following Curtis's orders, to the appointed place on Sugar Creek. All of the previously scattered Federal troops concentrated there. The pursuing Confederates had been marching for three days on empty stomachs and, in many instances, on bare feet.

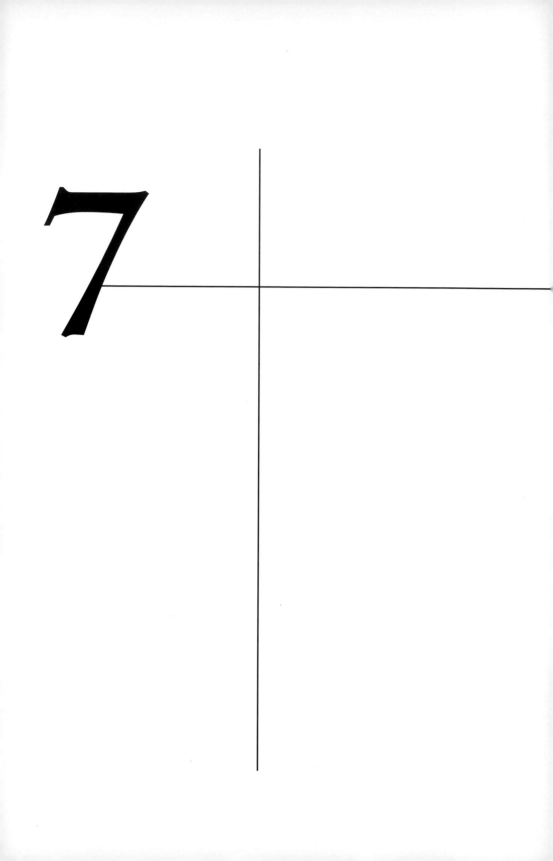

The Greatest Battle of the Trans-Mississippi

Curtis drew up his ten thousand men from northern Missouri, Iowa, Illinois, Indiana, Ohio, and the city of St. Louis on the north bank of Sugar Creek in northeastern Arkansas. Behind him a mile away was Pea Ridge, a large 150-foot-high ridge named for an abundance of peas that grew there. It curved northeast and then southeast for more than a mile. Its abrupt south side rose sheer in spots and sloped at others. Below the east end, along Telegraph Road, stood two-story Elkhorn Tavern.

Most of the St. Louisans were German immigrants under Brigadier General Franz Sigel. His regimental commanders were Colonel Peter Osterhaus, a fellow German immigrant, and a Hungarian, Colonel Alexander Asboth. Colonel Eugene Carr led the Third Illinois Cavalry, and the Third Division served under Colonel Davis of Indiana, whose parents, like their Kentucky cousins, had named their son for President Jefferson Davis.

Against these, Van Dorn had Price's Missourians, McCulloch's Arkansans and Texans, the Third Louisiana Infantry under Colonel Louis Hebert, and pro-Confederate Cherokee from Oklahoma under General Albert Pike. As the Federals dug in, Van Dorn decided to leave a token force building fires in front of the Union troops while the Missourians led the way across the creek and around Pea Ridge to attack the Union lines from the rear at dawn. The Texans, Arkansans, Louisianans, and Native Americans were to follow and come in from the northwest flank of the entrenched Union forces. It was a great plan. But Van Dorn had failed to scout the road. Had he done so, he'd have found that the Federals had already blocked the road in several places.

Father Bannon usually wrote one or two lines in his diary. To the events of March 7, however, he devoted thirty-eight lines, and to the following day thirty lines. When the Missourians set out, the chaplain rode with Generals Van Dorn

and Price, Colonel Henry Little, and Colonel John Q. Burbridge, a St. Louis banker whose regiment led the night march.

Father Bannon noted the many times felled ashes and poplars blocked the road. One occurred four hours into the march. The thick woods delayed Wade's guns. The next stop that Father Bannon recorded held the advance until 7 A.M. The Missourians finally rounded the ridge after the winter dawn, but met little resistance. The movement of the Confederates had presumably gone undetected. Price's men pushed on toward the Elkhorn Tavern. Victory seemed in sight.

But all the while, things were too quiet on the western front. Nothing happened until the afternoon. Then Pike's Cherokee attacked and captured an Illinois battery. Instead of advancing, the Indians war-danced joyfully around the conquered cannon, allowing the Illinois troops to regroup and drive Pike's men back.

Then double disaster struck. General McCulloch walked out of a grove of trees to survey the battlefield. His colorful uniform and flamboyant Texas headpiece caught the eye of Peter Pelican, an Illinois squirrel hunter. One shot rang out, and McCulloch fell. General James McIntosh, second in command, came toward the slain officer. Pelican shot again.

In the meantime, Union colonel Thomas Pattison outflanked the Louisiana troops and captured their leader, Colonel Louis Hebert. That left Pike the only leader on the Confederate west wing. Unfortunately, Van Dorn had not briefed

Facing Left: General Pike led his Cherokee into battle without a briefing on Van Dorn's strategic plan. During the fighting, he became the only surviving Confederate general west of Pea Ridge. Confusion followed, then disaster.
Facing Right: General Ben McCulloch led the Texans and Arkansans successfully at Wilson's Creek, but lost his life at Pea Ridge.
Right: Elkhorn Tavern, reached by the Missouri Confederates on the first day of the battle.

him as to his battle plan. Pike knew little of what was going on, or why it was going on.

On the other side of the distant field, the Missourians had marched all night and had been fighting from eight in the morning. They reached Elkhorn Tavern by four in the afternoon. Van Dorn made his headquarters there.

After seven and a half hours of fighting, the Confederates bivouacked on the field. Father Bannon met with General Frost and Colonel Little and then visited the wounded at Elkhorn Tavern. The battle on March 7 ended with both commanders uncertain. The Union officers did not appreciate the strength of their position and wanted to retreat. Curtis would not move.

The fight resumed at 7 A.M. with both sides giving their artillery the command to fire. The firing continued with varying intensity until 10 A.M.[1] To the trained ear of the Union commander, the Rebel fire sounded tentative. In truth it was. General Van Dorn had not brought along his supply train. Brigadier General Martin E. Green had gotten his wagon train within a mile of Elkhorn Tavern when he received orders to go to Elm Springs, a town twenty miles to the south and a little west.[2] The Southern gunners could fire only a few rounds near Elkhorn Tavern, and the exhausted and starving foot soldiers lacked the physical and mental strength to launch a new attack.

At this juncture, General Sigel, who had irritated Curtis by delaying on the previous day, now gave the Union commander reason to forget the past. The

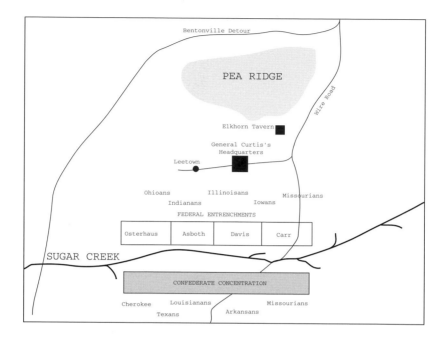

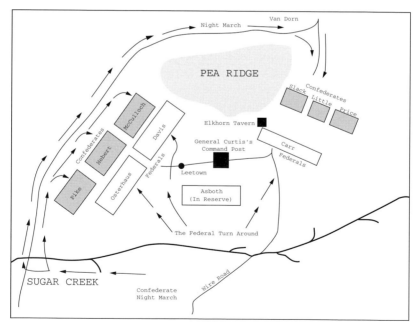

Top: Positions before the Battle of Pea Ridge, March 1862.
Bottom: The Battle of Pea Ridge, March 7–8, 1862.

German ordered his foot soldiers to lie prone on the ground while he moved his batteries several hundred feet ahead of them. They opened fire, smashing the Rebel batteries. Then he moved his infantry forward in a snakelike movement that seemed to come from Chief Crazy Horse rather than from General Von Clausewitz's manuals. As Sigel's men moved forward on the right, Curtis gave the signal to advance to Carr's Illinois troops on the left. They had borne the main thrust of General Price's men on the previous day. Now they had their moment. The Rebels fell back before the overwhelming advance.[3] By 11 A.M. the battle was over. Curtis had lost 10 percent of his force—203 dead, 980 wounded, and 201 missing—a total of 1,384 out of 10,000. The Confederate losses reached 8 percent. The killed and wounded numbered roughly 1,000. Approximately 300 were captured out of a force of 16,000.

The outcome had long been "touch and go." Curtis had lost a greater percentage of men but saved his army and Missouri for the Union. Van Dorn could not threaten Grant's rear and delay his sweep to the South.

When Father Bannon saw the batteries retire by the Bentonville Road, he rode east with the intention of joining General Price and Colonel Little. These officers had withdrawn with the left wing by another road. Instead, the chaplain fell in with Colonel Patton and moved on the presupposition that the Rebels held the roads ahead.

At this time he learned of the serious wounds of General William Slack and of a soldier named Charlie Peng. He baptized the latter and then went on to the home of a family by the name of Mitchell, where he and his comrades had supper. They slept that night in the woods by the Mitchell residence.[4] Thus ended the last day of Father Bannon's first battle. There would be more. But these would be far away from the border of southwest Missouri and northwestern Arkansas.

Left: The Confederates fire on the Union lines.

Reminiscing About Pea Ridge

A painting that hangs on the wall of the White House of the Confederacy in Richmond shows Father Bannon attending a wounded Confederate in front of Elkhorn Tavern during the first day of the Battle of Pea Ridge. The painter, Wilson Hunt, was the son of a prominent St. Louis fur trader, Wilson Price Hunt. Wilson Hunt left two memorials of the Battle of Pea Ridge, an account in writing and a painting of the battle around Elkhorn Tavern. Hunt does not mention Father Bannon in his account, but in the painting, he depicts the priest in the foreground, comforting a wounded soldier.[1]

In reminiscing about the Battle of Pea Ridge at a Confederate veterans' reunion in 1885, Colonel R. S. Musser closed with these remarks:

> I ought not to forget to mention the gallant and meritorious conduct of Father Bannon. . . . He had the general care of souls throughout the whole army. He was everywhere in the midst of battle when the fire was heaviest and the bullets thickest. He was armed with a tourniquet and a bottle of whiskey. Whenever there was a wounded or dying man, Father Bannon was at his side, supporting his head; with his tourniquet he staunched his blood flow, with the spirits he sustained his strength till his confession would be told, or if necessary, till he could baptize him from the waters of the nearest brook. . . . Father Bannon was an Irishman of splendid physique, full of grace and personal manliness, learned and eloquent, social and genial. . . .[2]

Father Bannon told the story of two men he met during and after the battle. One was an artilleryman who blundered into serious injury. Father Bannon called him "McGolfe," an unusual Irish name. That man's name may have been, in reality, James Gillespie. In a series of reminiscences of the Battle of Pea Ridge that appeared in the *Missouri Republican* at the time of a Missouri Confederate reunion in 1885, a contributor told an identical story of the circumstances of Gillespie's fatal injury.[3]

The former St. Louis pastor recalled his procedures the night before a battle and how enthusiastic the men were to go to confession and prepare their souls for whatever might happen. He wrote years later:

> I only remember two instances of men refusing to avail themselves of my services on an occasion such as I have described. The next morning an engagement took place, and we drove the enemy back a couple of miles. In this fight we had but two men killed, and these were precisely the two I spoke of as refusing my services the night before. By God's mercy, however, I was in time to give each of them absolution before their death. I will speak of these two cases in more detail.
>
> One of the men was named McGolfe, a dashing, rollicking fellow in the Artillery. He had been long from the Sacraments and was afraid of confession; and say what I would I could not prevail on him to come.
>
> "Come, man," I said, "I know what a soldier's confession is." And I went through the usual catalogue.

Above: The Missouri Confederates come down Telegraph Road to attack Union troops near Elkhorn Tavern.

"You have it all there, Sir," he replied.

"Well then, come and kneel down, and we will finish it off at once."

No, he would not; and as time was precious, I had to leave him, and attend to others. The next morning his battery was engaged; it was a battery of six guns, drawn up across a road, and was making excellent practice on the enemy. McGolfe's duty was that of rammer and sponger. He had just rammed a charge home when the gun next to his own was fired. The guns were rather nearer together than usual, and McGolfe mistook this discharge for that of his own gun. Running forward to sponge it, he had just brought the sponge to the muzzle when the gunner pulled the string. The rod was spun round with fearful violence upon the unfortunate man, broke both his arms and legs, and fractured his skull frightfully, the bone of the forehead being driven in more than an inch.

After the enemy were driven back, I came upon him lying in a barn, a horrible object, close to a Northern soldier, likewise mortally wounded. Strange to say, he was in his full senses, and kept roaring out, "take away this Yankee boy; I can't lie quiet here with this Yankee by me."

I went up and spoke to him; he knew my voice, but his sight was gone; and on my mentioning his confession to him, "Oh!" said he, "time enough for that. I'm not so bad as that goes to; I shall be right enough again in a day or two."

"No, McGolfe," I replied, "you are dying. Your skull is split open, and your legs and arms are smashed; you cannot live out the day, and you must prepare to meet God's judgment."

"Well, take away this Yankee; I can't make my confession with this Yankee close to me. He disturbs my mind; take him away!"

"Never mind the Yankee; attend to your own soul."

The Yankee, I found, was a poor German, who understood no English; so I induced McGolfe to make his confession at once. I then went to the German, and from the few words which I understood, I made out that the poor fellow was a Catholic, and recently enlisted. He was evidently in the best dispositions, kissed fervently the crucifix, which I held to him, and seemed intensely grateful at meeting with a Catholic Priest. I did therefore all I could for him, and went to see if any other cases wanted help. But before speaking of the second man, let me finish with McGolfe.

The next morning I was riding on to overtake the staff when I came upon an ambulance wagon.

"Whom have you got in there?" I asked.

"McGolfe," was the reply.

"What! is he still alive?" I exclaimed, and rode up to the wagon.

"Ah, Father Bannon, is that you?" called out McGolfe. "Come here til I shake hands with you!" The wretched man had neither hand nor foot that he could use. I was delighted to find him still sensible, for my heart rather misgave me about his treatment of the poor German, and I was apprehensive that his dispositions yesterday were not as good as they might have been. My delight was increased when McGolfe went on to say: "I can't help thinking of that poor Yankee. I behaved like a brute to him. He died last night, but after you left him he never stopped saying his prayers, and he prayed like a good one. He made me think, I can tell you. I'm just sorry for the way I treated him, and if you can give me any more penance for it, do. Now, if you'll stop by me, I'd like to make my confession again."

And he began to accuse himself out loud before all the men about, so that I expostulated with him, and told him to speak lower.

"No," he said, "I have been a bad man, and they all know it. I have given bad example, and I want to do some penance for it;" and he continued his confession at the top of his voice. When he had finished, I consoled him, telling him I should give him no penance, for he had done enough. I then gave him the last absolution, and in about an hour he was a corpse. On quitting McGolfe and the German the day before, I had directed my steps to where a surgeon was employed with some wounded men.

"Have you any here for me?" I asked.

"Yes," said the surgeon, pointing to one of the wounded. "I think he must be one of yours, for he is an Irishman."

I stooped down to the man and asked if he was a Catholic. He was; and of such a regiment, such a company. He was shot through the stomach, and the bullet had broken his spine. He had not long to live.

"Why," I said, "I was with your regiment last night, but I don't remember you. Were you with me, or how was it?"

"No, Father," he answered. "I knew you would be coming, and I watched to keep out of your way, for I did not wish to meet you."

"You unfortunate fellow!" I exclaimed; "do you see now how the devil deceived you; and how nearly he had you by the throat?"

"Indeed, I was a fool, Father; and I am sorry for it with all my heart."

He made a good end, poor fellow; and I was careful to take down his name and the address of his family in Ireland, as I always did in similar cases; for I knew how great a consolation it is to Irish fathers and mothers to hear from a priest that their child died well. He was the son of a small farmer in Meath, and his family had heard nothing of him for several years. . . . I sent a letter to his mother, as I did to some fifty or sixty others, telling her that her son had been mortally wounded at the battle of Elkhorn Tavern, that I had attended him at his last moments, and could give her the consolation of knowing that he died happily.[4]

In a public address many years later, Senator Champ Clark said he would like to see a novel about Missourians in the Civil War. He wondered what Robert Louis Stevenson or Arthur Conan Doyle could do with "Fighting Jo" Shelby, or Major Emory S. Foster and his mysterious band of Federal freelancers that never appeared on the Union muster rolls, or "Rock" Champion's daredevil hard-riders who charged an entire regiment of Federal troops to let Guibor's battery, "recruited mainly from among young St. Louisans with a large sprinkling of hard-fighting Irish in its make-up," get away from a flanked position. "I would like to see your true story-teller," he went on, "take such a character as that of Father Bannon, the Catholic Priest, who accompanied the artillerymen of Guibor's command . . . who joked and laughed with them in bivouac and went with them into action . . . and who prayed with the dying on the battlefield."[5]
Another veteran recalled:

A Catholic priest . . . accompanied Guibo's [*sic*] battery. His clerical robes were often seen where missiles of death fell thick and fast. His

Above: Curtis's Bluecoats camp along Sugar Creek, with Pea Ridge at their backs.

mission was to comfort the dying, and assist the wounded, and he never flinched once, but responded always with alacrity, and in the midst of carnage and the roar of battle his self-possessed, gentle and pleasing demeanor never left him.[6]

While not specifically referring to his actions at Pea Ridge, St. Louis historians William Hyde and Howard L. Conard wrote of a tribute to him. They stated:

> His influence, in a religious sense, was felt by all who associated with him, and his presence wherever he went repressed the rude manners of the camp. Not that he objected to gaiety and mirthful pleasure, for he had the most affable manners and genial nature, but he always frowned upon the soldiers' unrestrained expressions and rude jests.
>
> He was physically large, handsome, dignified, refined and cultured. While his mission was one of peace, he became noted for his bravery in the field in attending the wounded and dying in various exposed places. He was both a pious and practical man, and became a ministering angel wherever broken and bruised humanity needed help and consolation.[7]

Above: Father Bannon wore a beard during the conflict.

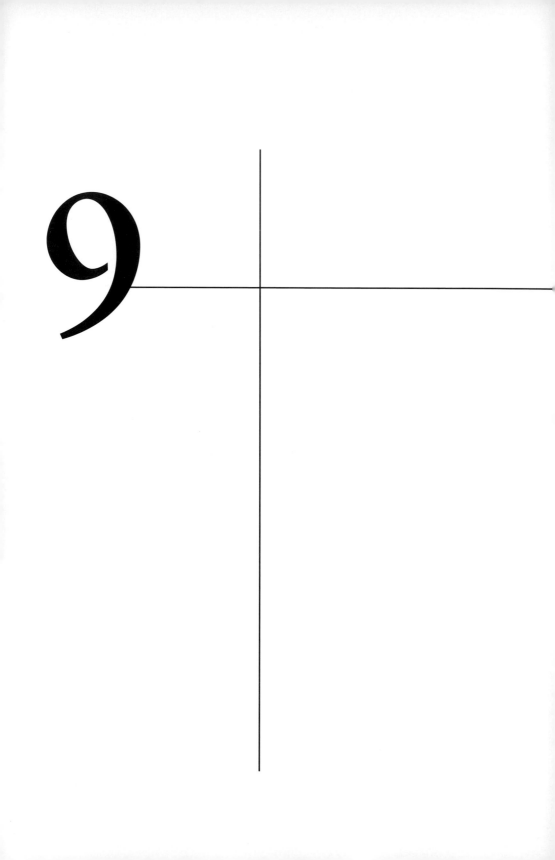

Changing Fronts

After the Battle of Pea Ridge, the Confederates split up, filtered through the mountains, and regrouped at Van Buren, near Fort Smith on the west-central border of Arkansas. Father Bannon celebrated St. Patrick's Day, March 17, with Father Patrick Riley, the vicar general of the Diocese of Little Rock.[1]

The Arkansas Catholic clergymen at the time numbered many natives of Ireland. Even the bishop of Little Rock, the Very Reverend Andrew Byrne, came from County Meath. Father Bannon did not note whether he had met Father Riley before. A sense of brotherhood had long existed among Catholic priests. This mutual acceptance was even stronger when both men shared a common homeland. No doubt Father Riley had many questions of Pea Ridge and the next stage of military action.

Several days later the chaplain joined the troops moving down the north bank of the Arkansas River past the Mulberry River toward Clarksville, roughly forty miles downstream. Gradually, as the army began to move, Wade's and Guibor's batteries provided the site for Sunday masses. The priest left his vestments and altar equipment in the care of Wade's men. While this gave Catholics in all units a focal point for Sunday services, it had at least one drawback. On Sunday, March 23, 1862, for instance, Father Bannon rode in the line of march ten miles ahead of Wade's men and had to cancel mass.[2]

On March 28, Father Bannon recorded in his diary that he swam in Piney Creek.[3] The troops then left the river and moved through the towns of Springfield and Greenbrier, forty miles north of Little Rock. Price's men slowly pushed their way along secondary roads through hilly country, without uniforms or sufficient equipment and with limited food supplies. In contrast, across the Mississippi, the well-equipped Bluecoats of General Grant—some of them

Missourians or former residents of Missouri as Grant himself was—brought all the supplies they needed up the Tennessee River in steamboats as they prepared to press the Confederates near the Mississippi border in southwestern Tennessee.

Father Bannon reached the capital of Arkansas on April 3.[4] Bishop Byrne had taken seriously ill and had gone to Helena, Arkansas. As a result, Father Bannon could not pay his respects to his fellow Irishman. But he did see Pastor Peter Clark and remained in the town several days. He offered Mass at the Convent of the Sisters of Mercy on April 4–5.[5] These nuns belonged to a congregation founded only a short time before in Ireland. They had come to America in 1851 to open an academy for girls.

The Confederates set up an emergency hospital in a brick building owned by the sisters, adjacent to the convent. Twenty-five wounded men moved in immediately. The history of the Sisters of Mercy states: "Owing in a large measure to the meager supply of rations and clothing allotted to the sick and wounded, the death rate was very high. Forty coffins, it is said, were the daily output of the coffin factory. . . ."[6] Father Bannon had seen the work of the Sisters of Mercy in St. Louis. This newly formed Irish religious community had not yet opened a hospital in St. Louis, but the nuns had worked in a variety of areas, including visiting the sick in their homes. Two Mercy nuns had nursed the wounded with an Irish regiment in the British army during the Crimean War (1854–56), then nursed the sick at a hospital in Cincinnati. Now these two Mercy nuns served with the Army of the Cumberland that the First Missouri Confederate Infantry was soon to face in northern Mississippi. Father Bannon visited the sick and wounded at the makeshift hospital and still had time to do needed shopping.[7]

From Little Rock it would not have been all downstream, even if they had had boats. The Arkansas River flowed to the southeast, while the troops were heading for Memphis a little north of due east. In his diary the priest wrote of swamps, submerged horses, and rain all day on April 9.[8]

After slogging through rainy Arkansas, Father Bannon and the western army finally reached Memphis at 2 P.M. on a damp and cloudy Friday morning, April 11,[9] four days after the bloody Confederate defeat at Shiloh in southern Tennessee. The next day the tired and wet Rebels boarded the Memphis and Charleston Railroad cars and started for Corinth, Mississippi.[10] They arrived at Corinth at 5 P.M. on April 13.[11]

Rightly, the strategic rail center of Corinth in northeastern Mississippi, four miles from the Tennessee border, had become a prize sought by both armies,[12] still powerful but shaken by the shocking casualty lists at Shiloh. At Corinth, the railroad, coming south from Chicago through Cairo, Illinois, and Jackson, Tennessee, and going on past Corinth through Meridian, Mississippi, to Mobile, Alabama, on to the Gulf of Mexico, crossed the line east from Memphis to

Chattanooga, Tennessee. At that point one branch went northeast through the Cumberland Gap to Richmond, Virginia, the capital of the Confederacy. Another swung southeast to Atlanta, Georgia, then east through Augusta to Charleston, South Carolina, or through Macon to Savannah, Georgia.

The value to the Confederacy of holding Corinth would become dramatically clear at the end of 1862, when Jefferson Davis decided to visit the state where he had his plantation. After inspecting troops in southeastern Tennessee, he had to follow a roundabout way, because the Federals occupied Corinth.[13] It would be even more significant in June 1863, when some Southerners wanted divisions of the Army of Northern Virginia to come west and try to relieve the siege of Vicksburg. The Federals' grip on Corinth cut the most direct route south and west from Richmond. Instead of sending General Longstreet to hit Grant's forces in the rear, Lee would gamble all on an invasion of the north.

While Corinth was strategic for ultimate victory or defeat in the war, the countryside in southwestern Tennessee and northern Mississippi hardly lent itself to successful military movements in force. Dense forest covered the region. The marshy and soft soil stretched away in gentle rolling hills. Small, sluggish creeks abounded in the area, but their water was unfit for drinking purposes. Nature had not intended the area to welcome more than 150,000 able-bodied men, much less the many thousands of Confederate veterans wounded a short time before at the bloody battle at Shiloh Church.

Appropriately, Father Bannon mentioned the Sisters of Charity of St. Vincent de Paul first in his diary on the day of his arrival.[14] Corinth was more than a town under siege. It groaned under the endless wounded who had rolled in from Shiloh. To add to the eight out of every ten amputees who were dying from tetanus, shock, or other aftereffects of the surgery, the sick jammed the railroad station, hotel, residences, and stores in numbers that would have challenged a city like New Orleans or Memphis. To add to the horrors, lack or ignorance of sanitary precautions had contaminated the water supply. Dysentery, typhoid fever, and measles soared toward epidemic proportions. With the arrival of the Trans-Mississippi troops, the Confederates had eighteen thousand sick.[15]

To compound the health-care problems on both sides of the battle line, the country had only six hundred trained nurses at the start of the Civil War. All were Catholic nuns. This has been one of the best-kept secrets in our nation's history. The prevailing attitude among American people, North and South, had been that a woman nursed only the sick in her own family home.

The Confederate government had repeatedly asked nursing help of the Sisters of Charity, who ran Charity Hospital in New Orleans. The mother superior sent out several teams, one of them to Pensacola, Florida, another to the military hospital at Holly Springs, Mississippi. When the Federals took Pensacola, the sisters moved to Corinth, Mississippi, shortly after the Battle of Shiloh. Sister Regina Smith, the leader of this team, wrote to the mother superior of terrifying numbers of wounded and dying. At the same time, Sisters Cyril Ward, Philomena Pitcher, and Jeanette Murrin at the military hospital in Holly Springs came the thirty miles east to Corinth to take care of Confederate wounded and Northern prisoners.[16] Father Bannon had been aware of the work of the Sisters of Charity at the Mullanphy Hospital in St. Louis, and he knew the high regard the people of St. Louis had held for them.

"In the Confederate Army," Father Bannon stated, ". . . any religious community who chose to volunteer for the work (and there was not a Congregation that did not send its quota), had transport, lodging, and rations supplied to it by the Government, with a chaplain for the sisters. Some had the care of stationary hospitals; others followed the different armies in charge of the camp hospitals." [17]

As in all aspects of wartime life, the actual living conditions of the nun-nurses did not always match the stated policy of the government. But the nun-nurses in the Confederacy did not have to put up with the prejudgment of Dorothea Dix, director of the Federal Nurse Program, who had little understanding and less appreciation of the life and dedication of the sisters serving with the Northern armies.

Father Bannon had some astounding recollections of the religious influence of the nun-nurses. "More than eighty percent of the Protestants who entered the Sisters' hospitals became Catholic," he wrote. "And scarcely a man died among them who they did not win over before his death. Their tender care and charity was the talk of the Army: the soldiers swore by them, so to speak and no man who had been to one of their hospitals, would willingly go to another."[18]

Father Bannon then related scenes he witnessed that bear out these words:

> A soldier ill, or wounded, but able to walk, would come and hand his billet to the Sister in charge:
>
> "But this billet is not for our hospital," said the Sister.
>
> "Oh, now, look here, Sister! I'm not going to any other place. I'm going to stop here."
>
> "Well, but there is not room for you."
>
> "There's room in the passage," was the reply, "and I won't give any trouble, indeed."
>
> And the man would spread his blanket in the corridor, or by the door, and lie down; well knowing that he would not be turned away. I have seen the corridors so full, that it was difficult to make one's way along, without treading on the men. They looked on the Sisters almost as superior beings, and it is something incredible how they submitted their will and

their reason to them,—these men who from their cradles had been reared in intellectual pride and spiritual independence. The way in which they swore by what the Sisters said cannot be better illustrated than by the following incident.

One of Sisters told me one day that she had a patient willing to become a Catholic, that she had given him some instruction, but that it would be better if I would see him at once. I went to his bed-side, and after a few introductory questions, I asked if he had ever professed any religion.

"No," he said, "I have not: but I have made arrangements about that now; I have settled it all with the Sister."

"Quite right," I replied, "but it will be well for me to have a little talk with you."

Above: Because of the excessive casualties at Shiloh, the midwestern governors temporarily "un-horsed" General Grant in 1862.

"Now, I tell you what it is, Mister," replied the patient, "it's no use any of you coming talking to me. I belong to the Sisters' religion, and that's enough."

"Exactly, and so do I. I am a Priest of their religion,—the Catholic religion: and I have come to see what I can do for you."

He would not however be satisfied until he had called the Sister and learnt from her that all was right and proper. While I was instructing him, something or other I told him seemed too much for his good will.

"Oh, come now," he said, "you don't expect me to believe that!"

"Yes," I said, "that is what the Catholic Church teaches, and we are bound to believe it."

"Well," he replied, "we'll see. Here, Sister!"

The Sister came, and the patient addressing her said, "Sister, this man tells me so and so. Is that true?"

"Oh yes," said the Sister smiling; "quite true."

"Do you believe it, Sister?"

"Yes certainly; we all believe it."

"Very well," he said, turning to me, "all right, I believe it. Go a-head, Mister; what next?"

The man's language may seem flippant and off-hand; but he was thoroughly in earnest, and received everything I told him: it was however necessary to make a few appeals to the Sister now and then, and when she confirmed what I said, he accepted it at once and finally. He only remarked once, "He says some very hard things, Sister!" But he took all the hard things in directly he had the Sister's word. In the end I baptized him; though it might be said perhaps to be rather in *fidem Sororum*, than *fidem Ecclesiae* (in the faith of the Sisters rather than in the faith of the church).[19]

While the sisters, doctors, and their trained and untrained coworkers were caring for the wounded and ill, fifty thousand able-bodied Confederates were facing twice that many well-fed, well-shod, and generally well-equipped Bluecoats. Steamboats had taken many of the Union wounded down the Tennessee River to the Ohio and up the Mississippi to well-established or newly opened hospitals in St. Louis. If the Confederates were to hold anywhere west of Chattanooga, they had to do it at the giant infirmary that was Corinth.

Both of the armies facing each other on the Tennessee-Mississippi border had lost their commanders. The Confederate general Albert Sidney Johnston had bled to death from a wound on the first day of the Battle of Shiloh, and General Pierre Beauregard, victor at Bull Run, took charge. Grant had driven the Confederates back, and he survived the carnage but not the onus of having lost

Above: With General Halleck so cautious, General Pierre Beauregard was able to pull his troops safely out of Corinth.

Left: Like McClellan before Richmond, General Henry Halleck vastly overestimated the size of the Confederate forces at Corinth and hesitated to attack.
Facing: The Missouri Confederates retreat from Corinth.

10,162 killed or wounded. Of the 100,000 men engaged in this first great blood-letting of the war, one out of four had been killed, wounded, or captured. Only President Lincoln's support kept Grant anywhere near the top. The aura that his victory at Fort Donaldson had given him was now gone.

General Henry W. Halleck, head of the Department of the Mississippi, put General George Thomas in charge of the veterans of Shiloh, made Grant his assistant commander with a fine title and little power, and took personal charge of front-line operations. The hesitant Halleck believed the rumor that 200,000 men defended the northern Mississippi town of Corinth.[20]

As historian Shelby Foote has observed, 200,000 of anything, even rabbits, seems formidable. As a result, Halleck moved cautiously, with a great amount of digging and trenching.[21] This was the situation when the Army of the Trans-Mississippi reached Mississippi.

The First Missouri Brigade received orders to bivouac at Rienzi, about ten miles south of Corinth on the Natchez Trace. Father Bannon accepted Colonel Little's invitation to quarter with his staff. On the road through pine forests

drenched in rain, the chaplain's horse fell while crossing a creek and gave the priest a rude dunking. This event brought comment in the diaries of both Bannon and Little. The former jotted. "Crossing the creek—went under—horse fell."[22] "The Chaplain," Colonel Little wrote, "having tried to swim at Corinth had to stop and dry."[23]

Shortly after Father Bannon offered Mass at Corinth on April 15, two prominent Catholic clergymen came to visit the sick and wounded—the Very Reverend John Quinlan, bishop of Mobile, and Father Patrick Coyle, vicar general of the Diocese of Mobile and pastor in Pensacola, Florida, a city in the Alabama jurisdiction. Early the following year, incidentally, the thirty-four-year-old bishop, a native of County Cork in Ireland, would write to Stephen Mallory, secretary of the Confederate navy, the only Catholic in Davis's cabinet, in a successful effort to clarify Father Bannon's service status.[24] The bishop's companion, Father Coyle, had just completed a six-month tour of duty as chaplain of the Third Florida Regiment. His path would cross that of the Missouri chaplain regularly in the next few weeks.

After reaching the Rienzi encampment, the chaplain, who now wore a dark beard, talked a local businessman by the name of Bennet into making available his warehouse for religious use. Bannon turned the storehouse into a church, offering the Catholic soldiers a welcomed refuge. Colonel Little assisted by issuing circulars to the troops announcing the opening of the "new St. John" church.[25]

With disease striking great numbers of unacclimated Missouri soldiers, the already-taxed emergency hospitals soon overflowed with newcomers.[26] Father Bannon spent much of his time giving the last rites and conducting funerals for those killed by malaria, diarrhea, and pneumonia.[27]

Father Bannon had a disappointing Holy Thursday. His circulars announcing the time and place of the services had not reached the men. As a result he had no congregation.[28] That afternoon he rode with Colonel Little and Captain Schaumburg to the old town looking for a parade ground. By the time they returned, Colonel Little received orders from General Beauregard to prepare camp for twenty-five thousand men. "Colonel B and 6 regiments of Mississippi Infantry arrived that night."[29]

Before the quest for camping space was over, Little, Captain Petry, and the chaplain had ridden twenty-five miles to look for a campground. Rain and thunder marked that Good Friday. Colonel Little sent out circulars announcing the vespers service. But the storm kept the attendance down to thirty or forty. Father Bannon preached on "redemption."[30]

Rain continued over the days of the great religious feasts, keeping Catholics from their Easter duties of confession and communion and holding down attendance. With the return of the sun on April 22, Bennet, who had allowed Father Bannon to use his empty warehouse for religious services, now filled his building with cotton bales.[31] The priest had to look elsewhere.

Throughout those April days of checkered shade and sunshine, the Missourians moved back and forth from Rienzi to Corinth. Father Bannon looked in vain for a building to serve as a chapel but went back to Wade's battery on April 27.[32] He would suffer recurring headaches during these days, one on April 28,[33] a bad one on May 9,[34] and another on June 2.[35]

General Henry Halleck's huge Union army cautiously eyed the troops of General Beauregard throughout the spring. But the anticipated battle for Corinth still had not come. During the stalemate, rumors, right and wrong, filtered in from other fronts. On April 26, Father Bannon had recorded a report that, two days before, two Federal gunboats had passed Fort Jackson and approached New Orleans.[36] The truth was more deadly. Farragut had run the fort with twenty-seven ships and fifteen thousand foot soldiers and would soon take the largest city of the Confederacy.

Four days later, the rumors overreached reality. Forty-five thousand Federal troops allegedly had been trapped and captured at Yorktown, but General Lee had been killed.[37] It was true that Union general George McClellan had put that many troops in the vicinity of Yorktown, but they had not done enough by the last day of April to merit capture. And by mid-June, the still much alive Lee would take command of the Confederate forces facing McClellan's mighty army and drive him back up the peninsula between the James and York Rivers east of Richmond.

On April 28, Bannon took the hour-and-a-half journey to Corinth and visited the sisters' "hospital." Afterward he shared supper with Father Coyle.[38] The following day he visited General John B. Bowen's camp.[39] The chaplain had been with Bowen and General Frost on the southwestern expedition to the Kansas border in the late fall of 1860. But at the outbreak of hostilities, the Carondelet architect had been assigned to Albert Sidney Johnston's command. He was one of the wounded at Shiloh who survived. Father Bannon met several friends at Bowen's camp, among them Scott Elder and Henry Ivory. He also met a colonel with the unusual name of Belzoover—if the priest heard and spelled correctly—who had been a professor of mathematics at St. Mary's College in Emmitsburg, Maryland. Because of the rain, the chaplain did not return to his own quarters, but stayed at Father Coyle's that night.[40]

On the last day of April, Father Bannon took the eight o'clock train back to Rienzi. He received a donation of $430 from Catholics in "St. Digit"—wherever that was.[41] He noted a $60 donation May 1[42] and a $50 gift on May 3. At last he could catch up financially.[43] Captain Patrick Coniff went to the battery to arrange for Mass on May 4.[44]

In the meantime, on the Corinth front, now–Brigadier General Henry Little took sick on May 5 and went to the hospital the following day. By May 7, he felt better and slowly recovered. Father Bannon visited him regularly, as well as other patients. Hospital visits, work with the brigade, and baptisms kept the chaplain up all night regularly during these early May days. On May 9, he himself had a bad headache.[45] Before the headache put him on short bounds, the priest baptized Colonel McRae[46] and another officer identified only as "Colonel P."[47] Presumably he referred to Colonel Pritchard. At least once during the following months the chaplain would preach at that officer's headquarters.[48]

Three companies of the First Missouri Brigade went into action on May 9, taking three hundred prisoners and large quantities of arms and supplies. Among the captured stores, Father Bannon singled out "blankets."[49] Several other times during May, the Federals in northern Mississippi probed the Southern lines, and Price's men rushed forward to reinforce Corinth. As one might expect, each time the men went to the front, the Missouri chaplain accompanied them and recorded the operation in his diary.[50]

Beauregard knew that he could not hold off for long the overwhelming number of Bluecoats facing his battle line just north of Corinth. But he could keep some of his units alert and mobile to strike at sections of the enemy who moved into untenable positions. Federal general John Pope was the first to reach such a position near Farmington, six miles east of Corinth. Bragg hit the Union troops head on, while Van Dorn swept in from the flank. Bragg's men did their part, but Van Dorn got confused in the tangled countryside. John Pope escaped. In the long run, that success would prove unfortunate for Pope. Had he been badly defeated, he would probably not have been in charge of the Union troops who had to face Lee and Jackson at Second Bull Run that August.

After the Confederates' fruitless effort at Farmington, Father Bannon took the train with General Little's staff to Prairie Station, Mississippi. He left them there and went on to Mobile.[51] He purchased needed supplies and went back to Corinth in time for the total evacuation of the key rail city. It was a masterpiece of escape on Beauregard's part. He told his infantrymen to prepare to attack. As a result, a few men, fed up with dodging Yankee lead, surrendered to the enemy and told of the coming attack.

All the while, the move was steadily south. The ill and wounded went first, then the artillery, then Forrest's cavalry. As the infantrymen began to move out, bands marched up and down behind the trenches, and the last few soldiers erected dummy guns and set straw men in ragged gray outfits. One train moved in and out of town, while the same small group of veterans cheered the arrival of imaginary reinforcements. The Bluecoats steeled themselves for a frightening yell and swarm of fierce attackers.

They heard no Rebel yell. They faced no charging Rebels. In the ensuing days the frustrated Halleck, bereft of a major victory in battle, sent out papers of a great Confederate defeat. This brought only ridicule and clouded the fact that the Federal troops had cut a main Confederate lifeline, while suffering few casualties.

South of town, the First Missouri Confederate Brigade defended the rear of the retreating army. Father Bannon had noted earlier in the month that General Dabney Maury had taken command.[52] Now Maury moved a step higher to take command of General Samuel Jones's division.

While Maury commanded the rear guard during the retreat from Corinth, he had an interesting meeting with Father Bannon. He told about it in his *Recollections*. Like Price, the forty-year-old Maury had been born in Virginia and served in the Mexican War. But while Price entered civilian life, Maury stayed in uniform. He taught at West Point and served in the West until the firing on Fort Sumter. He had been with Price at Pea Ridge.

At 11 one night during retreat from Corinth, Maury slept on his saddle blanket under a bush. A horseman rode up. He had orders for General Maury to turn over the rear guard to the next officer in charge and to assume command of the First Division and march punctually at 2 A.M. It was the general's third successive night without sleep.

Maury wrote:

> The good and great Father O'Bannon [sic], Chaplain to Price's Missourians, was near me. He promptly said, 'General, you are very tired; take a drop of the 'cratur'; twill do you good and then you can get a nap til half-past one.' The good Father never drank a drop himself, but was indefatigable in his care for the wounded and wearied people, and always carried into battle a quart canteen full of good whiskey.[53]

By that time, Father Bannon had developed his own battlefield procedures. He described them in this way:

> As I was attached to the staff, I always had early notice of an intended battle sometimes as much as a fortnight beforehand. My practice then was to go round to each regiment over which I had supervision and, addressing every Catholic soldier, either satisfy myself that he had gone to his duties, or hear his confession myself. In the Southern armies there were many regiments entirely Catholic, and probably there were none without a greater or smaller number of Catholics in them. After thus making sure of each man, I would begin another round on the eve of the expected battle; taking those first who would be first engaged, the light troops and skirmishers.
>
> I would go up to a watch-fire, and waking one of the men, call him aside, hear his confession, and send him to summon others. The whole night would be spent thus in going from fire to fire. The men were always willing to come, generally too glad of the opportunity: some would even be watching for me. After the light troops, it was the turn of the heavy artillery, of whom about half the men were Catholics. Then as the day dawned and the troops were drawn out, I would go along the line, and hear the men as they stood in the ranks, and when the time came for advancing, I made a sign for them all to kneel, and gave them absolution *in globo*. I then went to the second line, or the reserve, till it was their turn to advance.
>
> The Catholic chaplains were much respected by all the men, whether Catholic or not. . . .[54]

At veterans' reunions after the war, officers and foot soldiers alike would recall Father Bannon's presence on the battlefield. The recollection of the routines he followed jibed with theirs.

One of the many Confederate veterans who looked back at the memory of Father Bannon with appreciation, Captain Joseph Boyce of St. Louis, described the chaplain's attitude on the battlefield. "Frequently," Boyce stated, "[Father Bannon] would be urged to go to the hospital during the time of battle. But he replied, 'I can attend there later. I must attend now to those who are not able to be removed from the field.'"[55] When asked if he was afraid during the battle, Father Bannon replied: "Certainly not. I am doing God's work."[56]

Captain Boyce recalled that General Price remarked, "I have no hesitancy in saying that the greatest soldier I ever saw was Father Bannon. In the midst of the fray he would step in and take up a fallen soldier. If he were a Catholic he would give him the rites of the church; if a Protestant, and if he so desired, he would baptize him."[57]

There would be similar remarks from other men after other battles. A Northern Jesuit chaplain, Father Peter Tissot, had different experiences and a different attitude toward the work of a chaplain on the battlefield. A native of Savoy, a province of Italy when he was born but part of France by the time of the Civil War, he was procurator at Fordham College in New York before the war. He became chaplain of the "Irish Rifles," the Thirty-seventh New York State Volunteers, in June 1861.

In his diary for April 5, 1862, during the Peninsular campaign, Tissot wrote:

> We often read of chaplains flying about on the battlefield from one wounded man to another through the thickest of the fight. I doubt whether it was ever done; at all events it should never be done. It is customary at the beginning of a battle for surgeons to choose a place—a house, if there be one, or a cluster of trees, where they hoist a red flag to show that it is a hospital, where the wounded are gathered. It is an understood thing that the guns of both armies respect the red flag. That is the post of the chaplain. He would expose himself as little as possible. If he does expose himself he may be of service to a few—which is doubtful—but if in so doing he is killed, he will deprive numbers of others of his services after the battle. . . .
>
> My experience has taught me that there is not much good to be done the day of a battle. Most of the wounded are left scattered on the field. Even when they are gathered in one place the first thing they want is a nurse or surgeon, someone to attend to their wounds. Then they are generally packed so close, especially if it be in a room, that it is out of the question to hear a confession, independently of the din, shouts, yells, "Confusion worse confounded." It may be easier in an army wholly Catholic, where the chaplain wears a cassock and is recognized by all at once. There is a better chance of doing good after the battle, when the wounded are distributed in houses or tents. The place for a chaplain to do good is in the camp. If he does no good there, he had better stay at home.[58]

Both Bannon and Tissot talked from experience. Both were born elsewhere, but Bannon had an advantage in that English was his native tongue and that many of the men were of his nationality. Tissot had been in North America for a longer period of time, but much of it had been in the Jesuit seminary in Canada. Further, few of Tissot's men were French; most were Irish. Bannon had been with his men before the war. He knew many of them—some were his own parishioners.

Tissot dealt with larger numbers of men. While regimental strength might have been the same, Bannon's first battle had seen fewer than twenty-five thousand men engaged on both sides. In the Peninsular campaign, the Southern army was over twice that large and McClellan had four times that many men advancing toward Richmond. Further, Bannon had a visible place in the line of battle, near Wade's and Guibor's batteries.

10

Iuka and Second Corinth

The giant Federal army dispersed after the conquest of Corinth. Price's Southerners, meanwhile, retired fifty miles farther south along the Natchez Trace to the Tupelo, Mississippi, area.[1] Once again, a calm settled over the western theater that would last most of the summer. But this period proved a busy one for Father Bannon—visiting hospitals, saying Mass, giving sermons, and conducting funerals.[2] One unpleasant chore on July 13 consisted of seeing to the spiritual needs of a soldier in the Second Tennessee condemned to death for desertion.[3]

General Braxton Bragg had ordered Price to harass the Federals in northern Mississippi. Van Dorn, not under Bragg, planned to raid through western Tennessee, bypass Memphis, and drive for Paducah, Kentucky. He wanted Price to go with him. Price wisely declined. Van Dorn appealed to President Davis to assert his superior rank. Van Dorn got what he wanted, recognition of his superior rank. But the Missourian had already moved on his own, following Bragg's recommendations, in early September.

Price seized an opportunity to strike General William Rosecrans's isolated forces at Iuka, Mississippi, near the Alabama border, on the rail line twenty-four miles east and a little south of Corinth.[4] On the night of September 13, Father Bannon sensed the impending engagement: "Three miles from Iuka—troops ordered out at 5 P.M."[5] Price had ordered a night attack to take Iuka by surprise. Rosecrans sensed the impending movement, abandoned the supply depot at Iuka, and withdrew.

After overrunning the town, the half-starved Rebels feasted on Federal plenty. The priest joined in the fun, explaining how we got "our share of the plunder." He must have missed seasoning on the fare at General Little's mess more than anything else. He listed "mustard, catsup and vinegar" as well as "carrots and pickles" among the captured "treasures."[6]

Above: Missouri Confederates move toward Iuka east of Corinth.

Grant, now in charge of the entire Federal operation in the West, moved his headquarters to Burnsville, Mississippi, halfway between Corinth and Iuka. He sent General E. O. Ord with two divisions to strike the Confederates from the northwest while Rosecrans hit them from the southeast. Before the Federals sprung the trap, however, Grant told Ord to notify the Confederates under a flag of truce that the Union forces had destroyed the Army of Northern Virginia on September 17, the day before, at Antietam Creek in Maryland. General Grant suggested that to avoid useless bloodshed he would accept the Confederate surrender. Price answered that he believed Lee's army could still fight.[7]

The battle would go on. Grant ordered Ord to halt his troops four miles from Iuka until he should hear firing from Rosecrans's men on south of the town. Sensing that Ord was not going to advance immediately, Price shifted his main forces to the south. Rosecrans had called Price "an old woodpecker"—an expression that meant "a cautious old bird who would not be surprised." The "old woodpecker" would get his men out to the southwest on September 19.[8]

Two miles southwest of Iuka, Little rallied his troops against a fierce Union attack. While he conferred with Price, a minié ball struck him in the forehead. Little fell dead. In the meantime, Father Bannon was on his way "out to the field with a canteen of water for General L[ittle],"[9] as he recorded in his diary that night. On the way he met Captain John Kelly, one of Little's staff, with the ambulance that bore the body of the general.[10] Kelly told Father Bannon what had happened, and the priest brought the remains back to Iuka.[11]

Price ordered the town evacuated on the night of September 19. While the sounds of creaking wagons, braying mules, and marching feet echoed from the road, Father Bannon hurriedly conducted the solemn burial ceremony for General Little. In a small garden behind the Converses' house, which had been Little's headquarters, the chaplain held services by torch and candlelight. The priest's last words about the popular commander affected all present.

Years later, St. Louis historians William Hyde and Howard L. Conard would recount the chaplain's message as hearers had recalled it for them: "Father Bannon made the oration and in a feeling manner spoke of the character and virtues of the dead General, not, as he said, in the capacity of a priest, for he was not of his [the general's] church, but as a warm admirer and friend."[12]

The historians then painted a vivid picture: "The intense darkness of the night, the dim flame of the torches, the bowed and uncovered heads of the dis-

Right: Father Bannon held graveside services for General Henry Little.

tinguished group of officers, and the touching words of the speaker, made an impressive and weird scene, that will remain in the memory of those who witnessed it."[13] Weary Confederates soon pushed southward down the Fulton Road throughout the night, slipping out of Iuka to safety.

Southern strategists had only begun to set plans in motion. They ordered Price's army of the West to link with Van Dorn's army for a combined strike on Corinth before the end of September.[14] A disappointed Father Bannon recorded in his diary on Sunday, September 28, how there would be "no Mass [for] we would march today to unite with Van Dorn."[15]

Price moved his troops westward, Van Dorn pushed his to the east, and they combined at Ripley, about twenty miles southwest of Corinth. Van Dorn had one division under Mansfield Lovell, an excellent horseman. Just as Van Dorn wanted to make up for his defeat at Elkhorn Tavern, Lovell had to try to make the South forget that he had failed to hold the Bluecoats out of New Orleans, the city President Davis had sent him to defend. Given the casual spirit of the people there and the limited trained manpower at Lovell's disposal, one wonders if Robert E. Lee or Andrew Jackson himself could have held the city. But now Lovell saw his chance, as did Van Dorn. Two veterans were present, General Dabney Maury, whose rise to the head of the division has already been noted, and General Louis Hebert, a clean-shaven Louisianan. This veteran of Pea Ridge, with the broad forehead of an Indian chief, recently had taken Little's place.

The two commands would move north along the west bank of the Hatchie River, presumably to threaten Bolivar, Tennessee, where General S. A. Hurlburt held Grant's reserve force. When the Rebels had marched thirty miles to reach the Memphis and Charleston Railroad at Pocahontas, just across the Tennessee line, however, they would swing east and south to Corinth. Once Van Dorn had cracked the linchpin of Federal defenses in northern Mississippi, he could move at will on Memphis or follow his earlier plan of pushing on to St. Louis.

Only a dreamer like Van Dorn could have imagined that three divisions of soldiers could have pushed their way through thirty miles of woods, along a one-way road, without alerting the enemy. About halfway to Corinth from Pocahontas, the Rebels clearly knew that Rosecrans was ready for them. The element of surprise was totally lacking. The wily Ohioan actually had consolidated his forces at Corinth in readiness to aid Hurlburt if needed. Grant had gone to St. Louis to confer with General Samuel Curtis, the Confederates' nemesis at Pea Ridge. In Mississippi Rosecrans stood ready for Van Dorn and Price behind fortifications actually constructed by the Confederates under Beauregard after the Battle of Shiloh. Even Van Dorn had had his part in preparing these fortifications.

With the dread hour of attack approaching, many soldiers gave serious thought to the hereafter. Father Bannon baptized Clay Taylor and a number of soldiers in a creek. The water may not have been good for drinking but it could symbolically indicate spiritual health. On October 3, the Confederates probed the city's outer defenses. That night the chaplain led prayers in the dark, piney woods for former friends killed in action.

While the soldiers slept, Father Bannon toured the front lines and skirmish positions, heard confessions, and instilled hope in men who might meet their Maker with the sunrise. Indeed, the clergyman had quite a mission to fulfill. Almost five hundred of the Missouri Brigade would shortly become casualties on that October day when the temperature rose to ninety-four degrees. Indian summer had become July-like. Father Bannon wrote in his diary of the start of the battle in the predawn hours of October 4: "We were assailed with artillery at 4 1/2 o'clock in the morning—24-pound shells passed us for 2 hours."[16]

The crescent-shaped Union line stretched for a mile and a half at the crest of a gently sloping hill, covering the northern and western approaches to the town. On the outside of the crescent Van Dorn and Price were to attack simultaneously. Whether he had planned it that way or not, Price's attackers went forward in the shape of a wedge. As the Butternut column swept forward, volley after volley of grape, canister, and shell tore gaps in the formation.

Right: Father Bannon baptized Colonel Clay Taylor before the Second Battle of Corinth.

The Confederate charge captured a parrot gun called the Lady Richardson a few minutes after it had cut down Lieutenant Sam Farrington of Wade's battery. Father Bannon carried Farrington's body to a quiet place of interment. The body later was taken by his relatives to Bellefontaine Cemetery in St. Louis.[17]

In spite of desperate resistance, the Union center gave way. Price's men drove their opponents back and stormed into the town square. Union general Jeremiah C. Sullivan sent forward his unit stationed in the town and drove Price's spearhead back from the town square. Federal reinforcements converged and drove hard against the Confederate left. Federal artillery went back into action. By 1 P.M. the fight on the Federal right was over.

The Missourians' attack had been underway for a half-hour before Van Dorn finally unleashed his troops. Nonetheless, under Colonel W. P. Rogers of Maury's division, the Second Texas Regiment led the Rebels well into the defensive positions at Battery Williams and Battery Robinett. But the lack of proper timing between Van Dorn's and Price's attack proved fatal. One of the Federal officers defending Corinth was the one-armed Lieutenant Thomas W. Sweeny, who had held the arsenal in St. Louis against threats of some of the men facing him that day. He eventually became a major general.

Had the two prongs of the Confederate Army hit the Union lines at the same time, as Van Dorn had agreed to do, they might have swept the Union

Right: With Lieutenant Tom Sweeny, a one-armed veteran of the Mexican War, in charge of the arsenal, who needed Captain Nathaniel Lyon? Sweeny rose to the rank of major general, fought at Corinth, and marched with Sherman to the sea.
Facing: Confederates move toward the Union lines at the Second Battle of Corinth.

defenders back through the town. But the Confederate pressures came at varied times, allowing the Union reserve troops to move wherever needed. An Ohio brigade and the Eleventh Missouri Federals came up to throw volley after volley into the Texans' front line. A ghastly photograph taken a day after the battle and before a mass burial shows the body of Colonel Rogers and many of his brave men in front of the parapet. When Rogers fell, the battle was over. Rosecrans's Federals, in turn, were too worn out by the battle to pursue. After the war, friends of Colonel Rogers would erect a monument to the intrepid Texan on the courthouse lawn.

As had so often occurred during the Civil War, the mass attacks of infantry across open fields toward well-set defense had little chance. Corinth again showed the futility of the obsolete tactics and the unwillingness of the generals to open their minds to reality. The Union forces had lost 2,359 men—315 killed, 1,812 wounded, and 232 missing. The Confederates lost an appalling 4,233, with over one-third of them listed as prisoners or otherwise missing.[18] Tears came to old "Pap" Price's eyes as he saw so many of his troopers go down in this useless carnage. The South had gained nothing.

During the dismal withdrawal, Father Bannon lingered too long with the ambulance train in giving aid to injured soldiers and in hurrying stragglers down the road, and barely escaped capture. In the priest's own words, he was "chased by Fed[eral] cavalry last night at Rockford."[19] His horse had gone lame the pre-

vious week.[20] He did not get to take the mare to a veterinarian until the twelfth of that month, two days after he escaped capture.[21]

Both armies settled into winter quarters as fall gave way to colder weather. The Missourians remained in northeastern Mississippi during this period. On December 13, Father Bannon noted in his diary that "B. Martin"—presumably French-born Bishop Augustus Martin of Nachitoches, Louisiana—was at the hotel in Grenada, Mississippi.[22] Two days later the chaplain secured a pass for the bishop to visit the soldiers in camp, many of them from his diocese.[23]

Slightly more than a week later, Father Bannon left for Mobile to visit friends and assist the priests there during the Christmas celebration. Father Bannon had met the head of the Mobile Diocese, Bishop John Quinlan, the previous April in northern Mississippi.[24] The bishop must have learned of Father Bannon's unusual status with the army—an unpaid chaplain-at-large for Missouri Catholics. Now he decided to write to Richmond to help clarify the status of his fellow Irishman.

He directed his plea to the one Catholic in the Confederate cabinet, Stephen Mallory, secretary of the navy. He began by wishing the secretary and his family a happy New Year and thanking him for earlier kindnesses. He continued:

> With this preliminary, there is a little matter I would urge on your consideration, affecting a large body of brave Catholics, and indirectly, as far as it goes, the welfare of the Confederacy itself: it is, in reference to Reverend John Bannon of St. Louis. This reverend gentleman was chaplain (state) to the Missouri State Guard, when, in May 1861, it was dispersed at Camp Jackson, by the Federal Government. Father Bannon's devotion to our cause was so well known at the time in St. Louis, that it earned for him at the hands of the Lincoln officials much persecution and in one instance nearly cost him his life. When General Price was gathering his noble band of patriots, more young men (Catholics) from St. Louis left that city to join him: tho' separated from family and home, they murmured not, but fought on unflinchingly for the cause of the South. There was one thing, however, they cannot do without—the ministration of a Catholic Chaplain. They wrote to Father Bannon of St. Louis, for assistance; and he with a noble sacrifice of all self interest, relinquishes his comfortable position as Pastor of St. John's Church, in that city, and thro many dangers, succeeded in reaching Price's army, which he has followed faithfully ever since January 1862. Ever since then he has been the faithful Apostle to about 1,800 Catholic Missourians of Price's army; has been in the trying conflicts of Elkhorn, Farmington, and Corinth, and is yet with the same army. During all this time, he has not received a cent of the public money. He started from St. Louis with 300 dollars in gold and

has been serving since without any remuneration, depending entirely on the courtesy and generosity of the officers. He is now without funds, 1000 dollars in debt—and unable any longer, unless assisted, to continue his services in the army. I would most earnestly request, then, Hon. and dear Sir, that you would procure for him a chaplaincy, with orders to report to Major General Price, and if possible, to have it antedated so as to report his services from Jan. 1862 to the present. I know it does not belong to your Department, but I am sure, for the sake of our cause, and the spiritual interest of so many men you will do all you can to obtain the granting of his request. Thanking you again and again for your kindness, and lately that shown to Major Barry of Western Virginia, I am Honorable and dear Sir Yours most faithfully, etc.

P.S. If granted, let the Commission of Father Bannon be directed to me, for him.

So wrote his Excellency of Mobile.[25]

On the first day of the year Father Bannon recorded in his diary the news of Bragg's victory at Murfreesboro, Tennessee.[26] At least General Bragg claimed a victory before he retreated. One of the priest's companions on the journey from St. Louis to Springfield, late in 1861, P. B. Garesche, no doubt would hear sad news in a few days. A cousin of his father, Union colonel Julius Garesche, aide-de-camp to General Rosecrans, had ridden into a cannonball aimed at the commander of the army.

The priest visited hospitals in Vicksburg on January 2 with Father Peter Imsand, a Jesuit home missionary, and Father Patrick Gibbons of the Diocese of Mobile. The next day Father Bannon prepared to preach on the first Sunday of the year, January 4.[27] On Monday, he met again with Father P. F. Coyle, his coworker at Corinth.[28] He distributed prayer books in camp at Lumkin Mills, books he no doubt had purchased in Mobile.[29] He had one misfortune at this time. Bob, the late General Little's manservant, went away with the chaplain's mare.[30] Father Bannon got the animal back in early February.

General Price's greatly weakened division was ordered to Vicksburg. Price left for Richmond to see President Davis and clarify his position and that of his few surviving Missourians.[31] Either those facts or the continual rain brought the chaplain another severe headache.[32] Price left the Confederate capital with orders to return to the Trans-Mississippi, but without the remnants of the brave band that had come east the previous spring. Father Bannon would never again see his old commander. On the last day of January, Father Bannon saw another of his friends from the prewar militia. General John S. Bowen reviewed the division at Jackson, Mississippi.[33]

The frugal War Department of the Confederate States was still using 1862 printed forms on February 12, 1863—incidentally, President Lincoln's birthday—when Secretary of War James A. Seddon, to whom Mallory passed the bishop's letter, notified Father Bannon that he had been appointed chaplain to date from "the thirtieth day of January 1862 and was to report to General Price."[34] The secretary had scratched through the line requiring advice and consent of the Senate.[35] Seddon, further, had clearly written "three" over the printed "2" in the date of his letter. But he wrote "the thirtieth day of January 1862" in the open space reserved for the retroactive date for returning to day-to-day activities.[36]

Now that he had his status cleared not just for the future, but also for his past service, Father Bannon took a train for Mobile on March 5, no doubt to thank Bishop Quinlan for his efforts. He had to stand all night.[37] The train reached the southern Alabama city at 8 A.M. The priest returned to Jackson on March 12[38] and preached at St. Peter's Church on March 19.[39] This would be his last respite. Bowen's men headed for Grand Gulf on the Mississippi, about fifteen miles below Vicksburg.

RAILROADS OF THE CENTRAL SOUTH 1863

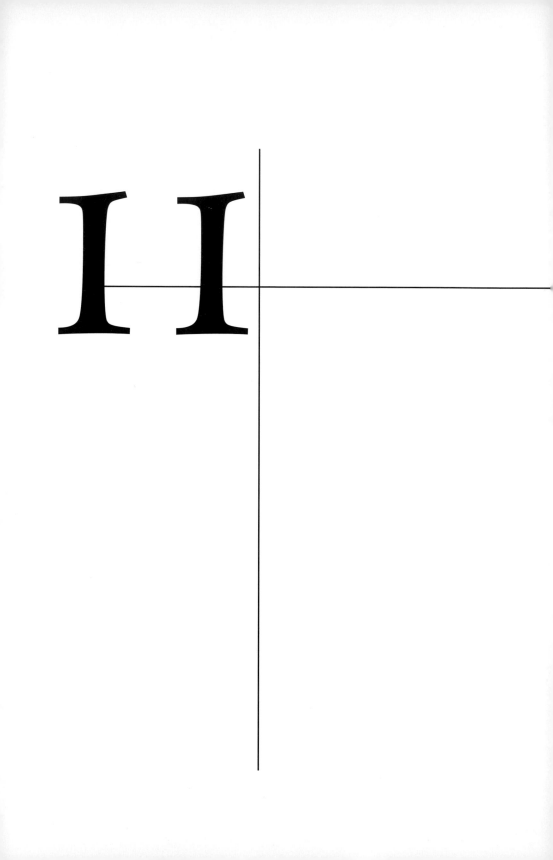

II

Vicksburg: Citadel above the River

By the time the azaleas and the camellias were in bloom, it had become apparent that the calm had ended. The hurricane would soon strike. General Grant was moving his mighty army against the Confederate citadel above the river. The First Missouri Brigade had taken positions at Grand Gulf, on the river fifteen miles south of Vicksburg.

Nature may have molded a more relentless man than Grant, but American history had not yet come across his equal. He tried and threw away several plans to take Vicksburg, including one that might have rerouted at least some flow of the Mississippi down the bed of the Tensas River to the west in Louisiana. The conqueror of Fort Donelson finally came up with a plan that might work, if the head of the naval units, Admiral David Porter, was able to do what Grant hoped. If Porter ran the gauntlet of Confederate fire and sped south of the city, Grant could move his troops through the Louisiana lowlands to the west, bypassing the city's fortifications. Then Porter's boats could bring the mighty army across the river below the town.

The two commands were independent of each other. Porter ran the fleet. Grant led the army. The admiral believed he could get his boats down the stream, but he knew he could not get them back against the strong current in the face of the Rebel batteries on the bluffs. If the Confederate general Pemberton held the city against Grant's onslaught, Porter's isolated gunboats would be wingless geese for hungry Southern hunters. The admiral faced a double gamble: that he could run most of his boats down the river past the powerful Rebel batteries, and that Grant would ultimately take the city. He chose the double gamble. That meant that the initial Union blow would strike the First Missouri Confederates.

When that brigade reached Grand Gulf, Father Bannon rejoined an old friend from the days of the Southwestern Campaign in the winter of 1860–61.

General John S. Bowen had slowly recovered from a serious wound at Shiloh and now had to guard and fortify a strategic position on the "Father of Waters."

The last Sunday in March seemed like just another peaceful day for Bannon at the Grand Gulf bastion. The priest offered Mass at the brigade's encampment, preached, and distributed forty-three communions.[1] An early Southern spring— by Missouri standards—had already brought its beauty to the lush countryside of western Mississippi. Dogwoods and redbuds sprinkled the Mississippi River bluffs with white and red blossoms. Daylight quickly passed to darkness on a leisurely day in camp.

Father Bannon conducted vesper service by the light of a campfire at 8 P.M. A soldier interrupted the psalms, shouting the alarm that Federal warships approached. "The Fed Boats surprised us," Father Bannon wrote in his diary.[2] Confederate signalmen upriver had failed in their duty to alert the garrison. Rolling down river with the swirling current, three Union gunboats pounded the fortifications, testing the new position's strength. Southern cannons answered. Neither side inflicted serious damage upon the other, but even minor casualties hurt. "One gun [a twenty-pound Parrott] burst in [William] Wade's Battery—2 killed & none hurt by the enemy's guns," recorded the chaplain's diary.[3]

Right: General John Bowen of St. Louis led the Confederates against Grant's mighty forces.

Father Bannon held funeral services at the church in Port Gibson[4] for the two dead artillerymen, Privates Claiborne D. Ferguson and John W. Underwood, both of St. Louis.[5] Father Bannon spent Good Friday, April 3, in quiet reflection in the country. After two Masses on Easter, April 5, he went to Jackson for a few days.[6] On April 12, Father Bannon offered Mass at Wade's battery. Six days later he attended a surprise party at that battery. Whether the surprise was for him or for Wade, he did not record. Bishop Augustus Martin of Nachitoches, Louisiana, visited Port Gibson on Sunday, April 19, and conferred with General Bowen on Monday.[7]

Grant, meanwhile, prepared for his invasion of Mississippi to reduce Fortress Vicksburg. Thousands of Federal troops maneuvered through Louisiana's swamps in preparation for crossing the Mississippi River. Grant targeted the landing site for Grand Gulf at April's end. But with Bluecoats waiting in transports, the Northern navy failed to reduce the defenses sufficiently to send troops ashore. In describing the fray, Bannon wrote: "Fed Gunboats engaged batteries at Gulf for 5 1/4 hours from 8 to 1 1/4 o'clock—Colonel Wade & Woods killed. . . . Fed Boats return . . . renewed fight & passed with their transports southward—2 Gunboats exploded—one transport."[8] The Union fleet continued southward, hunting for a suitable landing site on Mississippi soil. Grand Gulf had been checkmated.

Above: The gunboat *St. Louis*, built by James Eads in Carondelet, led Grant's attack on Fort Henry in Tennessee and ran into heavy fire from the Confederate artillerymen from St. Louis under Captains Wade and Guibor at Grand Gulf, Mississippi.

The bishop of the Diocese of Natchez, which included all of Mississippi at the time, William Henry Elder, a native of Baltimore and a former seminary professor, visited the battle area at this time. He kept a diary during the war. On April 24, 1863, while visiting a Catholic family, the Moores, who lived near Port Gibson, he met several officers of General Bowen's army. In the course of the day, Father Bannon arrived to visit.[9]

Two days later, on the third Sunday after Easter, the bishop offered Mass at the home of the Moores at dawn. At 9 A.M. he blessed the church at Port Gibson and placed it under the patronage of St. Joseph. Father Bannon offered the Mass, and the bishop preached. The chaplain and the bishop dined at the home of a family by the name of Ryan. The bishop noted in his diary that Father Bannon promised to preach at the church every Sunday afternoon while the army bivouacked in the vicinity.[10]

On the last morning of April, Father Bannon offered the funeral Mass for Private Edward Woods at St. Joseph's Church and blessed his grave at the Catholic cemetery. In the afternoon he conducted a memorial service for Colonel Wade at the courthouse in Port Gibson.[11] A Confederate officer, Lieutenant Colonel Alden McClellan, recalled years later that "Father Bannon delivered at the burial site of a Protestant soldier of the Missouri Command a touching and eloquent address, bringing tears to many listeners."[12] In a letter to a friend in St. Louis describing this funeral, Father Bannon spoke of meeting Mrs. Montrose Pallen, who was banished to the South and lived at the time in Mississippi. "She was with some Protestant friends and called on me after service."[13]

The time for conducting formal funeral services, for visiting friends, and for preaching to peaceful congregations went with the gentle breezes of May. Admiral Porter landed twenty-three thousand blue-clad foot soldiers from Illinois, Missouri, and neighboring states, south of Grand Gulf. They marched inland by an obscure road. The battle for Vicksburg had begun.

General Bowen turned his Missourians to meet Grant's veterans under the command of General John A. McClernand, a Kentucky-born former Illinois congressman. With anything like equal forces, Bowen might have outdueled the Union politician. But Bowen's 5,500 men could not hold indefinitely against four times that number. The Confederates fought well on May 1. Father Bannon recorded in his diary that "the Brigade held the Yankees in check until night."[14] But the sacrifices in Southern lives had been in vain.

Outmanned Rebels withdrew northward toward Vicksburg. The priest trudged along in the column until "night when we fell behind Bayou Pierre."[15]

It may well have been at this time that the following incident occurred. A friend heard it from Father Bannon at a Jesuit seminary in Dublin shortly after the war and then went on a mission to Australia as a priest. He later read the story in an American magazine that came into his hands. He related it in a letter to an American historian in St. Louis in the 1930s:

> Upon one occasion when both armies were stationed and entrenched on either side of a river . . . he was on the extreme right of the Confederate line. He learned that an officer had been mortally wounded on the extreme left and was anxious to see a priest. Father Bannon immediately mounted his horse and before the firing had ceased, started to gallop more than a mile to the position to which the officer was stationed. His commanding figure, of course, enabled him to be recognized, and the troops on both sides, Federal and Confederate, struck by his heroism, started up from their trenches, ceased firing, and cheered him loudly. The same recognition of his devotion and courage was repeated on his return journey.[16]

But the brown bayou failed to provide protection. A dejected priest merely scribbled how "no reinforcements [arrived] to check Feds who flanked us on

Right: A grim Grant resumed command and planned the Vicksburg campaign in the spring of 1863.

both [sides]—fell into the line of march at midnight."[17] There would be more retreats before the end of the campaign. The priest half-expected capture as he lingered along the crowded road to assist stragglers and the wounded. He noted in his diary that the "enemy's cavalry & artillery [were] in pursuit."[18] But Bannon and the Missouri troops escaped capture, withdrawing in early May.

As part of Grant's grand strategy, General Nathaniel Banks would come up from Baton Rouge with fifteen thousand men, capture Port Hudson, and continue upriver to take part in the final assault on the last Confederate stronghold. But in the meantime, disturbances in western Louisiana had grabbed Banks's attention. Undaunted, Grant saw the good in the new situation. He would have had to delay a month waiting for Banks. It was better to be on his own.

Further, Colonel Benjamin Grierson's raid north to south through Mississippi from Memphis, Tennessee, to Baton Rouge, Louisiana, during the last half of April had rocked the South, startled the entire nation, and derailed many Southern units that would have aided beleaguered Vicksburg. It also destroyed many Confederate lines of communication. It had an added feature for General Grant. It proved to him that he did not need to bring along provender on his various moves. Mississippi was rich in food for the taking. He needed to bring only ammunition. Grant could move freely without a base of supply, as General Winfield Scott had done in Mexico less than twenty years before.

When Grant moved, Sherman predicted disaster. To add to the trouble, the Rebels sank several Union boats. Sherman took some satisfaction in the news that four newspapermen went down with the boats. In his view of the "Inferno," only politicians placed lower than newspaperman. To Sherman's dismay, however, some misguided Confederates pulled the journalists from the brown waters.

When General John C. Pemberton called for help, General Joseph E. Johnston at Tullahoma, Tennessee, hesitated to act. Down in Charleston, South Carolina, General Pierre Beauregard spoke enthusiastically, but he made few preparations to come to Vicksburg's relief. General Lee had beaten Hooker at Chancellorsville in the first days of May. Would he send help? Had the Union not held Corinth, the trip on the railroad from Richmond through Chattanooga to Holly Springs, Mississippi, and then down to Jackson would have been easy. But the Federals had cut Confederate communications, and Lee was looking north. Johnston did come by mid-May, just in time to be driven out of Jackson by Grant, who had rushed east to meet him.

Grant now turned west. The Confederates had a strong line on Champion Hill, a commanding seventy-foot ridge named for the owner of the plantation. A thick pine forest stretched along its southern end. Pemberton put Major-General Carter Stevenson on the hill itself, at the left of the Confederate line, Bowen in the middle, and Loring on the right. While the Union left under McClernand lingered, General James B. McPherson on the Union right pushed forward against Stevenson. A group of Bluecoats under Alvin P. Hovey reached the top of the hill. Bowen saw the need on his left, came to the rescue of Stevenson with the First Missourians, and drove the Federals back down the hill. But eventually the indecisive McClernand moved, and Loring gave way on the Confederate right. McClernand captured eleven cannons and many prisoners and forced a general Southern withdrawal. In spite of the Missourians' courage, the Rebels barely escaped destruction. Pemberton lost the battle and 3,624 men to Grant's 2,441. The First Missouri Brigade lost six hundred men—killed, wounded, or captured. Father Bannon stayed close to his men in the battle and in the retreat across the rain-swollen Baker's Creek to the west of Champion Hill.

Confederate defeat along the banks of Baker's Creek sealed not only Vicksburg's but also the Southland's fate in May 1863. Another Southern fiasco came on the following day, May 17. Bowen's mauled division and a Tennessee brigade manned the defenses spanning a bend of the Big Black River. Here, General Pemberton had ordered a stand to allow troops cut off at Champion Hill to rejoin his army. A Federal attack easily smashed through the lines, causing a rout. The chaplain and most of his brigade members escaped in the stampede over the river's bridges. Pemberton's shattered army limped into Vicksburg the next day.[19]

Above: The north end of Vicksburg was unready for the approach of Grant's army.

Above: A Confederate platoon regroups at Vicksburg.

The stage was set for the final struggle for Vicksburg's possession. Located atop the Mississippi River bluffs, the South's "Gibraltar" gave Grant his greatest challenge so far. He had bottled up twenty thousand Rebels in Vicksburg's nine-mile-long network of defenses running along ridgetops. The fight would prove hard and long.

The Battle of Vicksburg took place in an area unlike any other battlefield of the war. Only a visit to the scene can give a real picture of what it must have been like. It was as if the battle of the crater that would take place the following summer at Petersburg, Virginia, were duplicated a hundred times along the front. Attacking troops had to go down a steep hill thirty yards and then immediately climb an equally steep hill in the face of enemy fire all the time, without the slightest undulation of the surface and the only cover a growth of cane at the bottom of the ravine. The two ridge lines were less than fifty yards apart.

Grant, nonetheless, would try. Thousands of Bluecoats charged. The Confederates were ready. The First Missouri Brigade, as part of Bowen's division, held a reserve position in the rear. When the Federals charged on May 19, the Missourians rushed to defend the left-center during Grant's assaults. Thousands of Bluecoats charged en masse to carry Vicksburg by storm. As could be expected, Father Bannon had gone into the trenches with the reserve troops. The priest described the bloody day's activities: "Feds press us on left: repulsed 6 times."[20] The Union legions had been hurled back, after suffering nearly one thousand casualties. Other generals might have given up the impossible assault, but not Grant.

The Union commander gambled again on a quick victory only three days later. Blue masses swarmed forward on May 22 to meet a comparable defeat. Another decisive repulse ended with more than three thousand killed and wounded. Hundreds of wounded Bluecoats lay before the Confederate defenses, tortured by the summer sun and the pain of their wounds. All around them the bodies of their slain comrades began to swell grotesquely. The wounded men who had fallen in the first assault remained unattended for six days. Pemberton suggested a truce of several hours to allow the Union troops to rescue their living and bury their dead. Grant agreed to this generous offer at 6 P.M. on May 25.

Grant changed his strategy to a "python policy." He would tighten the blockade around the city and shell the city into starvation and submission. In his typical cryptic way, Father Bannon reflected this new approach. "Sharpshooting resumed next morning: Shelling during the day."[21] An unceasing bombardment pounded the city.

When not in the trenches, Father Bannon spent much of his time at the city hospital. Perched atop one of Vicksburg's highest hills, it offered a fine target for Federal artillery on land or boat. On May 27, the St. Louis priest was horrified when the Union fleet's "Mortars threw in incendiary shells [into] the city [which passed] over my [quarters]: fire on the roof of hospital."[22] Even while attending the wounded, Father Bannon risked his life as Federal guns riddled the hospital. On one occasion a shell burst between him and Doctors John A. Leavy, a member of the St. Vincent de Paul Society in St. Louis, and J. H. Britt, a graduate of Saint Louis University's School of Medicine. The shell stunned Leavy and tore away part of Britt's leg.[23]

The siege continued as spring passed into summer. With no Confederate succor able to hit Grant from behind, the Vicksburg garrison faced inevitable starvation or surrender. As casualties among the doomed defenders rose with each passing day, the chaplain's chores and responsibilities grew on his daily visits to the trenches. Father Bannon came close to death on numerous occasions. One such close call came on June 23—the siege's thirty-seventh day. On that hot day, Bannon described how there was a "Furious assault on our Right . . . at 10 P.M. Parrot (sic) shell passed thru the house about 3 P.M. 6 feet over my head."[24] And only two days later, a shell barely missed the priest, when it plowed through the hospital, hurling debris and killing some of the wounded.[25]

Father Bannon had great regard for the Sisters of Mercy who nursed the sick: Mother De Sales Brown, Sister Vincent Brown, Sister Ignatius Sumner, Sister Agnes Maddigan, Sister Philomena Farmer, and Sister Xavier Pursine. They had come from Baltimore to Vicksburg in 1859 and opened a school in a large brick building. Shortly after the firing on Fort Sumter the school closed, and the building became a hospital for soldiers. The nun-teachers became nun-nurses.[26]

Other Sisters of Mercy nursed the wounded at Oxford, Lauderdale Springs, Jackson, Shelby Springs, and other places. As Grant's forces approached, the sisters moved the disabled to places of safety.

Before Grant encircled the city, three Daughters of Charity, Sisters Martha, Philomena, and Scholastica, all trained nurses who had cared for the wounded at Natchez in 1862, brought their skills and experience to beleaguered Vicksburg.[27]

Writing from the seclusion of a Jesuit residence at the University of Louvain in Belgium three years later, Father Bannon would recall his experiences at the "Sisters Hospital." He wrote:

> Within the lines of Vicksburg during the siege, we were under a tremendously hot sun, and a tremendously hot fire, and had to live for six weeks on wretched rations of mule beef, that I went one day to visit the ward for the mortally wounded. This ward was naturally not so well cared for as the others, for the cases were all hopeless as far as nursing and surgery went; but for my purposes they were perhaps more hopeful than many others. On this occasion I noticed a group which struck me more than usual. A wounded man, about forty years of age, lay insensible on one of the beds, and two other soldiers, one about the age of the dying man, the other a lad, but both bronzed with hard service, were standing sad and silent by his side. I went over to them and asked the elder of the two if the wounded man was a relative.
>
> "He is my brother," was the reply, "and this boy's father." They were all three "patriot soldiers," as the first Southern volunteers were called; they served in the ranks at their own expense, and took not a farthing of pay.
>
> "I fear," I said, "that there is no hope of his life."
>
> "Do you think so?" said the brother anxiously; and turning to the lad he added, "How shall we tell your mother?"
>
> "Well," said I, "perhaps he was prepared for death. Did he profess any religion?"
>
> "No,—but he thought a deal about religion, and was fond of hearing preaching."
>
> "Do you know if he was ever baptized?"
>
> "He was not. But I have heard him say quite lately that he wished he had been; and that if God spared him through this war, he would get himself baptized at the end of it."
>
> "Well," I replied, "it is a pity that if he wished for baptism he should die without it. From what you tell me he certainly believed in God. Did he believe in the Trinity?"

"Yes, he did."

"Did he believe that Jesus Christ was God?"

"Of course he did."

"Well, I'll tell you what I think. I think you ought not to let him die without being baptized, since he wished for it himself, and now cannot help himself. Besides it would be a consolation to his wife and all his family at home to know that he was baptized before he died. It would take off some of the pain of losing him."

After saying so much as this I went away, and left them to talk the matter over between them. It is often well not to seem to push things, but to allow something to come spontaneously from the other side, though it may be in answer to one's own suggestions.

I visited some other cases and came back after an interval. I saw the two were in some perplexity.

"I am a Catholic Priest," I said, "but if you wish it I will myself offer to baptize your brother; for from what you tell me I find in him all the conditions requisite for me to do so in his present state. Think it over, and let me know."

I then left the ward. It was not long however before the two men came to seek me, and finding me in one of the corridors of the hospital, the elder of them said, "Mister, we think he ought to be baptized. And we should like you to baptize him rather than anybody else, for all the boys speak well of the Catholic priests and Sisters."

"Very well," I said, "I will keep to my word."

We went back to the bed-side, and taking off the damp cloth that was laid over the dying man's forehead I prepared to baptize him. It was an affecting thing to see those two rough soldiers drop on their knees instinctively, and to see the tears roll down their bronzed cheeks as I administered the Sacrament.

"Mister," said the brother, seizing my hand when I had finished, "I should like to be a Catholic too, if you will have me. If you will only teach me all about it, I will be thankful to you for ever."

The dying man never recovered his senses; and the brother became a Catholic. The younger man did not offer himself at once with his uncle, and the surrender of the town took him out of my sight, but I trust his case was only reserved for more worthy hands than mine.[28]

The appreciation these Southern Protestants had for the sisters stemmed from two causes: the nuns' dedication and their expertise. Many other American women had such dedication, but few had their nursing skills.

Grant still thought he could break the stalemate. On June 25, the Unionists implanted two thousand pounds of powder under the Third Louisiana Redoubt, near the Jackson Road. The resulting explosion blew a gaping hole in the Rebel lines. But reserves of the Missouri Brigade dashed to the scene in time to help beat back the infantry attacks. Bannon wrote of the day's fighting by describing how the foe mounted a "charge on our lines after blowing up positions. Feds driven back with great loss."[29]

The June 25 repulse finally made Grant realize that he would not take the citadel by storm. The steep decline immediately in front of the Rebel trenches made attack a mad venture. But it was only a matter of time before the defenders would run out of food and bullets. Further, any hope of help from the Army of Northern Virginia died when word came that Lee was moving up the Shenandoah Valley to strike at the North after his great victory at Chancellorsville in early May.

Father Bannon scheduled Mass for June 28 at St. Paul's Catholic Church on one of the city's most prominent hills. An injured brigade member, Sergeant James Hogan of St. John's Parish in St. Louis, wrote to his father a short time later:

> On Sunday, the 28th, my wound being well enough to walk around, I went to six o'clock mass in the Cathedral. I had just gotten inside the door when a 132-pound parrot shell from the batteries on the peninsula struck the railing outside the church, taking off the arm of a citizen who was coming in. Another shell as Father Bannon was commencing Mass, went in one side and out the other of the church, however, hurting nobody, but badly frightening the women, who all left.[30]

Father Bannon continued with the ceremony of the Mass. In his diary that day, he named the man who lost his arm as "Mr. Donovan."[31] Not long thereafter, according to Sergeant Hogan's letter, "another shell had whistled close by Bannon's head, while he continued saying Mass as if nothing had happened . . . ."[32] Indeed, risks were taken in simply performing the regular duties of a priest.

Grant attempted to blow up the Rebel works near the Jackson Road once again on July 1. As before, the Missourians charged into the tempest to plug the breach. But Grant had held his troops back. Nonetheless, Vicksburg was doomed. Bannon understood as much on July 3, when he noted that "Pemberton & Bowen went out on a flag of truce—Vicksburg to be surrendered tomorrow."[33] The Union troops marched on the Fourth of July.

Bannon witnessed the sad ceremony. He recorded the day's activities in his diary: "surrendered at 10 [o'] clock. Went out to see our men stack arms—General

Grant entered [Vicksburg] at 10 1/2 o'clock—Yankee troops & officers scattered thru town—Several Brigades marching at noon: Yankee flag over [the city]—122 Guns . . . fired salutes."[34] The North had for all practical purposes gained control of the Mississippi River, a harbinger of the eventual fall of the Confederacy. But the nightmare of Civil War would continue for almost two years.

The Union fleet could not take fifteen thousand prisoners north. As a result the Missouri troops were to be exchanged in September 1863 and to continue fighting to the end. But Father Bannon would not be with the Missourians upon exchange.

Vicksburg proved to be Father Bannon's last battle. President Jefferson Davis asked him to undertake a special mission for the Confederacy in his native island. The memory of his presence on the battlefield remained with the men of the First Missouri Brigade over the years.

Father Bannon undertook his new call with enthusiasm. He would never return to the battlefields.

Left: The Missouri Monument at Vicksburg stands at the point on the Confederate line where the First Missouri Infantry Brigade waited in reserve before being sent into the battle.

12

How Great a Chaplain?

In order to put Father Bannon's war record in focus, a look at the experiences of other priests who wore the blue or the gray will give perspective. While no authoritative survey of Protestant chaplains has yet appeared, a Benedictine scholar, Aidan Germain, gives basic facts on Catholic chaplains on both sides. He doesn't evaluate the work of these men. Instead, he names their units and the battles these units took part in during the time of their chaplains' service.[1] All these men were volunteers who left their college or parish and were willing to face the hardships and dangers of the battlefield.

In the section on the Civil War, he lists thirty-nine Union chaplains. Most served part-time. Eight saw full-time service, six in the eastern theater and two in the Tennessee sector. With the Southern armies he found records of seven full-time and twenty-seven part-time chaplains. Father Bannon was the only full-time chaplain in the western theater. The other six full-time chaplains served with the Army of Northern Virginia under General Lee, even those with the Louisiana regiments, the two French Jesuits, Darius Hubert and Hippolyte Gache, and the two Redemptorists, the Irishman James Sheeran and Aegidius Smulders, a native of Holland.

While colleges were losing students to the battlefields, parishes were flourishing. This put extra pressure on bishops with a small number of available priests. As a result, most archdiocesan priests served only for short periods. Three, Fathers William T. O'Higgins of Cincinnati, Thomas Brady of Detroit, and Bannon, served full-time. Father Bannon alone gave up a large city parish to be with the men in the field.

Religious congregations provided most of the other chaplains. The Congregation of the Holy Cross sent eight priests to the Union armies, the Jesuits three, and the Franciscans and Dominicans one each. Two Jesuits, two

Redemptorists, and one Dominican rode with the men in Gray. The only
Catholic chaplain killed in action was a Benedictine, Father Emmeran Bliemel of
the Tenth Tennessee Infantry.[2]

Far more material on the members of the latter-mentioned religious orders
has come down to us. They were more likely to write letters to their friends in
the brotherhood. In turn, these communities often published the letters in such
magazines as *Notre Dame Scholastic*[3] and the Jesuit *Woodstock Letters*.[4] These publications memorialized the exploits of such Union chaplains as Holy Cross
Father William Corby and Jesuits Peter Tissot and Joseph O'Hagan.

On the Confederate side, no such publications came out. Fortunately, Father
Bannon's diary was available for Philip Tucker in telling the story of the great
chaplain's war years, *The Confederacy's Fighting Chaplain: Father John B. Bannon*.[5]

Above: One black-cowled Benedictine priest, Father Emmeran Bliemel, served the Confederates of
the Tenth Tennessee Infantry. A sniper killed him while he assisted a wounded man.

Father Hippolyte Gache, S.J., wrote letters to his fellow Jesuits at Springhill College in Mobile. Historian Cornelius Buckley translated and annotated these letters that throw light also on the ministry of another Jesuit, Father Darius Hubert.[6] Father James Sheeran, C.S.S.R., kept a journal that historian Joseph T. Durkin edited.[7]

Father Darius Hubert, a French-born Jesuit, became chaplain of the First Louisiana Infantry Regiment in May 1861 and served on the Virginia battlefields or in the Richmond hospitals until Lee's surrender. A tribute to his work came from a fellow Jesuit, Father Peter Tissot, a captured Federal chaplain. "When the First Regiment Louisiana Volunteers left New Orleans for Virginia battlefields, Father Hubert marched with them as their chaplain," Father Tissot wrote. "He was in every battle they took part in. President Davis considered him the model chaplain, and General R. E. Lee never met him without a respectful bow."[8] Later, because of recurring ill health, the priest requested assignment to hospitals in Richmond, where he worked until the end of the war.[9] After the conflict, he did parish work and spoke at veterans' reunions and at the funeral of Jefferson Davis in 1889.[10]

James B. Sheeran, a short, trim man, looked like the typical stern, uncompromising schoolmaster of Irish fiction. When his wife died and his children joined religious orders, he entered a Redemptorist seminary. In October 1861, while doing parish work in New Orleans, he signed up with the Fourteenth Louisiana Infantry and began service at Yorktown, Virginia.

Chaplain Sheeran kept notes during the time of action and elaborated on these notes in quiet times.[11] He preached to large congregations that included others than Catholics, often at other Christian churches, such as the Orange County Courthouse Methodist Church. Conciliatory with all Christians, he berated scoffers and officers who blasphemed. He was frank and fearless, even lecturing General "Stonewall" Jackson on the rights and duties of chaplains.[12] On April 28, 1863, he won from General Lee a pass to move freely from the front to the hospitals in Richmond.[13] On May 27, 1863, shortly after the Battle of Chancellorsville, Lee singled him out for recognition.[14]

Father Sheeran was at the Louisiana Hospital in Richmond at the end of the conflict. Returning to the Redemptorist parish in New Orleans, he found the rigidity of community life stressful and joined the Diocese of Newark. He served as pastor of Assumption Church at Morristown, New Jersey, until his death in 1881.[15]

Two Federal chaplains saw extensive action with the Army of the Cumberland. Father Thomas Brady of the Diocese of Detroit joined the Fifteenth Michigan Infantry on March 13, 1862, and took part in the Battles of Shiloh and Corinth, and he was on hospital duty during the siege of Vicksburg.

He was with the Fifteenth Michigan at Kennesaw Mountain and the Atlanta Campaign. After the capture of Atlanta, he did not follow Sherman to the sea but was sent to the Trans-Mississippi, where he was mustered out at Little Rock, Arkansas, in August 1865.[16] Father Peter J. Cooney, C.S.C., of the faculty of the University of Notre Dame, served with the Thirty-fifth Indiana Infantry in every battle from Perryville, Kentucky, in 1862 to Nashville[17] in December 1864. After the South's surrender, Father Cooney returned to Notre Dame. Neither Brady nor Cooney received special recognition for their services.

Father Joseph J. O'Hagan, S.J., another native of Ireland, became chaplain of the Seventy-third New York Infantry, a ragtag outfit from Manhattan's east side. Captured during the Peninsular Campaign, O'Hagan was paroled and back with his men. The carnage of Fredericksburg (Union forces lost 12,653, and Confederate losses were half that many) appalled him.[18] He served at Chancellorsville and at Gettysburg. Superiors then sent the young priest a few miles away to Fredericksburg, Maryland, for his final year of spiritual formation according to the program of the Jesuit founder.

At that time, Colonel William Brewster, commander of Unit A of the Seventy-third, approved this order of the Jesuit superior and wrote, "During his two years of service, Father O'Hagan has performed the duties of his office in a most faithful manner, enjoying the respect and love of all."[19] After the year, he went back to the battlefields and marched with his men into Richmond in April 1865.

The finest tribute to Father O'Hagan's work on the battlefields came from the pen of a friend and associate in the service. At the time of the priest's death, Chaplain Joseph N. Twichell, a Congregationalist minister from Hartford, Connecticut, wrote:

> Father O'Hagan has been for seventeen years one of my dearest friends. . . . We were chaplains in the same brigade of the Army of the Potomac, and for the space of two years worked side by side. . . . He was one of the best and kindliest of men, and one of the most delightful of comrades. He had a bright, happy wit; no discomforts could overcome his cheerful temper, and his generosity was boundless.
>
> He was as brave as he was tenderhearted and faithful.
>
> I saw every reason to believe, that the motive of his earnestness was his desire to serve God.[20]

Father O'Hagan exercised a strong, good influence among the soldiers, especially those of his own faith, and he was widely known and much respected throughout the army. His abilities and acquirements were of a high order. He had as rich a career in peacetime as he had in the time of war. He became president of Holy Cross College in Worcester, Massachusetts. While enjoying a period of rest on a cruise, he took ill and died at sea near Acapulco, Mexico, on December 15, 1879.

In the summer of 1861, Father Peter Tissot, S.J., a native of the Province of Savoy on the border of France and Italy, became chaplain of the Thirty-seventh New York Volunteers, known as "the Irish Rifles."[21] During the Peninsular Campaign, he had felt that a chaplain could do little effective work on the battlefield, and he concentrated on retreats during encampments. As the war went on he changed his attitude, if we may credit the "Reminiscences" of General James R. O'Beirne:

> Father Tissot was with us in the Army of the Potomac, and in my mess. He was saint-like in his uncomplaining endurance of suffering, and while almost continually in ill-health, the hardships of camp life and exposure to danger had no terrors for him.
>
> . . . He was always in the front rank line to hear confessions and to administer, as he oftentimes did, the consolation of the Blessed Sacrament to the wounded soldier or officer as he fell under the hottest fire of bullets. Father Tissot was, and is known today among veterans as the model Chaplain of the Army of the Potomac, and this well-earned reputation is still accorded to him in the War Department."[22]

On completing his term as chaplain, he became vice president of Fordham College. During 1864, he was acting president of the school. After the war, he gave retreats and parish missions in the New York area, until illness immobilized him a few years later. He died of cancer in June 1875 at the age of fifty-two.[23]

Michael Nash of the Sixth New York Infantry ranks with the greatest of the chaplains for persevering in dedication to duty in a unique way in places ranging from New York to Key West to Texas. A newly ordained clergyman, he faced a task that called for a veteran, not a beginner. He was present at fifty-two engagements of his unit far from Antietam or Vicksburg. The Sixth was rarely out of sight of enemy forces in the Gulf area. Once, during Mass, a Federal sniper cut down his drummer-boy acolyte. Nash barely escaped in this and other instances. He turned many soldiers to full Christian living. Since many naval units lacked a Catholic chaplain, Father Nash had to provide for them as for parishes without priests at many places along the gulf. During four long years he never saw another priest. He performed his routine functions with full dedication and was heroic on countless forgotten battlefields.[24]

Father William Corby, C.S.C., was the best known of all Federal chaplains, and the only one born in America. He entered the University of Notre Dame at age nineteen and, a year later, joined the Congregation of the Holy Cross. Ordained on Christmas Day in 1860, he served on the faculty of Notre Dame for a year. In the fall of 1861, he answered the call to go to the front as chaplain of the Eighty-eighth New York Infantry, made up principally of soldiers of Irish ancestry. Eventually the Eighty-eighth joined with Massachusetts, Pennsylvania, and other New York volunteers to form the Irish Brigade under General Thomas Francis Meagher. Corby saw action in all the major engagements of the Army of the Potomac from Yorktown, Virginia, in April 1862, through Malvern Hill, Antietam, Fredericksburg, Chancellorsville, Gettysburg, Wilderness, Spottsylvania, and Cold Harbor to Petersburg in 1864.[25]

Father Corby shared the dangers and hardships of the foot soldiers without complaint, and when the battle was on, he was always found among the men of his command comforting and inspiring them, binding their wounds, and giving them the consolation of religion by example, word, and sacrament.

After each battle, Father Corby had other work. Colonel James J. Smith of the Sixty-ninth described it thus:

> The Father's lantern was often seen glimmering during the watches of the night on the disputed battlefield between the two armies where, braving the shot of pickets of either army, his services were given to the helpless—the cordial and help for the wounded, the rites of the Church for the dying. . . . The Father's love for his men was equaled only by the love and reverence they had for him.[26]

"He was a soldier, a hero, a saint," wrote General St. Clair Mulholland of the 116th Pennsylvania.[27] On another occasion, he wrote at length:

> I see him now as if it were but yesterday, the most sublime figure on all that glorious field, standing amid the smoke and carnage; he alone, among the two hundred thousand warriors with uplifted hands, like Aaron the High Priest of Israel, prayed and gave the last rites of religion to his comrades. . . . Brave men and great generals were there, each fighting for victory and thinking how to gain it; but the priest of Jesus Christ, alone of all that mighty host, was battling not only for his country, but for the souls of those who were dying to save it.[28]

Father Corby returned to the University of Notre Dame in late 1864. He became president of the university and raised it to new life after a disastrous fire.

Later his fellow members of the Congregation of the Holy Cross elected him to the office of provincial. He also served as the commander of the only legion post consisting of members of a religious congregation. He died at Notre Dame on December 28, 1897. In the meantime, a group of alumni of St. Joseph's College in Philadelphia began a campaign to erect a statue in Father Corby's honor on Cemetery Ridge at Gettysburg—on the spot where he gave general absolution to the entire Irish Brigade as General Hancock ordered them to counterattack Anderson's Confederates on the second day of the battle. The response was enthusiastic.

The North erected no monument to any other chaplain; the South erected none at all. In his book on Union chaplains, *Knights Without Armor*, author Robert S. Hall mentions no chaplains with records to match those of Fathers Corby, Tissot, or O'Hagan.[29] In *Chaplains in Gray*, Charles Pitts praises several Episcopal and Methodist clergymen of the Army of the Tennessee who later became bishops.[30] None of them won acclaim from their commanding officers that matched the praise given John B. Bannon, Darius Hubert, and James B. Sheeran.

Among the many who spoke or wrote about Bannon, the Methodist pastor Enoch M. Marvin held a unique vantage. Like Father Bannon, he had served a parish in St. Louis, missionized the South early in the war, and then took Father Bannon's place with Price's command.

Shortly after the close of the Civil War, the conference of the Methodist Church chose Enoch M. Marvin as bishop. A man of consummate dedication, he soon gained a reputation as the most eloquent preacher of the Southern Methodist Church. He visited the mission fields in China and wrote several books urging greater concern for the foreign missions. In an unpublished treatise on Civil War chaplains, he singled out Father Bannon among the Catholic chaplains. Here are Bishop Marvin's words:

And now, that I have mentioned three efficient Methodist preachers from Missouri who served the Confederacy, I will mention one more good chaplain, whose name was Father Bannon, a young Catholic priest from St. Louis, who came down South with our command and served the Catholics as their chaplain.

We had a number of good Irish Catholics in our army who had been gathered up around St. Louis; and, wonderful soldiers they made. We all loved Father Bannon. Everybody who knew him looked up to him, for he was so faithful, good and efficient in every way in all of his duties.

Right after the siege of Vicksburg Father Bannon disappeared; and, it was a long time before we could find out what had become of him. We knew that there was some good reason for his disappearance; and, finally, we learned that President Jefferson Davis had sent for him, that he had gone to Richmond and had been sent off on a secret mission for President Davis.[31]

One might wonder if this evaluation represented an objective historical judgment or a chauvinistic accolade of one St. Louis pastor for another. By one of those ironies that history likes to indulge in, the congregation that young Pastor Marvin served in St. Louis built a stone church across the street from Father Bannon's shortly after the Civil War. By that time, Father Bannon's former parish, St. John's, had become the residence of the archbishop of St. Louis. These two religious edifices, incidentally, are both on the Register of Historic Buildings and are still active temples of worship.

Others besides Bishop Marvin praised Father Bannon. General Dabney Maury called him "the good and great Father O'Bannon (*sic*), Chaplain to Price's Missourians. . . . [He was] indefatigable in his care for the wounded and wearied people."[32]

Above: Guibor's artillerymen never had the neat uniforms such as this Confederate battery enjoyed until after the fall of Vicksburg.

Albert Danner, quartermaster of the First Missouri, recalled the arrival of the Confederates from St. Louis: "There came South with General Price's army from St. Louis, a fine battery, fully equipped, or Irishmen, fine fighters, and all members of the Catholic Church. With them came from St. Louis a young priest, Father Bannon, as their chaplain. Father Bannon was brave, courageous, energetic and liked by all in the Missouri Army, Protestants as well as Catholics."[33] As already mentioned, his own General Sterling Price spoke of him as the "greatest soldier he ever saw."[34]

How did Father Bannon's record rate with that of other chaplains? Both sides had chaplains who stood out for exceptional service to their men and who won recognition from their superior officers: Union chaplains William Corby, Peter Tissot, Joseph O'Hagan, and Michael Nash, along with Confederate fathers Darius Hubert and Joseph Sheeran of the Army of Northern Virginia, stood out for service to their respective causes. The records show that Father Bannon at least equaled if not surpassed each of them.

13

Confederate Agent

Since the Federal fleet could not handle the large volume of prisoners at Vicksburg, "Unconditional Surrender" Grant set down conditions for the surrendering Confederates. He paroled the survivors of the siege for three months. After that, they could return to military duty if they so wished. The Missourians decided to muster in at the end of the period at Demopolis, a town in west-central Alabama on the road to Montgomery. In the meantime, Father Bannon went to Mobile where he presumably met with some of the Jesuit fathers at Spring Hill College. Then he took a train for Richmond, to report to Bishop John McGill.[1]

He preached at the cathedral and came to the notice of Secretary of the Navy Stephen Mallory, who was in attendance at Mass. Mallory, the only Catholic in the Confederate Cabinet, had expedited Bannon's commission earlier in the year. The priest visited with the secretary. He and the bishop received an invitation from President Jefferson Davis to come to the White House.

The Confederate leader had already sent a young officer, Captain James L. Capston, a graduate of Trinity College, back to Ireland to explain the cause of the Confederacy. When Capston left Richmond earlier in July, President Davis had promised him that he would send him a coworker. Father Bannon seemed to be an ideal coworker. With the approval of Bishop McGill, he agreed to return to his native land.

When hostilities had begun two years before, Southerners had taken a contemptuous view of the Federal army as a handful of mercenaries, with officers untrained and unworthy. In spite of the consistent defeats in the East during 1862, however, the Union army had kept coming with greater and greater reserves.

The North had sent recruiters surreptitiously to many countries of Europe as well as to Canada. The Southern leaders had come to realize that the immi-

Above: Confederate president Jefferson Davis asked Father Bannon to take non-battlefield duties as a special agent in Ireland.

gration of a large mass from Europe would in itself decide the contest. So the South decided to act. Henry Hotze, the Confederate agent in London, had kept a close eye on Federal undercover campaigns of recruitment throughout the British Isles.

In Ireland the recruiters used two ploys. They offered work on a nonexistent railroad. When the penniless Irish reached the States and found no work, the recruiters lured them into enlisting in order to get enough to eat. The other procedure was to approach a prospective immigrant in the port cities of Cork or Cobh, offer them an extra drink or two, and sign them up. Some of these recruiters, further, received commissions from draft dodgers in the States who had agreed to pay for substitutes in order to avoid service. Immigration had always been far greater in the North, but these procedures speeded up the coming of men from Europe.

Both the Confederate president, Jefferson Davis, and the secretary of state, Judah Benjamin, knew the influence of priests among Catholics. Davis had gone to a Dominican school as a boy in Kentucky, and Benjamin, whose wife was a Catholic of French ancestry, represented Louisiana, a state with a large Catholic population. The two men readily saw the value of having a Catholic priest, a native of Ireland, work with Captain Capston. Father Bannon then agreed to transfer from the army to the special service of the State Department on September 1, 1863.

Secretary Benjamin sent a four-page letter to Father Bannon that included much of what he had previously written to Capston. As a private and confidential agent of the Confederate government, he was to enlighten the Irish on the true nature of the American conflict. In this way he was to counter the attempts of the North to recruit Irishmen.

Benjamin pointed out several topics that Father Bannon could address with his countrymen: the slaughter of Meagher's Irish Brigade at the Battle of Fredericksburg; the fact that Irish soldiers in blue uniforms would be facing their countrymen in gray; the treatment of foreigners in the respective areas; the anti-Catholic agitation by the Know-Nothings in the North before the war; and the desecration of Catholic places of worship by soldiers from New England.

The secretary gave a number of day-to-day directions. Father Bannon, of course, would respect the laws of England. The priest would not reveal the purposes of his mission, but at the same time he would use no dishonest disguises or false pretenses. The Confederate agent in London would supply day-to-day expenses entailed in the work. The secretary authorized the sum of $1,212.50 in gold for Father Bannon's travel expenses and salary. And, finally, the secretary authorized him to go to Rome to see the Sovereign Pontiff if the priest thought it would strengthen his hand to do so.[2]

With this generous subsidy in gold, Father Bannon slipped through the blockade from Wilmington, North Carolina. Bannon did not mention the name of the boat that took him to Bermuda. By chance he talked religion with a young Confederate seaman on the voyage and helped turn the young man toward the faith. The sailor's name was John Bannister Tabb. He eventually became a Catholic, a priest, and a poet of distinction.

From Tabb's life story one learns the name of the vessel, the *Robert E. Lee*. Originally the *Giraffe*, it had run the blockade twenty-one times. Father Bannon's trip would be one of its last. On November 9, 1863, the Federals captured it on the way to Texas. Explaining his conversion to the Catholic faith, Tabb stated, "I learned a few of the doctrines and practices of the Church while in Cuba and from Father Bannon who went abroad with us on our trip to England."[3]

After reaching Bermuda, Father Bannon went up to Halifax and over to London and arrived in October. He reported to Henry Hotze, the general planner of the strategy. Not quite thirty years old at the time, Hotze had served in the American legation at Brussels before the war. He returned to America and became a writer with the *Mobile Register* in 1859. By the time Father Bannon arrived, he had become, in an unassuming way, perhaps the most influential Confederate agent in Europe. He had developed a system of procuring and dispensing information that could have done credit to an astute diplomat of many years.

Above: The speedy Confederate blockade runner the *Robert E. Lee* took Father Bannon to Bermuda.

In the letter from Judah Benjamin, dated September 5, 1863, that Father Bannon handed to Hotze, the secretary of state introduced Father Bannon and wrote of his service as chaplain of the "Gallant Missourians" under General Price. Father Bannon "has consented to proceed to Ireland and there endeavor to enlighten his fellow countrymen as to the true nature of our struggle and to satisfy them, if possible, how shocking to all the dictates of justice and humanity is the conduct of those who leave a distant country for the purpose of imbuing their hands in the blood of a people that has ever received the Irish immigrant with kindness and hospitality."[4] The secretary authorized Hotze to provide needed funds. If any clergyman from the Northern states would assist Father Bannon, Hotze could also reimburse them for their efforts.[5]

The priest took up residence at the Angel Hotel in Dublin, a favorite resort of parish priests, politicians, and newspaper people. Here they discussed news of the world. Naturally, the appearance of such a colorful character as Father Bannon would cause a stir. He was both a successful pastor in America and a noted chaplain. Newsmen headed for the Angel Hotel to get the Southern version of the causes of the war. Later on, Father Bannon moved to a private residence at 24 St. James Place in Dublin.

Father Bannon had always believed that the basic struggle consisted of the capitalists of the Northeast trying to dominate the agricultural areas of the South and West for their own selfish benefit. He saw the abolitionists and nativists—strongly anti-Catholic—firmly entrenched in the Republican Party. They shouted "No Popery" as loudly as "No Slavery." Lee's army had invaded the North only twice and destroyed no Catholic schools or churches. Northern troops, on the contrary, desecrated Catholic churches. Even Northern newspapers carried accounts of these ravages.

In his first letter to the secretary, dated November 17, 1863, Father Bannon spoke of the heavy emigration from Ireland and blamed it on one thing: the failure of the crops in 1861 and 1862. He pointed out that the government of England tried to thwart every attempt at enlistment, but the exodus was continuing.[6] Five days later he wrote again, putting the numbers of people leaving between fifteen and eighteen thousand a month.[7] Father Bannon had an ally in John McHale, the archbishop of Tuam in County Mayo, a powerful writer and beloved figure. The archbishop denounced emigration.

Shortly before Father Bannon arrived in Dublin, General Thomas Francis Meagher of the Irish Brigade had pleaded the cause of the North. Another leader of the Young Ireland Movement of 1848, William Smith O'Brien, had sent a letter to *The United Irishman*, sharply criticizing the plea of the general. Though Meagher was a gallant soldier, the men in his unit had been so mauled in the Battle of Fredericksburg that it had almost ceased to exist as a working unit. This put Meagher's plea in a bad light. A friend of O'Brien, John Martin, also a leader of the 1848 uprising, had written to commend the stand of his friend. Father Bannon had supplied newspapers with items from the *Richmond Whig* and the *New York Freeman's Journal*, and he had written a letter to *The Nation* justifying the South. Bannon had written under the pen name Sacerdos (priest). Now he induced John Martin to write a series of letters for *The Nation* and promised to supply him with needful data.[8]

Eventually Father Bannon came to realize that other means were needed. The average immigrant probably did not read the newspapers. He decided, therefore, as Capston had done, to print a circular to be given to the potential immigrants and posters that could be tacked up in boarding houses of the seaport cities. Hotze approved this plan. Besides the writers already mentioned, he decided to add statements of John Mitchell, another Irish leader of the Rebellion of 1848, who had two sons who had died on the battlefield in defense of the South. Mitchell had written a letter two months before to *The Nation*, imploring the Irish people not to project themselves unjustly into a war against a young nation like themselves, struggling for freedom.[9] Bannon had two thousand copies of the poster printed. One thousand he sent to Capston for distribution in Queenstown, the port of Cork. Father Bannon requested Capston to see to it that every young man who came to that port for embarkation be given a copy. Five hundred more were sent to Galway.[10]

In the meantime, at Father Bannon's request, the Confederate State Department sent a representative, A. Dudley Mann, to the Holy See, to induce Pope Pius IX to interest himself in the situation in Ireland and by some authoritative word as the Father of Christendom, put a stop to emigration. The previous year, on October 18, 1962, the Holy Father had written to Archbishop John J. Hughes of New York and to Archbishop John M. Odin of New Orleans, begging them to use every effort to bring about a peaceful solution of the difficulties between the states.[11] Archbishop Hughes, incidentally, had earlier exercised great influence in winning Irish opinion for the North.

In January 1964, Father Bannon had twelve thousand copies of a second poster printed and two each mailed to parish priests of Ireland. It contained the Pope's letters to President Davis and to Archbishop Hughes, Davis's letter to the Pope, and a long commentary from the pen of "Sacerdos."

In a personal letter, Father Bannon asked the priests to place the poster where their parishioners could see it, in the hope that they would then hesitate to go to America and fight their fellow Irishmen of the South. He titled the poster "Address to the Catholic Clergy and People of Ireland."[12]

Father Bannon took it for granted that, in the Holy Father's appeal to Archbishop Hughes and in his prompt and generous recognition of the president of the Confederate States, he showed that Pope Pius IX took the same view of the war as Father Bannon did. The priest saw the war as a contest between the remnant of Christian civilization yet living in the South and the domineering materialism of the age personified in the amalgamation of Yankee descendants of Oliver Cromwell and recent anticlerical German immigrants. He justified secession by citing the example of America's Declaration of Independence from Britain in 1776. Factions of New England blighted the country as England had done a century before.

The Yankee manufacturers, Father Bannon wrote, pushed the war to enrich themselves at the expense of the farmers and planters of the South. Northern soldiers fought to restore the old fraternal union, but those in control sought only economic domination of the South. The old Union from the days of Washington flourished under the guidance of honorable Southern gentlemen. The Catholics and Irish of America owed their citizenship and preservation of equal rights to them. The few Catholic ranking officers in the armies of the North were, in Father Bannon's view, more decoys to lure other Irish into the service.

Nativists in Northern cities had hounded Archbishop Bedini, the representative of the Pope, and burned him in effigy in the public square in Cincinnati. Bannon claimed they had shot down women and children in the streets of Louisville before the war, and during the conflict plundered chalices from the tabernacles of Washington County and Frederick County, turned churches into stables, used vestments as horse blankets, and trampled on the Blessed Sacrament.

The men of the South, Bannon claimed, were friends of the foreigner, and many were Catholics, descendants of Spanish who settled in Florida, French in Louisiana, and Irish in Maryland and Kentucky. In the South, one did not hear the Irish Catholics referred to as beggarly, ignorant papists and low foreigners, as one did in the North. It was the South that crushed Know-Nothingism in the election of 1856. Northerners reduced Catholics to a status lower than slaves in the South and then expected Catholics in the North to hazard their lives to improve the status of ones better respected than they.[13] These were the only times Father Bannon ever referred to African Americans.

Father Bannon soon had evidence that his message had taken root. He attended a funeral of a prominent ecclesiastic that drew priests from all over the country. The one thing they talked about was the American war and the charges of Father Bannon against the North. It just happened that a pastor from a Northern city had just come back to his native Ireland and attended the funeral. He affirmed the Confederate chaplain's pubic statement, supplying many more particulars regarding the hostility manifested by the Union army toward Catholicism since the beginning of the war. He himself had been a victim of some of these outrages.

The funeral was presumably that of Monsignor William Yore, vicar general of the Archdiocese of Dublin and pastor of St. Paul's Church. He had taken an active part in the struggle for Catholic emancipation and fought for fair treatment of Catholic chaplains in the Crimean War. The *Freeman's Journal* devoted a full column and a half in its February 15, 1864, issue to an account of his achievements.[14] Father Bannon was assured that the bishops agreed with him and supported his efforts.[15]

A short time later, the bishop of Toronto, John Lynch, and the British government became aware of Bannon's excellent work in stopping recruitment of troops in Ireland. The *Times* praised the Irish agent whose noiseless industry, devoted zeal, and sound discretion had so successfully brought about a change in the emigration pattern.[16]

The January poster opened up a new avenue of approach. Now, Father Bannon began to receive invitations from those parish priests whose congregations had been dwindling fast due to emigration. In February, they wrote asking him to address their people at length upon the dangers incurred in the New World. In the first two weeks of February, he received three such invitations. He accepted them and hoped many more would come once the priests knew he was in the neighborhood. Throughout late February, he toured the country, lecturing on the American war four times.[17]

In almost every place the parish priests had become friends and supporters of the Confederacy, and signs of their influence was clear. Father Bannon wrote to Secretary Benjamin, recounting the remark of an Irish peasant: "We who were all praying for the North at the opening of the war, would now willingly fight for the South if we could get there."[18] Father Bannon wouldn't take full responsibility or whole credit for this change of sentiment. He found out that the warm advocacy of the North by Archbishop Hughes early in the conflict had had an effect on the Irish priests. But the archbishop had not said much or done much throughout the previous summer, and they began to see a connection between that and the letter of the Pope to the New York prelate.

Many of the priests previously had warmed to the courage of the South and its heroism but had been doubtful of the justice of its cause. Many letters came from disillusioned friends who had gone to America and hadn't found things so pleasant there. Quotations from the *New York Freeman's Journal* and the *New York Metropolitan Record* seem to bear out the statements of Father Bannon.

Father Bannon felt that, by this time, if the Union and Confederate recruiting officers could move freely in Ireland, within one month the Southern cause would attract four-fifths of the fighting men in the country.[19] In March, he went on another lecture tour after sending out another poster addressed to the young men of Ireland. He printed his own previous address as well as those of John

Mitchell, William Smith O'Brien, and John Martin. He pointed out the interesting fact that all of the surviving men of the Rebellion of 1848, the Young Ireland Movement, were strongly in favor of the South. He branded as false the rumors that 200,000 Irish served in the Union army, quoting the *Chicago Tribune* to prove that less than 40,000 were in Federal service. He challenged those Irishmen who recruited other Irish young men to fight for the North. They were doing Hessian work against the people of the South.

He appealed to the consciences of Catholics by pointing out that both St. Alphonsus Liguori and St. Thomas Aquinas, the greatest of all theologians, taught that a foreigner about to enter the military service of another country must, under pain of mortal sin, inquire as to the justice of the cause. As long as one continued to fight for an unjust cause, he could not gain absolution unless he got his discharge as soon as possible. If one fought merely for pay in an unjust cause, he could not receive absolution.[20]

The two circulars that Father Bannon had sent out came to the attention of the editors of the London *Times*. In an editorial on March 8, 1964, the writer remarked on "the cogency of the reasoning of Sacerdos, . . . (and) the able disquisition on the Right of Secession."[21]

During his lecture tour throughout Ireland in March 1864, Father Bannon arrived in Cork at the time Bishop Patrick N. Lynch of Charleston arrived in the city on the way to Paris, and eventually to Rome, as a special commissioner of the Confederate government. Accompanying him was a nephew, R. L. Lynch, who left a description of Father Bannon in action:

> I shall never forget Reverend Father Bannon, as I saw him the first time. He was then about forty years old, in the heyday of his magnificent manhood, standing over six feet two, with a finely shaped head, and most intelligent features, the whole set off by a full black, silky beard, which fell nearly to the waist. . . . There must have been more than one thousand sturdy Irishmen, with their bundles and packs, waiting on the dock for the arrival of the Cunard Steamer from Liverpool, to take them to Boston.
>
> In a few minutes Father Bannon appeared on the scene in his priestly garb. Mounting a box, he soon had all the Irish lads around him, as they recognized in him, at once, the Catholic priest. In a clear, ringing voice, he told them of the war that was raging in America, between the North and the South; how the Southern men, ragged and starving, were fighting for the protection of their homes; how he himself had served as chaplain for an Irish Catholic Regiment on the Southern side, until he and the whole regiment had been captured at the surrender of Vicksburg; and that he had remained in prison until exchanged.

He explained to them that, on their arrival in America, they would find no work; that after a few days, they would be arrested as vagabonds, thrown into prison, and be given a choice, either to remain in jail, or enlist in the army. "I, as a priest, tell you the truth," he said, "so that you may not walk blindfolded into the trap set for you. My advice to you, is for all of you to return to your homes, and not go to America until this cruel Civil War is ended." And then a most touching thing happened. All of those young fellows dropped to their knees, with the cry "Your blessing, Father." When it had been given, they quietly shouldered their packs and bundles and marched away to their homes.[22]

In early spring, Father Bannon came to the aid of a group called the Southern Independence Association, which Hotze sponsored. It lobbied in both the Upper and the Lower Houses of Parliament. To those in either house who were in favor of the Southern cause, Father Bannon sent clippings from Irish and American papers that would supply them with information and arguments on the question of Southern rights and interests.

Agitation in Parliament led to the unmasking of a mysterious agent, Finney or Feeny by name, who gave out that he was in charge of a railroad in America and needed workers for rail construction. In reality, he ran no railroad but supplied Irish immigrants for the Union army.

Left: Bishop Patrick Lynch of Charleston, South Carolina, presented Father Bannon to Pope Pius IX.

Above: Pope Pius IX remarked about Father Bannon's impressive physique and long black beard.

The *Dublin Evening News* in early July 1864 told of Confederate General Jubal Early's invasion of Maryland. While no word came from the Georgia front, Grant was obviously hung up before Petersburg, Virginia, after losing in a summer-long attack almost as many men as Lee had in his entire army. This fact provoked Captain Capston to refer to Grant as the "Great Butcher Lying in Front of Petersburg."[23] The South was hanging on, and the fall election might bring conciliatory leadership to the North.

Bishop Lynch had asked Father Bannon to accompany him to Rome. Secretary Benjamin had anticipated such a possibility in his initial directives before Father Bannon left the States. Bannon now felt that his work was done and wrote to Benjamin for the last time.[24]

Father Bannon traveled to Paris, where he again joined Bishop Lynch and his nephew, Robert Lynch, whom he had previously met in Cork. Lynch left a narrative on the stay in Paris and the trip to Rome as he earlier had described Father Bannon's meeting in Cork with would-be emigrants.

Bishop Lynch had used his fluent oratory to influence Napoleon III to recognize the Southern Confederacy. While favoring the South, Napoleon waited for England to move in the matter. From day to day, young Lynch anxiously awaited news that the French troops in Mexico had entered Texas to assist the South.

Father Bannon left for Rome in the company of the bishop, his nephew, and a priest from Charleston, Father Timothy Bermingham. Bishop Lynch hoped to win over Pope Pius IX to recognize the Confederacy. The Pope had unofficially recognized Southern independence by addressing a letter to President Jefferson Davis. The party left Paris for Rome.

Father Bermingham, incidentally, had a nose to match the prow of a blockade runner. Happy, he could laugh at remarks about the size of his prominent proboscis. Sensing that, Father Bannon remarked on one occasion: "Father Bermingham, if you had lived in France during the First Empire, Napoleon would have made you Marshall of France." "Why?" innocently inquired Father Bermingham. "Because," he answered, "Napoleon always selected his marshalls from men who had the biggest noses."[25]

At least during part of the journey to Rome, the bishop's party traveled with a group of tourists. In the rugged mountains of central Italy, a lady in the party insisted on riding her horse along the narrow edge of a frightful precipice, instead of walking and leading the horse over the dangerous stretch.

Father Bannon insisted on being allowed to lead the horse. It was good that he did. In the most dangerous spot, the horse's hind legs went over the edge, with the lady clinging to its neck. Father Bannon clung to a jagged rock with his left hand and his right hand grasped the bridle of the doomed horse. With amazing strength, he led the horse against the rocky wall until young Lynch pulled the lady to safety. The horse went crashing to its death, hundreds of feet below in the chasm.

The rest of the journey to the Eternal City was uneventful. Within a week of the party's arrival in Rome, Pope Pius IX invited Bishop Lynch and his associates to a private audience. Two open carriages with liveried attendants brought the four to the Vatican. Bishop Lynch and Father Bannon, as his chaplain, rode in the first, and Father Bermingham and young Lynch in the second. When they arrived at the Vatican, a cardinal directed them through the ranks of the colorfully attired Swiss Guards. The room for the private audience was large but simply furnished. Two attendant cardinals stood near the Pope, who sat in front of a small, plain table.

Pius IX wore the traditional white cassock and red skullcap. His face riveted attention. "Never before or since," young Lynch wrote, "have I ever seen such mobile and gentle features. The expression seemed to be changing every moment, so much so, that he was the despair of all photographers."[26]

When one of the cardinals started to present Bishop Lynch, the Pope anticipated the presentation and welcomed him. The bishop, in turn, presented Father Bermingham. This proved equally unnecessary, as the Pope had received him years before and remembered him from the enormous size of his nose.

Next, Bannon bent his knee to kiss the papal ring as all the others had done. As he straightened up to his great height, with his great black flowing beard, the expression of the Pope's face denoted wonder, then admiration.

Motioning to the two cardinals, "Stand aside," the Pope said, "that I may better see '*cet homme magnifique.*'"[27]

Of course Father Bannon felt twice as tall as he actually was. The Pope saw that he had caused this display of vanity, and the expression on his face changed. In a stern voice he demanded, "Who gave you permission to wear that beard?"

Momentarily flustered, Father Bannon relied on his Irish wit. Bowing low before the Pope, he said, "Holy Father, I am only a poor Confederate chaplain. What would become of me if in camp, I had one half of this enormous beard shaved off, and the bugle should ring out, 'to horse, to horse, the Yankees are here?' I, the poor priest, should have to ride away like a fool, with half my beard gone."

A heavenly smile gradually crept over the face of Pius IX, as he said, "My son, you may wear your beard."[28]

14

Whither the Call?

In America, the Confederacy hung by thin threads. Sherman took Atlanta and wasted the South's breadbasket. Relentless "Sam" Grant almost surrounded Lee's unfed and outmanned forces at Petersburg. A re-elected Lincoln spoke more confidently.

Too late the Confederate government had begun to face the issue of slavery. The South's ambassadors in London and Paris had long insisted that the two European powers would send no help as long as the South kept blacks in thralldom. At the outbreak of the war in 1861, "free men of color" in Louisiana had marched out to defend their homes as their fathers and grandfathers had done under Andrew Jackson in 1815. Mississippians, however, had refused to allow these Louisiana black troops to defend their sacred all-white soil. The rest of the South supported Mississippi's blunder. In 1864, to save Atlanta, General Patrick Cleburne had urged the freeing of all slaves who would join the Southern forces. His wise recommendation met a rebuff of fire as fierce as the wall of fire he and his men would meet that fall at Franklin, Tennessee.

The South could have made a case for peaceful secession had it not fired on the flag at Fort Sumter. Not until later did the Supreme Court point out that the Constitution looked to an indestructible union of indestructible states. But the Confederacy could not justify before world opinion its determination to keep human beings in bondage. In spite of the sacrifices of its people and the bravery of its soldiers, the South was going down.

Where did that leave Father Bannon? He was an agent of a government that was collapsing, a priest without a parish. Even if he had not known about the regime of vengeance that a small clique of anti-Lincoln "Radical Republicans" was bringing on Missouri, he faced uncertainty. If he tried to get back to St. Louis, the vindictive laws would jail him. What would Archbishop Kenrick say or do? How would those of his parishioners feel whose sons died for the Union? And the parents of Confederate veterans who might have blamed Father Bannon for misleading their sons South? He had run off from his parishioners four years before. Would they welcome him back if Archbishop Kenrick did?

Father Bannon had accepted assignment in Ireland with the blessing of Bishop John McGill of Richmond. No doubt the bishop would have welcomed him in his war-torn diocese. So would his friend from their Roman journey, Bishop Patrick Lynch of Charleston, South Carolina. Sherman had shredded the central part of his territory. The area needed help. Father Bannon could have done great work there. In either case, he could not get back to the South until peace came and Lincoln lifted the blockade. Further, he had no familiarity with any place there. Only St. Louis was his second home.

He could return to his native Ireland. Cardinal Paul Cullen, who had ordained him, still headed the Dublin Archdiocese. No doubt the cardinal still held in high regard the first priest he had ordained since becoming an archbishop. Young John Bannon had taken his early studies at the Vincentian College of Castleknock. Did he consider joining the Vincentians? No evidence exists to affirm or deny this possibility.

Father Bannon had little contact with the Jesuit fathers in his early years. In St. Louis he had joined the St. Louis Catholic Literary Institute that met at Saint Louis University, a Jesuit institution. He had invited a Jesuit orator, Cornelius Smarius, to speak at the cornerstone laying of St. John's Church and Jesuit Frederick Garesche to preach at the pontifical mass of dedication. The Jesuit president of Saint Louis University, Father Ferdinand Coosemans, had assisted the archbishop at the pontifical mass. Later on, it became apparent that a prominent Jesuit, Father Joseph Keller, whose father was organist at the St. Louis Cathedral, knew Father Bannon well.

Be that as it may, John Bannon made the Spiritual Exercises of St. Ignatius in Rome. At the conclusion, he conferred with the Jesuit-General Peter Beckx and asked for admission to the Jesuit novitiate of the Irish Province. The father-general welcomed him into the order.

Above: Father Bannon shaved his beard and entered the Jesuit Seminary.

15

Reorientation in Erin

On the day after Christmas, 1864, a six-foot-four clergyman, with broad shoulders and a long, black, silky beard, walked toward the door of the Jesuit novitiate in Milltown Park at Dublin's south end. The thirty-five-year-old priest was John B. Bannon.

Seventy years later, a fellow novice who spent most of his priestly years in Australia could still remember the day his former colleague with the black beard that hung over his chest had entered the postulancy. He recalled further that for a fortnight Father Bannon held the center of attention in the recreation periods after dinner and supper with stories of his memorable experiences.[1]

Father Bannon shaved off his beard and prepared to enter the novitiate on January 9, 1865.

His fascinating accounts of surviving cannonades and running blockades drew the attention of his ten fellow first-year novices from the central focus of their lives. They should have been hearing of Jesuit saints Ignatius of Loyola and Francis Xavier, not of Missouri Confederates Sterling Price and Daniel Frost. The Ignatian way of life and the methods of prayer, as outlined in the *Spiritual Exercises* of St. Ignatius, should have held their attention, not the successive strategies of General Grant at Vicksburg.

The veteran chaplain could readily see the reason for the associate director's strong recommendation that he refrain from regaling his young fellow novices with his colorful accounts of men at war. It was bad enough having Father Peter De Smet, the Indian missionary, come regularly and, with his tales of Sioux villages in the Black Hills, lure young Irish Jesuits to seek transfer to the missions of the distant Missouri province. Father Bannon's heroic stories might stir even more to sail for the American frontier.

As all novices at Milltown Park had to do at the time, Father Bannon wrote a short account of his birth, his education, his family, and his inclinations.[2] His father was a native of Dublin; his mother came from County Roscommon. He had been born there at the town of Rooskey, December 29, 1829, while his mother was visiting her family.[3]

Father Bannon wrote that he had always enjoyed good health during his early years in Dublin. Having attended the Vincentian College at Castleknock and the Royal Seminary of St. Patrick's at Maynooth, he had been ordained by Archbishop Paul Cullen in 1853. Then, with the archbishop's permission, he had gone to America that same summer to work in the Archdiocese of St. Louis.

"I feel inclined to do any duties imposed upon me," Father Bannon went on to say. "I have a disinclination for preaching, though none for teaching or foreign missions." Then, on second thought, he qualified his feelings regarding the pulpit. "My disinclination for preaching arises principally from dislike of all offices or duties which bring me prominently before the public. This disinclination does not extend to preaching to the poor and humble."[4]

The quiet routines and silence of novitiate life, the full schedule of work, study, and prayer, with only short periods of free time between each duty, contrasted dramatically with the clangor of encampments, the carnage of the conflict, and the challenging work of the Confederate agent. With a gray stone building several stories tall housing the novices and their directors, the Jesuit novitiate

offered a perfect place for calm reflection, situated as it was in parklike grounds in the southern environs of Dublin. The area abounded in walkways flanked by chestnuts, limes, and maples. The most impressive tree in the entire area, a two-hundred-year-old cooper beech, probably one of the first introduced from Germany in the seventeenth century, spread its wide branches just as the live oaks had done in the vicinity of Vicksburg that Father Bannon had so recently left.

On January 17, 1865, Father Bannon and his father, James Bannon, deeded to John's brother Michael "the lands of Slattagh Beg, situate (*sic*) in the Barony of Ballintubber North, with the town parks of Elphin, known by the names of Aughmagmane and Curraghmore."[5] By giving up these extensive land holdings, Father Bannon indicated his intention to take the Jesuit vow of poverty.

Even though the master of novices, sixty-year-old Father Joseph Lentaigne, had been the first provincial superior of the Irish Jesuits, he must have felt awed to have among his mainly teenaged novices this powerful personality. As the year went on, however, he came to realize that the class contained an unusual number of able young men. Several of Father Bannon's classmates were destined to stand out over the years. Patrick Keating became the father provincial of the Irish Province,[6] John Naughton won acclaim as a man "of great eminence and distinction" for his work as a home missionary,[7] and two members of the class became rectors of colleges: Philip O'Connell at Limerick and George Kelly at Tullabeg.[8]

Australia beckoned zealous Jesuits in those days. Father Joseph Lentaigne and Father William Kelly left the year after Bannon's entrance (1865). Three priests and two coadjutor brothers sailed for the South Pacific in 1866, and a third contingent would follow in 1867. Three of Father Bannon's fellow novices, George

Facing: The novitiate at Milltown Park at the south end of Dublin proved amazingly peaceful after the Battle of Pea Ridge and the siege of Vicksburg. Father Bannon entered the Jesuits here.
Right: Garden at the novitiate at Milltown Park, Dublin.

Kelly, Thomas McEnroe, and Charles Morragh, eventually moved Down Under, and Father Lentaigne's successor, Father Aloysius Sturzo, followed him and opened a novitiate at Sydney.[9]

Because Father Bannon's cousin, Father Joseph Higgins, went to Australia and became bishop of Ballarat, situated across the bay from Melbourne, and Father Bannon had indicated a willingness to go to the foreign missions, one might well presume that he gave thought to a ministry under the Southern Cross, but no extant records deal with this issue.

Only one out-of-the-ordinary event occurred during Father Bannon's initial year in the novitiate. In September 1865, his new superiors sent him to St. Stanislaus College in Tullabeg to open the annual retreat for 115 students.[10] No further comment accompanied the simple notation of fact.

The provincial superior sent Father Bannon and Philip O'Connell to Louvain University in Belgium in 1866 to review the latest developments in dogmatic and pastoral theology.[11] While Father Bannon was there, Bishop John McGill of Richmond visited him at the Jesuit residence. The Virginia prelate told the ex-chaplain that the Confederate Congress had passed a vote of thanks for his success in stopping Federal recruiting in Ireland and voted him a $3,000 bonus.[12] It seems unlikely that the welfare and whereabouts of the Confederate leaders, Jefferson Davis and Judah Benjamin, would not come up for discussion. Father Bannon probably had not heard that the ex-president of the Confederacy was imprisoned at Hampton Roads, Virginia, or that the ex-secretary of state had escaped to England. Bishop McGill may have spoken of the successful meeting of the American bishops at Baltimore, and no doubt mentioned the part Father Bannon's former superior, Archbishop Peter Richard Kenrick, had played in that meeting.

While Father Bannon mentioned his visit with Bishop McGill in a letter to a Southern historian some years later, we have no clear-cut record of any visit or correspondence with Archbishop Kenrick of St. Louis, who years before had invited him to America and appointed him pastor of a growing congregation. The priest had left a sealed letter for His Grace when he followed his militia command South. Anticipating the severe penalties Federal authorities in Missouri would have imposed on anyone who had sympathized with the Confederacy, Archbishop Kenrick had left the envelope unopened.

Father Bannon's ties with the Archdiocese of St. Louis ended practically with his commitment to the Southern army. No doubt he requested temporary leave in the unopened letter. Final canonical separation would have been mandatory before his acceptance into the Jesuit order in 1865. Courtesy would suggest more. The question naturally suggests itself: did the priest and the archbishop ever meet again?

In a speech many years later, a close friend of Father Bannon, Captain Joseph Boyce said they did. Boyce had some of the circumstances of the visit out of time frame, but his statement seems substantially correct, even though no other reference has surfaced.[13] Archbishop Kenrick went through Ireland in late June 1867, on his way to Rome. Records indicate that he came again in late September the following year.

The *Annals in the Irish Catholic Directory* recount the solemnity that marked the Feast of St. Michael, September 28, 1868, at St. Michael and St. John's Church in Dublin. The *Annals* state: "One of the most illustrious prelates of the American Church, the Most Rev. Dr. Kenrick, Archbishop of St. Louis, presided."[14] Under the date of October 6, the *Annals* state: "At High Mass in the Cathedral Church, at which His Eminence the Cardinal Archbishop presided, the Most Rev. Dr. Kenrick, Archbishop of St. Louis, preached a splendid sermon."[15] In the course of the sermon, Archbishop Kenrick called his native land "the martyr-nation of the world"—an often-quoted tribute.[16]

On the same October Sunday, the *Annals* noted, Father Patrick Ryan, secretary to Archbishop Kenrick and soon-to-be pastor of the church Father Bannon had built, "preached a magnificent sermon before a densely crowded congregation of parishioners drawn together by his fame as a pulpit orator."[17] One may presume that, during Archbishop Kenrick's stop in Ireland en route to Rome, or on his return stop in Ireland, Father Bannon met with him.

No doubt the former St. Louis pastor also visited with his friend Father Patrick Ryan. They would have had much to talk about besides events and friends in St. Louis. They had an added connection. As a civilian chaplain, Father Ryan had cared for the spiritual needs of Confederate officers imprisoned at the former McDowell Medical College in St. Louis. Some of them were Father Bannon's friends or acquaintances.

In the meantime, Father Bannon published an account of his experiences as a chaplain of the Southern army in *Letters and Notices*, an in-house publication of the English Jesuit Province.[18] He immediately captured his English readers' attention by contrasting his procedures on the eve of battle with the stories he had heard over the years of Crimean chaplains. He began in a formal style, but soon his narrative flowed as fast as the Mississippi River at the foot of Vicksburg bluffs. He concentrated on two soldiers: an Irish Catholic cannoneer badly wounded at Elkhorn Tavern and an unbaptized volunteer in the Vicksburg Hospital.[19] These experiences have been related in earlier chapters.

16

Into the "Heart of the Irish Church"

After Bannon's year in Louvain, the *Brief Chronological Notes* for the residence at St. Francis Xavier Parish on Gardiner Street in downtown Dublin carried this item for 1867: "Father John Bannon, who was to take such an important part in the work of this church, came to reside here about this time as a 'traveling missionary.'"[1] This assignment put him into the midst of the central thrust of the Irish Church.

In 1850, while Father Bannon was still in theological studies at Maynooth, the Irish bishops had held their first synod since the twelfth century at the town of Thurles. They chose the parish mission as the chief tool in strengthening the religious life of the people and challenged the Vincentians and the Jesuits to man the pulpits. Both groups responded enthusiastically, followed by the Redemptorists, the Passionists, and other congregations.

Under the leadership of Archbishop Paul Cullen of Armagh, the entire religious life of the people had taken a more devotional tone, popular in Italy. In various scholarly treatises, the leading American historian of nineteenth-century Ireland, Professor Emmet Larkin, called Cullen's influence "a devotional revolution."[2]

A descendant of prosperous farmers, Paul Cullen had gone to Rome in 1820 at age seventeen to study for the priesthood. He completed his studies in Rome. "He was to remain there in a position of increasing power and trust," wrote Church historian Patrick Corish, "until he was appointed bishop in Ireland. This Roman experience marked him deeply, but it always coexisted with his Irish family heritage."[3] An uncle had been executed in the uprising of 1798, and his father barely had escaped a similar fate.

The new archbishop was an austere but nervous man who found decisions difficult. Nonetheless, he drove himself relentlessly in spite of poor health. He never could get used to his native climate after his long sojourn in Rome and suffered continuous colds. He identified "Irish" with "Catholic," opposed English politics, and looked to the day when Irish Catholics would convert the world-empire of England. Pope Pius IX chose him as archbishop of Dublin in 1852 instead of any of the three prelates recommended by the Irish clergy. He had ordained Father Bannon shortly after his consecration.[4]

The Great Famine had marked a permanent change in Irish social structures. Laborers without land were few. The poor had suffered most. The "nation-forming" class, as historian Emmet Larkin called them, were now the farmers of small- to medium-sized holdings of thirty acres or more. They dominated constitutional policies. Most of the priests came from this group, too. Basic literacy was steadily improving because of the growth of the National School System.[5]

Left: Archbishop Paul Cullen ordained Father Bannon in 1855. Ireland's first cardinal, he called for a program of parish missions that challenged Father Bannon to preach in all parts of Ireland.

A new sense of the centrality of the Pope came to Church life. The postal system brought greater Roman supervision of the local churches. In turn, bishops more closely supervised the clergy, who were more disciplined, more professional in preparation, and more single-minded. "The priest was to regard himself as a man set apart," historian Patrick Corish wrote, "marked by his black or dark dress and Roman collar, prayerful, devoted, carefully nourishing his necessary learning, all this supported by regular retreats and clerical conferences."[6]

The bishops, too, came from a different source. It was less common for a parish priest to rise to the episcopate. Most likely the bishops would come from successful administrators or members of religious congregations. Archbishop Cullen did not like the seminary at Maynooth because of its ties with the British government and advanced few of its alumni to the episcopate. He fostered the Irish College in Rome and promoted its graduates when he could. He regularly put forward names other than those on the list of three, called the *terna*, chosen by the parish priests.[7]

The number of priests was growing—from one for every 2,000 Catholics in 1850 to one for every 1,250 Catholics in 1870. But the real expansion came with the Irish Christian Brothers and with the nuns, who grew from 120 in 1800 to 1,500 in 1850, to 3,700 in 1870 and 8,000 in 1900.[8]

Above: Oftentimes on remote missions, the priests shared the sparse accommodations of farmers, occasionally in a thatched-roofed cottage such as this one.

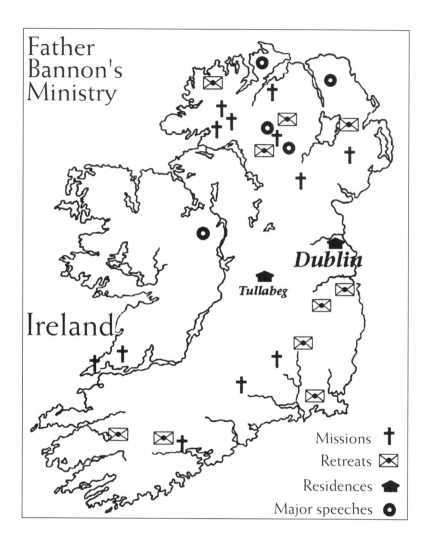

Father
Bannon's
Ministry

Dublin

Tullabeg

Ireland

Missions ✝
Retreats ✉
Residences ⌂
Major speeches ◉

While Father Bannon worked in America, churches, convents, and schools had been sprouting all over the green fields of Ireland. Father Bannon could see the optimism that had followed the years of famine. He would do his part to keep it alive and flourishing. Less than two years after Father Bannon returned, Ireland would welcome the first cardinal in its long Catholic history; that prelate was Archbishop Paul Cullen. Early in 1868, England got a new prime minister, William Ewart Gladstone. Just as Cardinal Cullen put new spirit into the religious life of the Irish people, so Gladstone improved their civic life and enlarged the scope of their freedom. Economic and social improvements began to match the religious advances.

Father Bannon's initial mission would prove almost as challenging as his first battle at distant Pea Ridge on the Arkansas-Missouri border back in 1862. He was to missionize Catholics on the Isle of Man in the Irish Sea starting in November 1867. He traveled by steamer with the veteran home-missionary and province pioneer, Father Robert Haly, to Holyhead in Wales. They attended a music program in Liverpool and then visited the Jesuit College at Stonyhurst. After this pleasant meeting with a group of fellow Jesuits that included two Irish scholastics, one of them Father Bannon's novitiate classmate George Kelly, they took the ferry to Douglas on the Isle of Man, halfway between Liverpool and County Down in Ireland. Archbishop George Errington welcomed them for dinner that evening.[9] A native of Yorkshire, Errington would make his presence felt at the First Vatican Council three years later as one of the two English archbishops who opposed the definition of papal infallibility.

The visitors from Ireland enjoyed two days of sight-seeing before the mission.[10] The Isle of Man had a Catholic history that dated back to the Irish monks in the years immediately following the death of St. Patrick. A bishop resided there when Norway controlled the island. But the Protestant movement of the sixteenth century made drastic changes. Only about thirteen hundred people were Catholic by the time of the arrival of Fathers Haly and Bannon, and these few did not attend Mass regularly. Not only men, but also many women overindulged in stout. In addition, some Catholics were married at the Kirkbradden Presbyterian Church.

On Sunday, November 10, 1867, the archbishop opened the three-week mission with mass at 8 A.M. Father Bannon faced an additional challenge in his well-prepared sermon to a large congregation. The cathedral was magnificent, but so were the echoes, and the poor acoustics made hearing difficult. Having faced the difficulty of preaching under poor conditions during General Grant's relentless bombardment of Vicksburg, Father Bannon met this new challenge undaunted, and his sermon earned Father Haly's warm approval. At noon that day a large group of people attended Mass but walked out before Benediction.

Father Haly noted happily in his record: "Father Bannon reprimanded them severely for it in the evening."[11]

Father Bannon catechized the children every morning and preached on Purgatory. Father Haly noted that no Catholic on the island requested a memorial mass for any reason. But he could record positively that many backsliders returned to the Church, several had their marriages blessed, and many prayed the Rosary.[12] Father Bannon had obviously impressed his hearers and his colleagues.[13]

Early in the New Year, Provincial Superior Edmund O'Reilly assigned Father Bannon permanently to the traveling mission team. With Fathers Haly and Fortescue, the former Confederate chaplain would give missions in many dioceses of Ireland.

His teammates enjoyed nationwide fame as preachers. The *Irish Catholic Directory* for 1869 spoke of the fifty-one-year-old Father William Fortescue as "famous throughout Ireland as a missionary."[14] The seventy-one-year-old Father Robert Haly had won fame even earlier. The one remaining portrait of this venerable priest shows a strong man with a rugged physique, full white hair, and severe visage. That aspect did not reflect his reputation as a fatherly and compassionate spiritual director. A native of Cork, he studied at Stonyhurst in England and became a Jesuit in 1814. He finished theology at Freiburg in Switzerland and was ordained there in 1828. Returning to Ireland, he gave his first parish mission in the town of Sellbridge in 1833. During the next quarter-century, he directed various Jesuit colleges. In 1859, he headed the newly established Province Mission Team.

Henry Brown, author of the book *A Roll of Honor: Irish Priests and Prelates of the Last Century*, published in 1905, included Father Haly in that illustrious company. He praised the venerable Jesuit for having given his energy "to apostolic work in almost every parish in Ireland, either by himself or as head of a band of missionaries."[15]

Father Bannon had the privilege of the tutelage, inspiration, and comradeship of this dedicated apostle. Describing the effort of the Haly team, a modern home missioner, Father Kevin Laheen, S.J., wrote: "The arrival of the missionaries was awaited with widespread interest. It was not only the Catholics who looked forward to their coming, but others awaited them and actually attended the mission."[16] Some Protestants came out of curiosity, some to get something to talk about other than the weather and the crops, others in the hope of stirring up controversy.

The usual mission consisted of a series of religious exercises during a three-week period. Each day began with High Mass and a sermon in the morning and at noon, confessions were heard in the afternoon, and a longer sermon, followed by Benediction, constituted the evening service. A team of two or three traveling

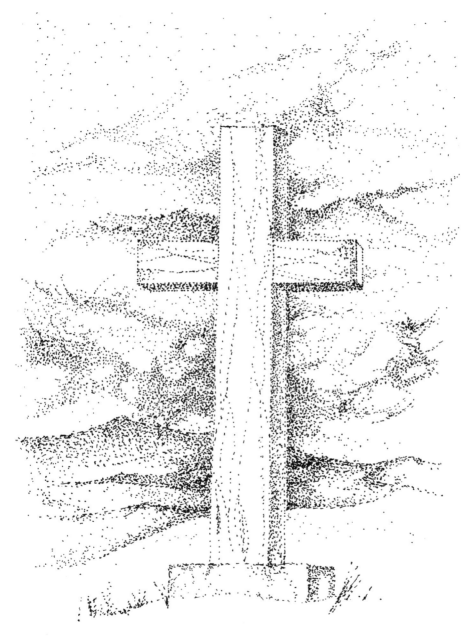

SHARRIS

Above: At the close of a mission, the Jesuits urged the parishioners to erect a cross of wood or stone to recall the message of their preaching.

missionaries had the assistance of the parish priest, his curate, and other priests from the vicinity who came to help with confessions.

Oftentimes the congregation would have only a minimal acquaintance with the truths of the faith, or the pastor had limited theological background. A leading historian of Catholic Ireland, Father Patrick Corish, wrote, "It may safely be concluded that his [the average Irish pastor's] Sunday preaching was essentially an extension of the catechism." [17] In such a situation, the missioners would concentrate on the basics of the faith.

Penal laws forbade Catholic processions, but the Orangemen could and did hold anti-Catholic parades. The missionaries felt that they should test the law, in various places, even if hostile neighbors pelted the pious pilgrims with rocks. Boys carried tapers, girls wore white dresses, and thousands of people marched in a public demonstration of their faith that some areas had not witnessed for a long time.

Forty years old, Father Bannon brought many qualities to this already splendid mission team: physical vigor, youthful enthusiasm carried in a voice of power and sweetness, an easy approach in dealing with people, the capacity for teamwork, a wide acquaintance with places and events, and a facility for telling illustrative stories. His two associates discussed with him the ups and downs of home missions, the enthusiasm and encouragement of the large crowds, as well as the tedium of travels between assignments.

Above: Father Bannon preached at St. Columba's Church on a hill in Kerry overlooking the River Boyle.

Posterity knows details of these missions because of the careful reporting by Father Haly. He left a written account of all the missions the team gave.

Father Bannon's first effort as a permanent member of the mission team came at St. Columba's Church on a barren hillside east of the River Foyle in Derry. "Father Bannon," the *House Diary* noted, "delivered a telling and persuasive opening discourse to the vast congregation that attended."[18] It was a promising start. A wooden bridge made access easy for those who lived in the town of Derry on the west bank.

April 1868 saw Father Bannon at two towns too small to make the standard map of Ireland, Boinabrina and Castle Jordan, in County Meath, about forty miles west of Dublin. The pastor, Father Kealy, met the missionaries with his carriage and took them to his rural parishes. This area almost rivaled the Isle of Man for difficulties. Countless Catholics had never attended Mass, had received no sacrament after Baptism, and had made bad confessions. Hostility, not peace, prevailed between two factions of the parish. People were moving away. Even while the mission went on, eighteen to twenty young people left the villages to seek employment elsewhere. Nonetheless, Father Bannon was able to organize a choir, and the missioners raised a modest mission cross in the yard adjacent to the church and rectory.[19] It had proved to be another challenging beginning for Father Bannon, but the veterans could see some good results.

In July 1868, Father Bannon gave the annual retreat to the priests of the Diocese of Cork.[20] The conferences of the retreat followed the *Book of the Spiritual Exercises* of St. Ignatius of Loyola, the Jesuit founder. The program began with such basic questions as why God made humans, and what could keep humans from God—the material the priest covered in the parish mission. During the other three-fourths of the retreat time, the director presented material from the New Testament on the coming of Christ, His message, His founding of His Church, and His death and Resurrection. The speaker would intersperse among these contemplations special meditations on the standards of Christ and of Satan, on Christ's call to His Kingdom, on the various ways people respond to this call, and finally, on methods of growing in love of God.

The *Londonderry Journal* for February 27, 1869, announced that Father Bannon would give a benefit sermon for a new rectory at St. Mary's Catholic Church in Stranorlar, in County Donegal, about forty-five miles southwest of Derry, on March 7.[21] A special train was scheduled to leave Derry at 9:30 A.M. and return at 8:15 P.M. The crowd was large, the sermon excellent.[22]

The gray stone church with its square Norman tower, where Father Bannon gave his benefit talk, still serves its congregation. The building holds seven hundred worshipers comfortably, while a four-foot levee protects it from the occasional rampages of the Finn River.

17

By Train or by "Bian"

The next mission assignment of three weeks in April 1869 took the mission team to Carrigaholt on the north side of the estuary of the Shannon River, near the southwestern tip of County Clare. It was the closest Father Bannon would get to America during the remainder of his life.

Fathers Haly and Bannon preached to the few people who lived near the church during the discouraging first week. By the second week the storms from the Atlantic had let up and the farmers could get their chores done and find the roads passable. The third week brought crowds. Nine hundred adults came, the priests of the area converged to assist with confessions, and Bishop Patrick Fallon of Kilmackdough confirmed four hundred children.[1] Even at the height of the tourist season today, it would be hard to find nine hundred adults within ten miles of the town.

During every long mission, Father Haly arranged a "rest day." The local pastor, Father Michael Meehan, brother of Father Patrick Meehan, who had worked in the St. Louis Archdiocese at the same time as Father Bannon, drove the missionaries the four miles across the peninsula to the villages of Kilrush and Kilkee, near the most spectacular coast in all of Ireland. Thirty miles to the north stood the sheer Cliffs of Moher, famous throughout the country. But the rugged coast across from Carrigaholt boasted an added feature. Several giant rocks had split off from the cliff and stood proud in the ocean a short distance off. Almost as high as the cliffs, they defied the mighty tides of the Atlantic. Even on cloudy days when the sea looked as gray as the stone on the Clare hillsides, the water, rushing between the towers and the cliffs, kept a sun-brightened blue, crested with white foam.

It was a long way to Tipperary from Carrigaholt in County Clare, to Golden, ten miles west of Cashel. Archbishop Patrick Leahy did not attend the mission but sent his blessing and the needed faculties. He might more readily have removed some restrictions, such as the requirement that all penitents go to confession in the vestry of the chapel, and avoid pubs on Sundays. Persons coming from a distance in hot weather found this a "quid intolerabile," Father Haly notes.[2] No priest could absolve such penitents, except during the mission, but had to send them all to the archbishop.

Heavy rain on Saturday evening caused the congregation to crowd into the little chapel on Sunday morning. Since all those in attendance carried lighted tapers, Father Haly feared disaster. But all went well during Father Bannon's sermon. On Monday, Father Bannon accompanied Father Haly on a visit to the Rock of Cashel and the Presentation Convent and schools in the town. Father Robert Kelly, who had taken Father Fortescue's place, stayed a day after the others at Golden and organized a sodality of Mary.[3] A two-horse carriage took the missioners back to County Clare, to the town of O'Callaghan Mills, for their next mission. Father Bannon again showed his versatility. Besides preaching and hearing confessions, he looked to the practical. Father Haly wrote, "The church is a glare of lights thanks to Father Bannon's ingenuity and exertions."[4] How Father Bannon improved the illumination, Father Haly hesitated to say.[5] The missionaries had three comfortable beds in three small rooms. In this instance, the pastor and curates had offered to dwell elsewhere.[6]

Their next destination, the town of Castlecomer, differed from most nineteenth-century mining communities, with their grim, soot-filled atmospheres. Thanks to a rich vein of anthracite—a hard coal that produced less smoke—Castlecomer remained attractive in a wooded valley in the hilly part of northern Kilkenny.[7]

While many of the parishioners worked in the pits,[8] Protestants owned most of the wealth in the town and had little love for their three thousand devout Catholic neighbors. The splendid parish church of Gothic style, begun in August 1841, could accommodate a large congregation but lacked good acoustics. The missionaries were able to put up a sounding board behind the pulpit to improve hearing conditions.

More men than women flocked into the mission at once and came to confession even before the assigned time of mission confessions. Two hundred altar boys in cassocks and surplices carried lighted candles and bells in the procession. Twice that many girls wore white frocks with blue sashes and garlands in their hair. Father Bannon started a young ladies' sodality in the village. Eventually, several thousand of the faithful received communion.

The figures for attendance and participation recorded by Father Haly awe one, but that was not the final note in the veteran missionary's words on Castlecomer. Three miles out of town, on their departure, the Jesuits came upon five hundred miners who had left their work to wave good-bye. Each carried a green branch. Their leader carried a banner with the words "Farewell to the Jesuit Fathers." Only reluctantly did the miners end their parade behind the priests' carriage and return to their duties. "We all agreed," Father Haly wrote, "that nowhere except in Ireland could such a spectacle be met with."[9]

To get to their destinations, the missionaries traveled by train or carriage. By 1870, almost two thousand miles of track criss-crossed Ireland, more than in the state of Missouri. Fares averaged a penny a mile. An enterprising Italian immigrant added carriage services to many other cities. Carlo Bianconi had come to Ireland in 1802 at age sixteen, an enterprising merchant and metal worker. At the end of the Crimean War (1856), he was able to purchase war surplus lorries from Britain. These horse-drawn conveyances took passengers from various railroad stations into the interior of the country. He routed one, for instance, from Clonmell on the Waterford-to-Limerick railroad to Mallow on the Cork-to-Limerick run. Another one went west from Mallow to Tralee, another from Athlone to Boyle on the Mullingar-to-Sligo railroad. The "Bians," as they were called, made it possible to go from Limerick to Tralee, and from Killarney toward the Ring of Kerry. So, between the railroad and the Bians, one could readily move around the country.

Each mode of transportation offered its unique challenges, with endless delays and missed connections. Regularly the priests spent hours in waiting rooms. Often, one or the other of the team, coming from a different direction, arrived a day after the others. On at least one occasion during Father Bannon's time with the mission team, no one met them at the station.[10] Most of the time, however, the parish priest met the Jesuits at the train, assured them lodging, and even, on occasion, moved out of his own quarters. The pastor helped as needed, and usually invited the neighboring clergy to assist with confessions.

In many places, the missionaries lived in the thatched cottages of the local people. Oftentimes, the priest felt he was imposing himself for a week or two on an already overfilled home, with the children sleeping on the floor so that the guest could have the other bed. Sometimes accommodations proved unaccommodating, as in Stranorlar, where a defective chimney spewed smoke back into Father Bannon's room while the other priests were comfortable.[11]

On one occasion all three members of the mission team had to bivouac with different farmers far from the town. With all due respect for the clergy, the cattleman had to have equal regard, but of a different kind, for his herd. The country folk were happy to have the priest bless their homes with his august presence, but cows had to come first. The needs of the missionary came second.

Sometimes a parish priest would plan a mission at a normally good time, only to have capricious weather keep the harvesters busy on their acres or holed up in their cottages. Downpours mired wagons on the dirt roads. In a surprising turn on one mission in October, Father Haly had to speak of "oppressive heat," a totally unprecedented complaint for an Irish autumn.[12]

Bad weather could cut attendance; churches were cold. The speakers themselves suffered from colds and sore throats, while members of the congregation coughed and sneezed. In some buildings reverberating echoes impaired hearing. Yet it was a rare day when the missionary felt the effort had gone for naught.

A newly ordained priest, or one totally accustomed to city living, might have found a lot to overtax his zeal. Father Bannon could draw on his wartime experience. He had endured the night march around wintry Pea Ridge, the endless bivouac in the rain at Iuka and Corinth, and the scorching summer at Vicksburg. He could survive long nights in the confessional and be up and going early the next day. He might have an occasional cold or sore throat, but he could take those in stride.

The missioners revitalized the faith of countless people, as other home missioners were doing in various countries. While Fathers Haly, Fortescue, and Bannon were moving around Ireland, two fellow Jesuits, born on the continent—Arnold Damen, a Dutchman, and Franz Xavier Weninger, an Austrian—were matching their success in the vast regions of the United States.

Both Irish and continental Jesuits followed the fundamentals of why God made humankind and what it meant to ignore God's purposes. Many preachers focused on sin and confession and spent hours counseling their penitents. The common practice of speaking to the men one week and the women the next had the added value of always leaving an adult at home to spend time with the children. Perhaps on the third week all adults would come, leaving an older daughter to take care of her younger brothers and sisters.

Besides the routine spiritual improvement of fairly steady Catholics, the missioners always hoped for the "big salmon," the well-known individual who, instead of sliding back, definitely swam in the opposite direction. At Carrigaholt the priests brought back a heavy drinker after forty years in a spiritual bog.[13] Late in 1870, Father Haly could record the conversion of an "obstinate and nominal Catholic" who had lived in concubinage for many years, missed Mass for a quarter of a century, and in general, scandalized the neighborhood. He reconciled the parents with the Church, blessed their marriage, and instructed the children. On the "rest day," the renewed Christian invited the priests to his estate for dinner and a hunt. They enjoyed both, but their real joy came from the fact that one sinner had done penance.[14]

An invitation in October 1869 took Father Bannon and his coworkers once again to Waterside in Derry. On the way the missionaries stopped overnight at Strabane. The priests stayed with personal friends, Father Bannon with the O'Connors, Father Haly with the Gillespies. After Mass and breakfast at the

Mercy Convent, they took the train to Derry, where they paid their respects to Bishop J. McLaughlin.

The heat on the weekend of October 8–10 was oppressive. Noting the strange conditions of the atmosphere, Father Bannon warned his brethren of possible trouble. Father Haly noted in his mission record that Father Bannon expected an earthquake.[15] What Father Bannon probably feared was a good midwestern U.S. tornado. He was certainly more familiar with big winds than quakes of the earth. But neither came, even though the heat clung to the countryside. A lady of the parish provided fresh shirts and socks for the visiting Jesuits.

Fathers Fortescue and Robert Kelly joined Fathers Haly and Bannon on Monday of the first week of the Waterside mission. Father Bannon catechized the schoolchildren. Bishop McLaughlin came three times to hear Father Bannon's sermons. That said much. If a bishop comes once, he's checking up on the speaker's orthodoxy. If more than once, he's open to new approaches in theology. Many priests of the diocese came to assist with the numerous confessions. The missionaries welcomed eleven Protestants into the Church.[16]

Word of Father Bannon's talks for the benefit of the parish residence in Stranolar that March must have spread through the area. The pastor at Ballmoney asked him to speak to raise money for the beautiful school building. The pastor had planned well, having sent invitations for the tea to wealthy Anglicans and Presbyterians. Fathers Fortescue, Haly, Kelly, and McKea went to Ballmoney for the occasion. Even though the day was wet, cold, and stormy, a splendid number of people attended and contributed handsomely. The collection amounted to two hundred pounds.

While Father Haly rested after a tooth extraction,[17] Father Robert Kelly joined Father Bannon for a "little mission" of shorter duration in the town of Donegal.[18] This thriving market town at the head of Donegal Bay and at the convergence of roads from Derry, West Donegal, and Sligo, had an appearance that matched its lovely situation. It had been an important place from ancient times and the site of a fifteenth-century Franciscan friary until the arrival of English troops in 1591.[19] During their week in Donegal, the rookie missioners proved they could do well without the veterans.

After this mini-mission, Fathers Bannon and Kelly headed for Omagh, an important road junction in County Tyrone, where Father Haly met them on Sunday, November 7, with Father Fortescue arriving the next day. Omagh boasts a towering Catholic church on the crown of a hill. The taller of its towers looks down on the steeple of the Protestant church nearby—in the true spirit of nineteenth-century ecclesiastical rivalry. But the smaller church of St. Mary's at Killyclogher in the northeast section of the town was the site of the mission. The building was interesting on the outside and surprising on the inside, with the

Above: Father Bannon preached at the new church in Rooskey, where he had been baptized.

altar on the west wall at the middle of the church, and balconies on the other three sides.

The parish had three thousand communicants, but intemperance prevailed and young people were free in their conduct, according to Father Haly. Furthermore, only sixty girls attended the Loretto Sisters' school. A consistent complaint held that the priests were not sufficiently interested in the school. Father Bannon stepped forward and gave a rousing talk on the value of Catholic education. This message helped to fill the empty desks in the school.[20] In appreciation, the Loretto nuns sent their boarding students to Father Bannon's mass and sermon every morning at nine.

The missionaries invited the children who had not made their first communion to Father Kelly's catechism class at one each afternoon. Two priests from a neighboring town came every evening to hear Father Fortescue. But few other priests came to help with confessions during the first two weeks. In spite of his initial misgivings, Father Haly wrote positively as the mission went on. Ten Protestants came into the Church, including a Presbyterian girl who had been living with a Catholic man. The two came to see the missionaries and sanctified their relationship.

The last mission of 1869, at the port city of Cork, began inauspiciously. No one met the priests at the train,[21] and two of the five, presumably Father Naughton and White, who had joined the team in the meantime, arrived late. Father Haly had to reside with the Christian Brothers some distance from St. Finbar's Chapel, the site of the mission. The church was in a crowded part of a large city that provided many contrasts with the average mission in the farming areas. The long work hours of most of the parishioners affected the mission.

The newspapers of the time rarely gave a detailed account of a mission. But the *Cork Examiner* for Monday, December 27, 1869—two days before Father Bannon's fortieth birthday and one day after the close of the mission—carried a lengthy account of the three-week mission and evaluated the work of the missionaries.[22]

"Never," a feature writer stated, "have the elements of a successful mission been so happily combined than on this occasion, and it is impossible not to anticipate vast advantages to the parish and the community at large from the ministrations of the missionaries."[23] Frequently, the ordinary accommodation of the church proved inadequate for the vast number of people who came to avail themselves of the mission. The newspaper account emphasized the fact that the Jesuit fathers gave the sermons.

The missioners spoke plainly but with great fervor and often with splendid eloquence on matters of salvation. As a result, countless individuals thronged to the confessionals from 5 A.M. until midnight. The zealous clergy of the parish and the neighborhood seconded the efforts of the Jesuit preachers by assisting

with the confessions. The number of communicants increased in like propor-
tion, and "the spectacle the church presented at all its services was one that must
have impressed the most indifferent visitor."[24]

The writer of the news account gave special acclaim to Father Bannon who
"in a sermon of great power, fervor and eloquence summed up the labours of
the mission."[25] After vespers in the evening, the members of the congregation
renewed their baptismal vows and Father Haly gave the papal blessing. "The
good fruit of this mission . . ." the writer hoped, "will never die out in this city.
The gratitude and affection of the people for the holy and learned men who so
earnestly devoted themselves to its exhausting labours never will."[26]

After this heroic effort, a New Year's respite seemed wise. But it was not to
be. Father Bannon took the train to Belfast and then crossed the Irish Sea to
Glasgow, where he preached to the members of the St. Vincent de Paul
Society.[27] Interestingly, the men of the cathedral parish in St. Louis, Father
Bannon's first assignment when he went to America in 1853, developed the first
unit of the St. Vincent de Paul Society in the States. Father Bannon remembered this new and influential lay organization from his days in St. Louis.

The weather in Scotland proved abominable, and Father Bannon brought a
bad cold back to Stranorlar in Donegal, where his fellow missionaries had begun
a mission. On January 23, he resumed his place in the pulpit. In the course of the
mission, five thousand parishioners crowded the church where he had given a
benefit sermon the previous year.[28]

Occasionally the food palled. Father Haly complained that at Killeary it varied all week—between mutton with potatoes and potatoes with mutton. The
priests began to look forward to Friday, Father Haly wrote, when salmon provided variety.[29]

Sometimes other religious activities conflicted with the mission. At one
place, the bishop conducted official visitations of the surrounding parishes at the
time of the mission. As a result, few priests could come to assist with confessions.
At Killmacow in County Kilkenny, the priests stayed at various farmhouses and
met with several Protestant families who were friendlier than in other places
they had visited. Their drivers took a short cut each morning through the estate
of a certain Mr. Bartolucci—"an Italian gentleman who should have been a
Catholic," in the opinion of Father Haly.[30]

Father Haly found the Italian's story worth telling. He had sung on the stage
in England and taught music. He ran away with and married one of his pupils, a
young Scots lady of rank by the name of Wallace. Her irate father settled fifty
thousand pounds on her and her children on condition that she never reside in
England. Bartolucci built a spacious house on their beautiful estate where he,
two boys, and two girls continued to live after the death of Mrs. Bartolucci.

At first, the Italian landowner had been feisty with his neighbors, but a young man whom he had threatened to arrest for trespassing played a trick on him. After several other losing efforts in dealing with his poor neighbors, Bartolucci took himself less seriously and became more liberal and friendly.[31]   A jovial neighbor taught others to come close to pronouncing the landowner's name by saying, "Bad luck to aich of ye."

In his recollections of Killmacow, Father Haly had referred to a "Mass Tree." The region of Ballintra, the site of the next missions, also boasted a "Mass Tree." During the days of persecution, the priest often said Mass under such a tree in a hidden spot that allowed the watchman to detect an approaching enemy. Sometimes, no guard was necessary. The Catholic people might have lacked resources to build a church, or the landowners may have refused to make a site available. The local people revered these "Mass Trees," as they did "Mass Rocks" and "Mass Caves," and protected them. When a railway threatened the tree at Ballintra, the magistrates hesitated to cut down the sacred memorial. At this juncture, a Protestant magistrate, Hamilton by name, called for an ax to undertake the task. A friend brought the ax, but Hamilton lost his courage.

Father Haly prepared for a mission with a careful analysis of the background and makeup of the community. The small town of Ballintra, among many little rounded hills in Donegal, was such a place. In this town, an equal number of Presbyterians and Catholics dwelt on friendly terms. In fact, to Father Haly the Catholics were too friendly with their "heretical neighbors," and had "imbided their independent spirit." As a result, he wrote, "Their religion sets very lightly on many."[32] Two Protestant churches—Anglican and Presbyterian—stood in the town. Father Dan Kelly had to choose a site for St. Bridget's beyond the town in 1845. He chose a hillside that offered a view of Donegal Bay in the far distance to the west.

While Father Haly pointed to the good feelings between Catholics and Protestants in Ballintra, the editor of the *Ballyshannon Herald* did his best to trigger hostile attitudes. He had earlier made rude attempts to prevent Father Naughton from taking a seat in the railway carriage on his way to Ballintra.[33] On July 9, 1870, he regretted the presence of a party of "strolling Jesuits, or so-called Holy Fathers who were giving a mission in Ballintra."

"The disciples of Loyola," the editor pointed out, "under whatever guise they may appear, are the sworn enemies of Protestantism, and civil and religious liberty throughout the world."[34] He referred his readers to another page in his paper where he would describe some of their horrible and bloodthirsty principles under the title "The Jesuits, Rome's Blood Men."[35] "Satan has amongst them some of his most active, trusty and devoted servants."[36] He ended with a prayer that God would spare Ireland from the withering curse that followed the Jesuit teaching and would stir up the people to the sense of peril that surrounded them.

Nevertheless, the only misfortunes that faced the missioners were sore throats. Father Bannon's came early in the first week, Father Haly's in the third. A Presbyterian, Dr. Johnstone of Ballintra, so little heeded the words of the *Ballyshannon* editor that he offered his services to Father Haly. When the day of the Orange parades passed without incident, the parish priest, Father Kelly, felt that Catholic processions would entail no risk.[37] The entire mission went well.

In the meantime, the Catholic world prepared for the first Ecumenical Council since the one held in Trent in the sixteenth century. Pope Pius IX summoned the bishops of the world to Rome to consider the many evils of the time. The most obvious evil was the lack of freedom of the Church in most of the countries of Europe. Instead of centering on this major problem of religious liberty, the council avoided it and, at the Pope's urging, looked into the question of papal infallibility.

While no indication has come down to us as to Father Bannon's views on the great issue, the two prelates he was closest to, Cardinal Cullen and Archbishop Kenrick, stood farther apart than Dublin was from St. Louis. Cullen presumably had a part in the framing of the precise language of the final declaration. Kenrick, on the other hand, saw no compelling argument in Scripture or tradition for the doctrine of papal infallibility. He adhered strongly to the ancient tradition of the infallibility of a general council, joining the Pope and bishops in collegial harmony. When a critic said that every Catholic in Ireland believed in the infallibility of the Pope, Kenrick responded that all Irish Catholics believed in the infallibility of their pastors. This, Kenrick asserted, was a tribute to the piety of the Irish people, not to their theological expertise.[38]

Neither Cullen nor anyone else adequately answered Kenrick's objections then or since. Instead, Cullen launched personal attacks on the St. Louis archbishop. He called the opinion of Kenrick and other opponents an "ugly, futile protest."[39] In a letter to Bishop George Conroy, Cullen wrote, "I chastised Kenrick. He has asked permission to reply but cannot answer my charges. He is in a very dangerous position."[40]

So limited was true discussion of the issue that the chairman of the sessions did not allow Kenrick to answer such critics as Cullen. In that situation, Kenrick decided to have his say in writing. He sent his secretary beyond the censorship of the Papal States and had his speech, or *Concio*, as it was called, printed in Naples. He then made a copy available to all participants.

Cullen retorted that Kenrick's treatise was "altogether heretical."[41] He spoke of Kenrick's "perversity," and predicted: "Dr. Kenrick, I fear, will end badly."[42]

Whatever Father Bannon might have held on the issue, he wisely kept his views to himself.

18

"A Pulpit Orator of the First Rank"

After twelve missions during a year and a half, the provincial superior assigned another priest to take Father Bannon's place. Father Haly penned in his crisp script: "His services were judged indispensably necessary in Dublin."[1] While Father Haly seemed justly upset to lose such an outstanding member of the mission team, no mention of the reasons for the change appears in *Minutes* of the consultors, the provincial superior's board of advisers.[2] Such an important decision should have been a prime concern. At that time, however, the secretary of the board omitted the views of the participants.

What makes this decision even more mysterious is a proposal of the provincial consultors two years later. In view of the great demand for missions, among them one at the cathedral in Derry, the consultors discussed the establishment of a second mission band. They listed four possible candidates, but not Bannon.[3] The next day, the same consultors recorded the fact that a parish priest wanted Father Bannon to give a talk in place of a priest who had repeatedly offended the ladies in his audience.[4] The provincial did not set up a second mission team, but instead added four more priests to the existing band, including two who could and did give missions in Gaelic.[5]

It seems strange that the name of such an active and able man as Father Bannon appears in the *Minutes* only one time during the entire decade of the 1870s. Further, his name never appears in the list of men considered to have administrative ability. The same twelve names surfaced regularly.[6]

During his year in the mission band, Father Bannon had begun a ladies' sodality at Castlecomer. The sodality movement, then experiencing considerable growth throughout the country, was one more Jesuit tradition that Father Bannon came to cherish during his time with Fathers Haly and Fortescue.

The historian of the Sodality of Our Lady in Ireland, Father Charles O'Connor, later provincial, praised the veteran home missioners and one or two of their early associates for promoting sodalities.[7] The sodality, incidentally, was a way of life for lay people that followed the plan of the Jesuit founder, St. Ignatius Loyola, just as the Third Orders of St. Dominic and St. Francis followed the religious outlooks of those saintly founders. Under the patronage of the Blessed Virgin Mary, the sodalities had grown up in the early years of the Jesuit order, the late 1500s. With the approval of the father general, the promotion of sodalities came to be one of the major apostolic activities of the Jesuits. It soon became apparent that Father Bannon had gained a strong appreciation of the sodality.

Father Bannon "was the founder of the flourishing Ladies Sodality at Loretto College, Stephen's Green," Father O'Connor wrote, "as well as the founder of the still better known Sodality for commercial young men under the patronage of Our Lady Help of Christians attached to the Church on Gardiner Street."[8] Later on, Father Bannon would found a third unit, the Ignatian Sodality for university and other students.[9] Still later he would organize another sodality, this one for women.[10] With justice could the historian of sodalities call Father Bannon "a big name in conjunction with sodality work in Dublin."[11]

Even though no longer a member of the mission band, Father Bannon still traveled extensively—now to give Ignatian retreats. As mentioned above, while the mission talks centered on the first section of the *Spiritual Exercises* of St. Ignatius, the regular retreat proceeded beyond this to the conferences on the life of Jesus Christ. While still on the mission band, Father Bannon had given two retreats: one to the priests of the Diocese of Cork in July 1868, a second to Presentation nuns in Carlow in April 1870.

During the 1870s, Father Bannon would give retreats to priests of the Dioceses of Raphaoe and Ferns, to Loretto nuns in Dublin and Omagh, and once again to the Presentation nuns in Carlow, to men and women at the Rathfarnham Parish, and to the Ladies at Mount Anville Convent in suburban Dublin.[12] This was the occasion already mentioned when a local pastor asked for Father Bannon to replace a previously assigned retreat director who had alienated the women retreatants at two other places.[13]

In the meantime, New Year's Day 1871 brought a great change to Ireland. Prime Minister William E. Gladstone brought to a reluctant end one of the great failures of the British Empire: its attempt to foist state-controlled religion on the Irish people. Even though the government forced all people to pay taxes to support the so-called "Established Church of Ireland," that body soon became a collection of lovely medieval churches without worshipers, more like museums or other tourist attractions. Two hundred and eighteen parishes—nineteen of them in Dublin—did not have a single Protestant pew holder. Nonetheless, the absentee ministers drew substantial salaries. Protestant Irish bishops became wealthy by doing almost nothing except pontificating to small congregations. One left an estate of 600,000 pounds. His Protestant Lordship of Tuam, an almost entirely Catholic area, left 260,000 pounds to his heirs, while the majority of the Catholic clergy lived in poverty.[14]

The State Church ceased to have public support on January 1, 1871, in spite of what the *Dublin Evening Post* had called the "verbosity and flatulence" of the Anglican bishops' appeal to their "supreme head under Christ," Queen Victoria.[15] Catholics and Dissenters (non-Anglican Protestants) no longer had to support what leading Englishmen called "a political contrivance."[16]

All the while Father Bannon was preaching the word throughout his native land. Typical of his pulpit calls were these. He went to the far northwest corner of Donegal on May 7, 1871, to preach the sermon at the opening of the Convent of Mercy in the village of Cardonagh,[17] where his successful appeal brought donations of 250 pounds for the nuns.[18] During the fall of that same year, on November 26, 1871, he preached at the solemn consecration of the spacious and handsome Gothic church in Strokestown, twelve miles southwest of his birthplace, Rooskey on the Shannon, in his mother's ancestral area of Roscommon in west-central Ireland. Bishop Laurence Gilloly of Elphin blessed the new edifice.[19]

In this speech at Strokestown, Father Bannon spoke more formally and solemnly than he did in the other talk that has come down to us. His theme was the value of a church building as a symbol of eternal truth in an age that deified science and presumed that natural reason alone can meet all the needs of humanity. This thought-provoking speech lacked the flair and challenge of the other extant sermon, but accomplished its purpose.

The *Dublin Evening Post* for March 21, 1872, announced that Father Bannon would give the annual Palm Sunday sermon at St. Michael and John's Church for the benefit of the national school. This was the church on Lower Exchange Street where Archbishop Kenrick of St. Louis had spoken three years before.[20] Father Bannon's oratorical skill augmented his already splendid reputation as a pulpit orator.

Earlier that winter Father Bannon had welcomed to Dublin the most widely regarded Jesuit in America, the Indian missionary Peter Jan De Smet. The versatile De Smet, renowned also as a writer and a peacemaker between Indian tribes, visited the Jesuit residence on Gardiner Street in December 1871. On his many visits to Europe, he recruited personnel and secured supplies for the Jesuit provinces in America.[21] It is not clear whether Fathers De Smet and Bannon had ever met in St. Louis, but correspondence indicates a warm friendship. Further, they had many mutual friends, especially General Daniel Frost. Father De Smet

Right: Father Bannon urged the famous Jesuit missionary Peter De Smet to ask the pope to make St. Patrick's Day a holy day in the English-speaking world.

had baptized the general before the Civil War. Father Bannon went with General Frost on the "Southwestern Expedition" of the Missouri Guard to the Kansas border in 1860 and was chaplain in Frost's command at Camp Jackson.

Father De Smet's visit opened up another avenue of concern, the religious welfare of Father Bannon's fellow Irish in America. In a letter, Father Bannon reminded Father De Smet that St. Patrick had promised that the Irish would never lose the Faith. Still, one could not be sure that this promise went with the Irish beyond the seas to America. The celebration on St. Patrick's Day was becoming an occasion for parades and jubilation—not a holy day—in St. Louis, New York, and elsewhere. The only way the Church could ensure attendance at Mass was to make March 17 a day of obligation by declaring St. Patrick patron of foreign missions. After all, he was the first missionary to bring Christianity beyond the Roman Empire, after the death of St. Paul the Apostle. If the highly influential Father De Smet, the greatest American missionary, won the support of the American bishops, Pope Pius IX might respond favorably.[22]

At that time the Church had hesitated to name a universal patron of missions. As it turned out, that designation came only in 1927 with the naming of St. Francis Xavier by Pope Pius XI. When Father De Smet wrote to Father Bannon in August 1872, he mentioned nothing about the suggestion that he lead a movement to have St. Patrick declared patron of the missions. He offered no excuses but could have had one. He had suffered four serious hemorrhages that had weakened him considerably and confined him to his room at the Jesuit residence at Saint Louis University.

The missionary enclosed a clipping from the St. Louis newspaper, the *Republican*, published by a mutual friend, John Knapp, that told of Coadjutor Bishop Patrick Ryan's blessing of the Redemptorist church of St. Alphonsus Liguori not far north of the 1860 site of Camp Jackson. De Smet assured the Irish Jesuits that the three novices from Milltown Park were doing remarkably well and that Father John Power was missionizing whites at the former Osage mission in Kansas.

The great Belgian's main purpose in the letter was to convey to Father Bannon the thanks of Auxiliary Bishop Thomas Patrick Foley of Chicago for a gift of eleven pounds that Father Bannon had sent him, along with the name of the donor. Father De Smet had forwarded the name and address of the donor to Father Arnold Damen, the Jesuit pastor in Chicago. The letter never reached the rectory on the street that would later become Damen Avenue. As a result, Father De Smet was asking Father Bannon to find out the name of the donor and give him the receipt and the bishop's note of thanks. The letter ended with a greeting to the father provincial and to all the Jesuits at St. Francis Xavier's.[23]

Father Bannon answered shortly after he received Father De Smet's letter. In his sometimes scarcely legible script, he told of his joy at receiving a message from Father De Smet and his sorrow of learning of the latter's poor health. Since the cold of a midwestern winter would surely add to his already serious weakness, Father Bannon urged Father De Smet to go south in November and stay until May. "By this means," the Irish Jesuit insisted, "you may protect your days A.M.D.G. [for the greater glory of God], while remaining in St. Louis you will clearly shorten your life and end your usefulness."[24]

His own health, Father Bannon wrote, was so good that it almost inclined him to visit again the city on the Mississippi. He regularly met St. Louis friends on their visits to Dublin, such as J. J. Donegan; Thomas Finn and his wife; publisher George Knapp, a fellow Confederate veteran; and James Ryan, an official of Saint Louis University; yet he presumed that all his old friends had died or moved elsewhere. If he did return, he'd be like a newcomer.[25]

That is the last extant letter between the two. The versatile De Smet would die the following year, 1873, fifty years after his arrival in St. Louis. The repatriated Irish Jesuit, almost thirty years younger, was just entering into his most prominent years in the ministry.

It is not clear who suggested that Father Bannon would be a stranger should he return to St. Louis. Clearly, they had not looked carefully at the real picture. Many parishioners of St. John's Parish in 1861 still resided there. Further, almost all of Father Bannon's friends and associates in the clergy still worked in St. Louis.

Archbishop Kenrick had returned from the First Vatican Council and took up residence at St. John's, the church that Father Bannon had built. The pastor, Bishop Patrick Ryan, praised "the personal courage, self sacrifice and devotedness" of his predecessor and friend, Father Bannon.[26]

Among his Confederate associates, General Sterling Price, his army commander, had died in 1867, shortly after returning to St. Louis. General Daniel Frost, Father Bannon's militia chief, had received amnesty to return from his exile in Canada, thanks to the intercession of General Grant. Frost remained a leading citizen of the St. Louis area for many years. A son became a U.S. congressman and a daughter contributed generously to St. John's College in Belize and to Saint Louis University, by that time located on the former site of Camp Jackson.

Robert A. Bakewell and P. B. Garesche, the priest's young companions on his zigzag course to the South, had returned to St. Louis, as had other Confederate veterans who were his friends—Henry Guibor, Joseph Boyce, Frank Von Puhl, Dr. J. A. Leavy, W. Clark Kennerly, and Wilson Hunt. The latter painted a picture of the Battle of Elkhorn Tavern that showed Father Bannon in the foreground assisting a wounded soldier. The Confederate veterans organized societies to hold reunions and recall memories. Father Bannon would have been no stranger anywhere in the middle South, least of all in River City, but he never crossed the ocean again.

Father Bannon pronounced his final vows in the Jesuit order in 1876. In the fall of 1876, he accepted an invitation to give the sermon at the dedication of a new church in Gothic style at Castleberg in western Tyrone County, near the boundary of Donegal. Each Sunday from the time the pastor, Father James Connolly, had planned to build, he read the names of the men who were to bring stones that week from the quarry near Drumquin, about ten miles away, or sand from the banks of the River Finn. The gathering of these building materials took two years, and the pastor often rode his horse some distance to encourage the progress.

Father Connolly also organized a group of women, mostly single, to solicit funds both in the parish and from friends in the neighborhood and overseas. The ladies collected more than 380 pounds. The total cost would be 3,000 pounds.

Gradually, the church rose to its gable height of fifty-two feet. It was one hundred feet in length and sixty-nine feet at its extreme width. A newspaper account covering the opening day boasted that the church was capable of accommodating three thousand persons. A more conservative voice qualified this figure, saying "if they were standing."[27]

On August 30, September 27, and October 4, an announcement of the dedication appeared in the *Londonderry Journal*.[28] The bishop of Derry, Rt. Reverend

Francis Kelly, would solemnly dedicate the church on Sunday, October 8, 1876. At the solemn high mass at 11 A.M. the Very Reverend Father John Bannon, S.J., of Dublin would give the sermon. After the sermon, there would be a collection to aid in liquidating the debt of the church.

A recent history of this parish carried extensive quotations of Father Bannon on this occasion. These give us a taste of the many sermons of the great pulpit orator. Before the bishop, a large number of priests from all over the area, and a congregation that had been gathering for two hours, Father Bannon ascended the pulpit. He delivered his discourse—to quote a contemporary—"in his peculiarly striking voice . . . and . . . with that oratorical power for which he was so distinguished."[29]

Speaking to a generation that had endured the worst their persecutors could inflict upon them, Father Bannon compared his people to the Israelites in the days of the Old Testament. "Now that a breathing time had come again after the long centuries of persecution, the Irish nation, like Judas Maccabeus, turned their hearts, welling up with faith and love, once again to the rebuilding of their temples. . . . Ireland was full of ruined sanctuaries. Was she to remain so? Oh, no!"

His hearers would recall the scenes of desolation at Ardstraw and Scarvaghern, places they were familiar with—as he said, "The old churches of Ireland had many memories clinging around their walls, crumbling to the dust, scarcely traceable, their ruins hardly able to bear testimony to their grandeur." Referring to an earlier, happy time, he recalled ". . . the magnificent churches, and secluded cloisters and learned schools that added fame to our country and glory to God: that gave instruction to the world, and proved that very true, and ever faithful to their God was the warm-hearted, generous Irish race."

Father Bannon concluded, "They established forever the claim of Ireland to the proud title of Island of Saints and Scholars."

Bannon dealt with the Reformation and its results briefly and then proceeded to praise the missionary effort of the Irish in recent times: "Everywhere, in the hidden, half-unknown, little towns of England, as on the boundless tracts of America. . . . In the deserts or tropics or ice-bound regions of the wide world, everywhere the brogue of the Irish nation was heard . . . celebrants and worshippers had it alike."[30]

Father Bannon then discussed one of the great ironies of modern times: the "Empire of England," as he called it, had with the help of the United States and several of its self-governing colonies created a condition throughout a large area of the world that made fruitful the zeal of countless Irish missionaries: a common language that many Irish spoke so eloquently, a rule of law and order (not always true in its relations with Ireland), and the accessibility of distant places.

Father Bannon saw that the English Empire had become an unwilling instrument of salvation. He concluded:

> And thus a country, the greatest persecutor of God's Holy Word the world ever saw, this country so opposed to Catholicity, this country England, so full of opposition of the Catholic Church, Catholic priest, and Irish Catholic, thus under the protection of this very nation, the faith she dislikes so deeply has been propagated, the Church she persecuted so fearfully is being spread, the Irish nation she ground down so bitterly received fame and glory: and all this by the Irish Catholic people. Their hearts were true to their God and their land.[31]

A contemporary praised his manner and message in glowing words:

> Father Bannon dwelt on this theme with thrilling eloquence and moved many to tears. He appealed to his hearers to be mindful of the traditions, the fame, the fidelity of their nation; to remember the memories of their old churches; to be generous in aiding to erect new temples and so again beautify their land; to be true to their God, true to the faith given them by St. Patrick, and so by living for it to be able to die for it.[32]

Another commentator reflected that his was the classical style that Demosthenes and Cicero had exercised in ancient times, Bossuet and Bourdaloue in France of the seventeenth century, and the American senator Daniel Webster three decades before. The devout worshipers certainly appreciated it. They contributed the amazing amount of 625 pounds, more than one-fifth of the entire cost of the graceful structure.[33]

During the ensuing years, preaching home missions and giving retreats and public lectures remained Father Bannon's main work. That phase of his varied career deserves continued treatment. Perusing the contemporary records, one reads, for instance, that in early January 1877, Father Bannon gave a lecture at Gardiner Street on "Catholicity in the United States."[34] The proceeds of this lecture went to the opening of a reading room for the members of the St. Joseph's Catholic Total Abstinence League.[35]

The eloquent missionary spoke in the interest of other good causes during 1877, such as at St. Andrew's in Westlands, on behalf of the House of Mercy on Baggot Street.[36] With his former fellow novice, Father John Naughton, he appealed for the Christian Brothers School on Seville Place and for the schools of St. James Parish.[37] Speaking at St. Francis Xavier Church he urged support for the nuns who had come from New Zealand to collect for their distant mission;[38] again at St. Francis Xavier, early in the following year, he sought funds for a library for his Commercial Young Men's Sodality.[39] Regularly, right up to his final meeting with them years later, Father Bannon would urge the reading of good literature.[40]

The prelate who had ordained him, Cardinal Cullen, consecrated the new church at Greenore, on May 31, 1877. Father Bannon preached the sermon.[41] A thousand parishioners attended Father Bannon's closing talk and mass in Roscrea on October 7, 1877, along with three hundred members of the Catholic Young Men's Society who had finished a retreat under the priest's direction.[42]

When Bishop Thomas Nulty of Meath presided at the opening of the Castletown church, Father Bannon again took the pulpit.[43] On February 9, 1878, Father Bannon appealed for funds for a library for his Commercial Sodality.[44] Cardinal Cullen and Father Bannon combined on a significant project. The Jesuit missionary composed an address from Loretto Convent, beautifully illuminated by the nuns, that Cardinal Cullen presented to the Pope. The "Roman Letter" in the *Freeman's Journal* praised this gift of the Dubliners.[45] At the same time, the members of the Young Men's Commercial Sodality sent an address and a donation of one thousand francs to His Holiness, the newly elected Pope Leo XIII. The superior of the Jesuits in Rome, Father Torquato Armellini, wrote to Father Bannon relaying the Holy Father's gratitude for the sentiments expressed in the address.[46]

Father Bannon's magnificent record of pulpit appearances called forth a justified tribute in the *Irish Catholic*: "In the Seventies his name and fame as a preacher were well known, and his remarkable personality, his striking presence, his eloquence were familiar and appreciated in most dioceses of the country."[47]

As busy as the 1870s were, the 1880s were even busier. July 14, 1880, brought many of Father Bannon's relatives to St. Francis Xavier Church, including his cousin, the Very Reverend Joseph Higgins, rector of the seminary at Navan who became bishop of Ballarat in Australia. The occasion was the marriage of another cousin, Frances Gardiner Coffey, second daughter of Edward Coffey and Maria Gardiner of Mullingar, to a solicitor, P. J. Nooney, son of Patrick Nooney and Patricia Bolesty, also of Mullingar. On July 10, 1853, twenty-seven years before, one month after his ordination, Father Bannon had stood as godfather for Frances at her baptism at the cathedral in Mullingar.[48] Now he had the added joy of witnessing her wedding.

Even though the consultors of the province had never listed Father Bannon among those of the province with ability at administration, they placed his name third among those they recommended in August 30, 1880, for the position of rector of St. Stanislaus College in Tullabeg, Tullamore, King's County, a school that Father William Delaney had strengthened academically by his educational statesmanship. Instead of becoming rector of the community, Father Bannon combined the posts of pastor of the church, minister of the house, consultor of the community, and director of the sodality.[49] The position of pastor, for a man of Father Bannon's zeal, would have been a full-time task in itself. The consultor, along with three others, met with the superior at stated times to discuss affairs of the community. These men had, as the title implies, only a consultative voice. This, too, would have found Father Bannon a valuable contributor.

The minister of the community, like the quartermaster in the army, had to take care of material needs, food, clothing, and shelter. If the lights went out, members of the community went to see the father minister. If the cooking went bad, he heard about it. In short, he was on call at all hours of the day and night. It was one of two positions in the order that Jesuits could attain. Few men seemed made for this position. Father Bannon obviously was no more cut out to be a Jesuit father minister than he was to be a quartermaster in the Confederate army. His usually good health weakened under the constant pressure. He dealt gracefully with people, not with things.

Right: Father Bannon often graced this pulpit at St. Francis Xavier in Dublin.

The house physician, Dr. L. G. Moorhead, wrote at St. Stanislaus College, Tullabeg, on July 31, 1881, "the Rev. Mr. Bannon, Minister of this institution, is, I regret to say, very much broken down in health." The physician recommended an immediate change of location to a warmer climate. "I am further of the opinion," he wrote, "that the duties of minister in this institution will for the future be quite unsuited to him."[50] In a letter to the Superior Father Aloysius Sturzo, Moorhead repeated his recommendation with a specific suggestion of a place, possibly southern Italy, named but illegible, that would be more beneficial than any place in Europe.[51]

No document indicates whether or not Father Bannon took a rest elsewhere. But he was back at Gardiner Street shortly after, to the joy of many. One sodalist, Mrs. J. S. Fallon, wrote the Provincial Father James Tuite, expressing happiness that Father Bannon would "be able to resume his own work" with the women's and men's sodalities.[52]

In 1882, the Irish bishops asked the Jesuits to take over University College, the school begun by Cardinal Newman in 1854. The Provincial Father James Tuite chose Father Delaney, successful in educational work at Tullabeg, to direct the new institution.

Left: A portrait of Bannon in his late seventies.

After Father Bannon had given retreats in the novitiate in Dublin for a year, Father Tuite decided to make the same mistake twice. He sent Father Bannon to rejoin Father Delaney at the University College on 23 Upper Temple Street. Besides his earlier posts of minister of the house and consultor of the community, he was given the extra office of keeper of the financial books.[53] Again, Father Bannon would not last long at the minister's post. When he no longer resided at the University College the following year, however, he continued as director of the students' sodality.

During that time, Father Delaney was asking the English provincial to send to Ireland several men of established reputations as scholars and teachers to strengthen the Irish faculty. The English provincial responded that Father Delaney had asked for the stars of the English Jesuit constellation. Instead, the assistant to the father general for the English-speaking countries, Father A. Porter, wondered if the Irish headmaster could find a place for a shy, frail, self-effacing teacher of the classics "whose mind runs in eccentric ways."[54] Even Father Delaney, wise man that he was, failed to realize that he had gained the literary jewel of that generation of English Jesuits, eventually to be famous throughout the English-speaking world, the poet Gerard Manley Hopkins.[55] Whether or not Father Bannon got to know well the budding poet is uncertain.

Father Bannon may have tried his hand at writing once again in 1882. Editor John Denver of Liverpool published a number of inspiring pamphlets, one of them A Life of John Mitchell, by John Bannon.[56] Was the author Bannon the Jesuit?

John Mitchell had been one of the leaders of the Young Ireland Movement who tried to lead his people to freedom in 1848. Exiled to Van Dieman's Land (later Tasmania), he eventually escaped to the United States. After several years in New York, he had settled in Richmond and had become a strong journalistic supporter of the Confederacy. Losing two sons in the war did not mute his enthusiasm. He had published a letter in *The Nation* on September 30, 1863, urging the Irish people not to take part without justification in a war against a small nation struggling, like the Irish, for freedom.

Shortly after the publication of Mitchell's letter, Father Bannon had arrived in Dublin as special agent of the Confederate government. In a poster Father Bannon published to dissuade Irishmen from going to America, he quoted the letter of Mitchell.[57] Early the following year, he urged Confederate secretary of state Judah Benjamin to encourage Mitchell to write more letters. Many Irishmen disagreed with Mitchell's political views, but "all parties," Father Bannon wrote, "agree to regard him as an honest man."[58]

Did the Dublin Jesuit write this life of John Mitchell published in Liverpool in 1882? He obviously was acquainted with the general outline of Mitchell's career. The style of writing recalls the storytelling ability that Father Bannon had shown in his wartime reminiscences in the *Letters and Notices* of the English Jesuit province already discussed. The composition reflects his letters and the broadsides that he had circulated as a Confederate agent.

Father Bannon had the narrative skill and an interest in, admiration for, and knowledge of the subject. The limited scope of the publication did not require extensive research and would not have taxed the time of an otherwise busy man. Some might suggest that the absence of the "S.J." behind the name of John Bannon would indicate that a non-Jesuit had penned the script. On the other hand, that may simply have been the result of an editorial judgment. Further, no other Bannon surfaced at the time. Until one came along, the presumption held that Father Bannon authored this tribute to a fellow Irish Confederate.

By that time, Father Bannon was back at St. Francis Xavier with his loyal businessmen sodalists, this time as community minister. There, he was destined to stay for almost a third of a century until his death at this address on Upper Gardiner Street. The community building stood just west of the church that was so central to the history of the Irish Jesuits since the restoration of the Jesuit order early in the nineteenth century. A careful look at the background and beauty of the church belong to Father Bannon's story.

At the time of Catholic Emanicipation in 1829, the "Reverend Gentlemen of Clongowes College"—as the Jesuits were legally called at that time—wanted to purchase a building in Dublin called the "Free Church," which seemed to be free of a congregation at that time, although not free of an owner who offered the building at a heady price. When the landlord heard that the Reverend Gentlemen wanted to use the edifice as a "Mass House," he turned down their bid. One of these early Reverend Gentlemen, incidentally, was youthful Father Robert Haly, who was to head the team of traveling missionaries that included Father Bannon almost forty years later.

The Jesuits decided to build a new church and purchased a piece of property between the large convent of the Irish Sisters of Charity and gracious Georgian homes on Upper Gardiner Street. This thoroughfare on Dublin's near-north side ran a little west of straight north from the Customs House on the Liffey River, five blocks up a more than gentle slope. It was four blocks east of Sackville Street, which would eventually bear the name of the Irish hero Daniel O'Connell, who defied a British tradition that very year. Elected to Parliament from Kerry, the eloquent orator had refused to take the oath that violated the conscience of every Catholic.

To design the church, the Jesuits called on architect John B. Keane, who had planned the cathedral of Longford.[59] Keane chose the shape of a Latin cross with the main body of the church extending 135 feet, the width being 40 feet. The transept extended 90 feet. Side altars and confessionals flanked the central nave. It was, at the time of its construction, the only church in Dublin that used native granite in the construction of its impressive Ionic-pillared portico, blending with its neighboring Georgian houses.[60]

As early as 1836, the *Catholic Directory* called it "one of the most perfect, convenient and classical edifices in our city."[61] What a beautiful temple of worship it was for the Irish Catholic people who had seen all their ancient cathedrals and monastic churches destroyed by Nordic raiders or self-righteous "Roundheads" or stolen by foreign monarchs whose much-married predecessor had declared himself head of Christ's Church in the western islands. As more and more people crowded into St. Francis Xavier, fewer and fewer found their way into Dublin's medieval Gothic cathedral commandeered by the "established" church, but still bearing the name of Ireland's missionary patron, St. Patrick.

The large convent of the Irish Sisters of Charity, who had sold the property to the Jesuits, crowded St. Francis Xavier's Church on the southeast. The Jesuit residence, several stories high at the time, adjoined it on the northwest. The hemmed-in appearance of the church on the outside left the visitor unready for the spacious and bright interior. Countless panels with flowers in the centers covered the level ceiling. "The interior is richly decorated," a later art critic would write, "the Corinthian altar-screen . . . and the altar piece, commemorating the great missionary patron, being of exceptional artistic merit."[62] Such was the magnificent temple where Father Bannon offered Mass, preached, and heard confessions. Here, too, he gained the reputation that evoked from a writer in the *Irish Catholic Directory* this tribute: "As a pulpit orator, he had few equals, and St. Francis Xavier's spacious church was crowded whenever he preached."[63]

Above: Father Bannon spent much of his last fifty years at St. Francis Xavier Church on Gardiner Street in Dublin.

19

"The Only Possible Candidate"

During Father Bannon's first year back at St. Francis Xavier's, the new provincial superior, Father Thomas Brown, transferred the provincial headquarters from Milltown Park to Upper Gardiner Street and moved many veteran priests to other houses in the province. Father Joseph Keller, assistant for English-speaking countries to Father General Anthony Anderledy, was passing through Dublin at the time.

"This [action of the Irish provincial] caused a great uproar in the house and the city," Father Keller wrote to the father general on August 8, 1884.[1] "It was truly providential," Father Keller wrote, "that they [the displaced priests] had the opportunity to speak with me and so spit out the poison. They are now much more tranquil."[2] After hearing the complaints of the various senior priests, Father Keller concluded: "It seems to me that it was a good thing to change them, and now that it has taken place, it will be seen as having been a good thing."[3]

Father Keller thought that the easiest way for the general to bring peace to the community was to appoint Father Bannon superior. He urged Father Anderledy to make this appointment and to do so quickly. Father Bannon, he insisted, "was the only possible candidate."[4]

At first glance, this recommendation might baffle the reader. The consultors of the province had never listed Father Bannon as having the *donum regiminis*— aptitude for administration. What prompted Father Keller to make so final a statement? He seemed to know Father Bannon well. Yet they had never lived in the same province of the order. A look at Father Keller's background sheds some light. Joseph Keller had grown up in St. Louis, the son of a Bavarian-born organist at the St. Louis Cathedral. Father Bannon had served there during his first year in America. An unpretentious man with a keen mind, the Roman-trained

Keller had succeeded Father De Smet as assistant to the Missouri provincial shortly before Father Bannon left for the South.

If he had not met Father Bannon personally during those mutual St. Louis years—an utterly unlikely possibility—he would have been aware of his now fellow Jesuit's earlier work as pastor in St. Louis, as chaplain of the Washington Guards, and as director of the Temperance Society in the archdiocese.

Provincial of Maryland and Missouri, then rector at Saint Louis University and at the seminary for all American provinces at Woodstock College, Maryland, during the next two decades, Father Keller brought to the Jesuit general congregation a solid reputation, wide experience, and a fluency in seven languages that fitted him admirably to fill the post of assistant to the general for the English-speaking provinces and the Low Countries.

Seven days after Father Keller dated his recommendation, Father General Anthony Anderledy named Father Bannon superior of the residence on Upper Gardiner Street. Across the Atlantic, his friend and the pastor of his former parish, St. John the Apostle and Evangelist, Patrick Ryan, was leaving St. Louis to

Right: Father Joseph Keller of St. Louis, assistant to the general of the Jesuits, knew Father Bannon from his days at the cathedral in St. Louis, where Keller's father was organist, and advised the father general to appoint Bannon superior of the Jesuits at St. Francis Xavier Rectory.

become archbishop of Philadelphia. In the fall of 1884, Father Bannon became a consultor of the Irish Province.[5] In the community, he had the assistance of Father Michael Waters as father minister and consultor of the house. Father Waters also directed two sodalities: one for women, the other for altar boys. He also supervised the parish school for poor girls. The two teamed up well.

"At Gardiner Street during his superiorship," a newspaper writer pointed out, "Father Bannon had a field of work congenial to his zeal and activity. . . . His unostentatious charity and kindly paternal care were not limited within a narrow circle."[6]

The community residence was a large four-storied building with wide stairwells and about thirty rooms with high ceilings typical of the times. The lightsome library on the top floor contained many sets of volumes, old and new, including the *Acts of the Saints*, a multivolume *Library of the Fathers*, recently published at Oxford, and an earlier French edition, and the complete works of Jesuit philosopher Francisco Suarez, whose portrait hung on the wall.

Twenty-one men resided at the Gardiner Street residence besides Father Bannon and Father Waters. These included the father provincial and his assistant, the directors of various sodalities and of the Apostleship of Prayer, the editors of the publication *Irish Weekly*, the pastor of the parish, and the pastor's assistants.

With his many duties as superior, Father Bannon wisely turned over the directorship of the Ladies' Sodality at the Loretto Convent and the Ignatian Sodality to Father James Cullen, who would eventually have charge of all the Sodalities of the Blessed Virgin in Ireland.[7] Father Bannon kept his favorite group, the Young Businessmen's Sodality.

Lambert McKenna, author of the life of Father Cullen, seems to imply that the new director added a more apostolic emphasis to the sodalities, but he gives no evidence that Father Bannon had stressed unduly the devotional side of the sodality program.[8] Besides a program of prayer, Father Bannon urged the men in his sodality to carry Catholic ideals of justice and fair dealing into the marketplace and manufactories as their apostolic endeavor.

When Cardinal Edward McCabe passed away in mid-February 1885, Father Bannon led Matins and Lauds for fifteen Jesuits—seven from Gardiner Street and eight from Milltown Park, Belvedere, and other Jesuit residences—at the coffin in the cathedral on Marlborough Street.[9] Irish wakes among the clergy did not have the jubilating atmosphere they had among the Irish American laypeople. But the funerals seemed to offer a grand opportunity for the clergy to convene, honor the departed one, and see friends. Ordinarily close to a hundred clergy—bishops and priests—attended the Jesuit funerals on Gardiner Street.

Father Bannon had already attended the funeral of his mentor on the mission team, Father Robert Haly, in 1882.[10] During his term as superior, he attended

Left: Captain Joseph Boyce, Confederate veteran, visited Father Bannon in Dublin after the conflict, bringing greetings from his former comrade-in-arms. Boyce also contributed to the erection of the statue to Union general Franz Sigel in Forest Park.

the funerals of his master of novices, Father Joseph Lentaigne, who had returned from Australia;[11] Father John Curtis; and Father John Callan.[12] Father Alfred Murphy, not Father Bannon, was celebrant at most of these funeral Masses.[13]

On Friday evenings during Lent, Father Bannon gave himself and the other preachers a little respite. In place of the usual sermon, he began the Way of the Cross followed by Benediction.[14] On November 5–7, 1885, he led the spiritual retreat for the Young Businessmen's Sodality.

Seventy-year-old Father Patrick Duffy, a chaplain in the Crimean War in the mid-1850s, held posts of procurator and consultor of the house during Father Bannon's years as superior. "Father Duffy was entirely military in his ideas," a biographer wrote, "and when he met anyone who had distinguished himself in battle, he felt quite at home with him."[15] Among these fellow veterans, he met Governor Robert Hamilton of Tasmania, who remembered that Father Duffy had carried him, badly wounded, to a Crimean medical station."[16]

Even though no records indicated that Fathers Duffy and Bannon reminisced about the two wars, it would have been against the nature of these two vigorous ex-chaplains, working together in a Jesuit community, to refrain from comparing the all-night march to Elkhorn Tavern and the charge at Balaclava.

Father Bannon might have invited Father Duffy to meet Captain Joseph Boyce when the ex-Confederate officer visited Dublin in mid-July 1887. But Captain Boyce mentions no such meetings in his letters.

Boyce wrote to their mutual friend, Dr. John Leavy, of his visit with Father Bannon in Dublin. During this joyful reunion, he noticed that Father Bannon's hair was as black as it had been when he climbed to the pulpit at St. John the Apostle and Evangelist Church in 1860.[17] The priest had shaved off his familiar black beard of the battlefield, but his approach was as cheery as during the old times in St. Louis and on the battlefields of Arkansas and Mississippi. Father Bannon spoke familiarly of his old comrades, Generals Frost and Price, Little and Bowen, the battery leaders Henry Guibor and William Wade, and the other colorful individuals, regardless of rank.

Boyce found it hard to believe that twenty-five years had elapsed since the Battle of Vicksburg. The two men talked for hours, the brigades and batteries passing by like a panorama. Father Bannon recalled specifically the incident that involved two physicians, Doctors John A. Leavy and J. H. Britt. While the three men were busy at the Vicksburg hospital, perched on a high hill overlooking the Mississippi River on the west and the blue-clad army on the east, Grant's cannoneers bombarded the building. One shell landed between them, stunned Dr. Leavy, and tore away a portion of Dr. Britt's leg. Father Bannon escaped injury.

Boyce found out that his long-standing friend was considered the best preacher in Dublin. Physically and mentally, he was the same vigorous man the brigade had known a quarter of a century earlier.

Captain Boyce described the changes in attitudes that had come to Missouri and to St. Louis after the end of the military occupation of the South in 1876, the setting up of "home rule" in St. Louis, and the end of "Radical Republican" repression in the state. Many Missouri Confederates who had drifted elsewhere immediately after the Battle of Appomattox had come back, and those who had stayed took a clearer stance.

Confederate general John S. Marmaduke, son of a former governor of Missouri, was elected to the high post his father had held. George G. Vest, a former member of the Confederate Senate, and General Francis Marion Cockrell, the commander of the First Missouri Confederate Brigade in the later years of the war, represented Missouri in the U.S. Senate. Confederate veterans had begun to hold reunions, and the Southern Historical Association sank hickory-deep roots throughout the South.

Captain Boyce carried with him a resolution passed at the May 12 meeting in St. Louis of the Southern Historical Association that praised Father Bannon for his work. Boyce presented the priest with a collage of photographs of the survivors of Captain Henry Guibor's battery that included Father Bannon's likeness. Guibor had become a focal person among Confederates in the St. Louis area.

During his visit with Father Bannon, Boyce also showed the priest a sketch of the Battle of Pea Ridge. This may have been a copy of Wilson Hunt's widely distributed painting that pictured Father Bannon aiding a wounded soldier near Elkhorn Tavern on the eastern flank of the Confederate forces. A copy of the painting adorns the wall of the museum at the Confederate White House in Richmond. The entire visit, Captain Boyce concluded, gave the priest "inexpressible pleasure."[18] Father Bannon's gratitude was as warm as a Mississippi summer.

Father Bannon waited a day or two, while he prepared a stirring sermon on the Jesuit founder for the Feast of St. Ignatius, July 31.[19] Then, in early August, he wrote to his friend Captain Guibor and the other members of the Southern Historical Association. He thanked them for their kind remembrance and generous souvenirs. Time has passed, he wrote, since those eventful days recalled by the gifts. But no duties could overshadow those stirring memories or cause him to repent of the share he took in the various fortunes of the men whose care, here and hereafter, were the motives for his sacrifices and the objects of his concern.[20]

The veteran chaplain had read carefully the narrative on the war published by the Southern Historical Association in the *Missouri Republican*. Friends had forwarded the account to him. The events came back so vividly that it was a relief to awaken to the fact that it was a memory and no longer a reality. Yet for the spiritual consolation and the salvation of these same men, whether Federal or Confederate, he would willingly face again the weary marches, the long vigils, and endless privations. He remembered the warm grasp and kindly smile of the men of St. Louis and of other areas of Missouri and asked Captain Guibor to convey his good wishes to all the men of his battery and the entire brigade.[21]

The ever-dependable Guibor did just that two weeks later. He read Father Bannon's letter to those who attended the August 18 meeting of the Southern Historical Association, as it lay plans for a Confederate reunion to be held the following month at the town of Mexico, in the heart of Missouri's "Little Dixie,"[22] a strong pro-Confederate area.

Father Bannon had not lost hope of paying a visit to St. Louis, but the work he had on hand, looking after affairs of the Jesuit church, would, in all probability, keep him from making real this fond hope. Within the Jesuit community, Father Bannon saw to the enlargement of the available living space, with a large wing stretching north of the original section.[23]

During late 1885 and early 1886, Father Bannon arranged for a Dublin firm to build a new organ for St. Francis Xavier Church. The melodious instrument cost sixteen hundred pounds.[24] It replaced the one built for the great musical festival at Westminster Abbey that the Jesuits had purchased years before for eight hundred guineas.[25] Father Bannon also hired a new choirmaster and organist. John N. Glynn had earlier gained a reputation as a musician of high rank at the Vincentian and later at the Dominican churches. He also would prove "most generous in giving his services in the cause of charity."[26]

Right: Captain Henry Guibor headed the Confederate veterans of the St. Louis region.

Father Bannon planned a corridor to extend seventy-four feet along the length of the church on the left. Eventually to be almost twice that long, it provided parlor confessionals, a servers' room, and other facilities over the years. This "greatly admired" addition gained the name the Bannon Corridor.[27] He also added a wing to the Ignatian Chapel with a gift of $300 from the sodalists. Further, they were able to erect a marble statue of the Jesuit founder. On Sunday, June 21, 1888, the sodalists came in great numbers to the Communion Sunday Mass, celebrated by the visiting American, Archbishop Patrick Riordan of San Francisco.

Father Bannon invited five bishops for the solemn three-day celebration of the canonization of three Jesuit heroes. With Archbishop William J. Walsh of Dublin presiding, and Bishop James Donnelly of Clogher celebrating High Mass, Bishop Patrick O'Donnell of Raphoe spoke on St. Peter Claver, apostle of African Americans in Latin America. A night later, Bishop Francis J. MacCormack of Galway preached on the ever-faithful scholastic, St. John Berchmans. On the third evening, Bishop John Healey, coadjutor of Clonfert, described the dual career of St. Alphonsus Rodriguez, pious Spanish wool merchant in lay life, faithful keeper of the door as a Jesuit brother.[28]

Father Bannon continued to preach for good causes, such as the Passionist mission in Sierra Leone.[29] In the last months of his term as superior, he asked for help for the House of Mercy on Baggot Street in February,[30] for St. Clare's Orphanage in March,[31] and for St. Peter's School in May.[32]

A Jesuit superior normally got in touch with the general's office in Italy at regular intervals. It could have been that Father Bannon felt that the father general had enough pressing matters of a more important nature, now that, because of the Italian reunification, he had to leave Rome and reside in exile at Fiesole. Or perhaps with the mobility of the central office, records were lost. Be that as it may, only one letter from Father Bannon, dated 1888, remains in the Jesuit General Archives in Rome. In this letter, he apologizes for not having written more often. Even more interesting, a careful perusal of letters of the fathers provincial and consultors before he became superior shows no mention of Father Bannon at all.[33]

Only one letter from the provincial, Father Timothy Kenny, to Father Bannon has a place in the *Provincial Letters* in the Irish Province Archives. In that letter the father provincial routinely informed the Gardiner Street superior of a forthcoming Procurator's Congregation, and of the rules governing such a meeting.[34]

Above: Father Bannon opened a corridor adjoining the church, which bears his name today.

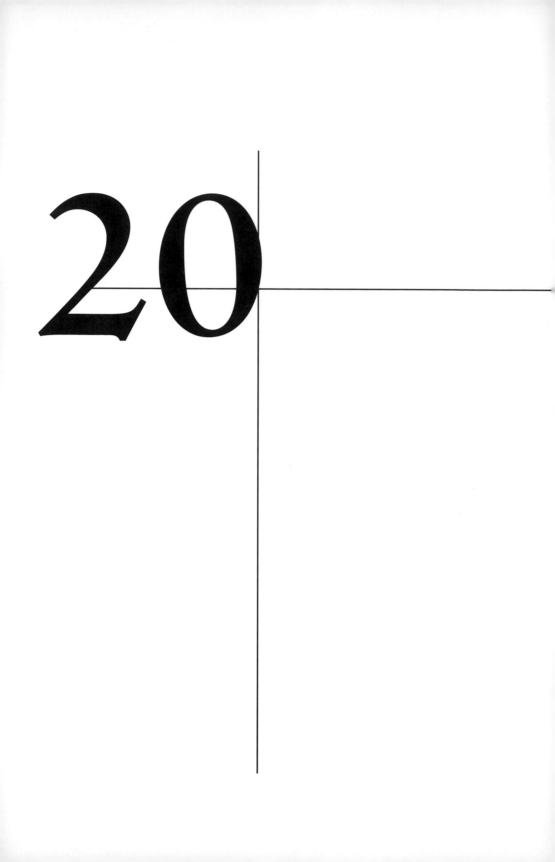

20

A Time of Jubilees

Father Bannon ended his term as superior in 1889, but he stayed in residence at Gardiner Street and continued to direct the Young Businessmen's Sodality. The records show, further, that he gave twelve retreats during the 1890s. A July 1890 retreat saw him at the convent of the Presentation nuns in Baltinglass, County Wicklow. He gave a July 1898 retreat at the Loretto Convent in Carlow. In Dublin, over the decade, he gave two retreats to Loretto Sisters, two to Carmelite nuns, and one each to Poor Clares, Presentation Sisters, and Carmelite Fathers.

In his sermons in St. Francis Xavier Church, Father Bannon began to team up with other speakers. On Good Friday 1891, for instance, he shared the pulpit for the Devotion of the Seven Last Words with Father Edward Kelly, his successor as superior.[1]

In October 1882, Father Bannon took a trip to France, and in September of the following year, he went to Brixton on the south coast of England, near Plymouth. After that, he seemed to leave Dublin rarely for any holiday.[2]

Sometime after 1894, Father Bannon may have become aware of the poetry of an American priest, John Bannister Tabb, whom he helped move toward the Catholic faith. Young Tabb had been a sailor on the blockade runner the *Giraffe*, later to be called the *Robert E. Lee*, that took Father Bannon from Wilmington, North Carolina, to the British West Indies in 1863. Tabb had asked the priest many questions about religion and was later to acknowledge his indebtedness to the Confederate chaplain.[3]

A London publisher, John Lane, put out Tabb's first important literary venture, *Poems*, in 1894. English critics praised the work more often than Americans did. *The Nation* and *The Spector*, for instance, carried favorable reviews in the spring of 1895.[4] The community library at the Gardiner Street residence had a copy of Tabb's book.

Left: Father Bannon may well have read the poems of Father John Bannister Tabb, whom Bannon started on the way to the fullness of faith back in 1863. A first edition of Tabb's *Poems* was in the Community Library.

In 1894, Father Bannon again shared the pulpit with another Jesuit on a major occasion. Father Alfred Murphy joined with him in conducting three days of devotions, called a *triduum* by the Jesuits, in honor of the Jesuit martyrs Rodolfo Aquaviva and his forty companions. While these Jesuits sailed to Brazil to Christianize Indians, a French Huguenot pirate captured their vessel. The corsair callously threw the forty Jesuits overboard in the South Atlantic. Father Murphy spoke in the morning and Father Bannon in the evening to a large congregation.[5]

In the summer of 1895, Father Bannon received a letter from the Confederate Association of Missouri penned by J. M. Barlow. The message "brought back memories of comrades and friends, faithful and generous, whose cherished names are still enshrined in my heart." Father Bannon asked Barlow to give to the members at the reunion his pledge of "lifelong fidelity to those early associations and hopes they will all be reunited in heaven."[6]

Father Bannon received a cherished Christmas gift in 1895: a graceful, tulip-shaped silver chalice, from a parishioner, Mary Teresa Crotty. Symbols of the Passion—the pillar, scourge, nails, hammer, tongs, ladder, and spear—mark the base, and a gold-plated Celtic cross adorns the stem just below the knob. This chalice is still in use at St. Francis Xavier.[7]

Captain Boyce came again in early June 1896. Father Bannon had just returned from visiting a sick member of the parish. On the following night, James McLoone, a first cousin of Boyce on his mother's side, and his wife Josie hosted a group of friends who enjoyed the reminiscences of the Missouri chaplain.

"It is remarkable," Boyce wrote in his diary, "how a man of his labors retains such great vigor and color. God keep him so."[8]

In one of the last letters (undated) that Boyce received, Father Bannon mentioned the city of St. Louis, Generals Bowen and Little, the batteries of Wade, Guibor, McDonald, Landis, and Bledsoe, and ended: "Tis a sad memory that 'Lost Cause' and all its varied incidents. Yet, tho' sad, I would not blot it out from my memory or expunge it from my life, for it made me acquainted with many brave and honorable men, of high spirit, great endurance and generous natures, whom I am proud to remember as companions and friends."[9]

In 1896, the year of Boyce's second visit, the parish began to put out leaflets that listed the speakers for the ensuing period—Lent, Advent, and the intervening months. Every list during the next ten years carried Father Bannon's name and topic at least once. Typical of these occasions, he would speak on Ascension Thursday in 1897, Easter Sunday in 1898, Christmas Day in 1900, New Year's and Holy Thursday in 1901, Trinity Sunday in 1902, and Quinquagesima Sunday in 1904. From 1906 to the last year of Father Bannon's life, the records are not available. We may presume he spoke less often during these years.[10]

Meanwhile, on April 28–30, 1897, the loyal director commemorated the Silver Jubilee of the sodality. He preached every evening, invited all to the communion rail, and intoned the *Te Deum* of thanksgiving.[11] In the celebration of the jubilee year at the beginning of the new century, the director marched with his sodalists in a religious procession.[12]

Father Bannon rarely absented himself from the monthly council meeting of the sodality. The regular meeting included matters of immediate business, reports of sickness or death in the family of a member, preparation for feasts, retreats, and special occasions such as Father Bannon's Golden Jubilee. When the council voted to present a chalice to him, present and past members were invited to con-

Right: The altar at St. Francis Xavier during Father Bannon's jubilee.

tribute. The sodality itself would provide what further funds were needed to reach the determined figure of fifty pounds. The sodality gave a donation of twenty pounds to the Jesuit community every month during the late 1890s. The sodality was also ready to come to the assistance of a member in need. On St. Valentine's Day in 1898, for instance, Charles Russell needed a loan. The sodality granted it.[13]

The novelist James Joyce, who joined the sodality as a young man,[14] made it the central focus of his short story "Grace." A group of Dubliners, business and professional men, brought a backslider to their retreat at St. Francis Xavier Church under the guidance of a fictional "Father Purdom." Joyce wrote:

> The transept of the Jesuit Church in Gardiner Street was almost full; and still at every moment gentlemen entered from the side door and, directed by the lay brother, walked on tiptoe along the aisles until they found seating accommodation. The gentlemen were all well dressed and orderly. The light of the lamps of the church fell upon an assembly of black clothes and white collars, relieved here and there by tweeds, on dark mottled pillars of green marble and on lugubrious canvases. The gentlemen sat in the benches, having hitched their trousers slightly above their knees and laid their hats in security. They sat well back and gazed formally at the distant speck of red light which was suspended before the high altar.[15]

In Joyce's story, Father Purdom gave a totally practical sermon on one of the most difficult of all New Testament parables, that of the mammon of iniquity. It was the type of sermon that Father Bannon could have given. The preacher dwelt on the careful accounting of the worldly businessman. He urged his hearers to keep equally careful accounts of their spiritual progress. At least one enterprising researcher, incidentally, studied another sermon quoted by Joyce. He found it surprisingly similar to a sermon by an Italian Jesuit available in Dublin at that time.[16] Perhaps, in this instance too, Joyce paraphrased a sermon he had heard or read.

If there were any particular occasion when Father Bannon should have gone back to St. Louis, it would have been in November 1898, when his former parish celebrated the fortieth jubilee of the church he had built. St. John's had been, in fact, the cathedral of the archdiocese for many years. Archbishop Kenrick had resided in the rectory there and four other priests as bishops there: his coadjutor, Patrick Ryan, who became archbishop of Philadelphia; John Hogan, bishop of St. Joseph, Missouri; John J. Hennessy, bishop of Wichita, Kansas; and Thomas Bonacum, bishop of Lincoln, Nebraska.

A *St. Louis Globe-Democrat* writer spoke of Father Bannon as "a most successful rector" and added: "There is scarcely anyone of prominence in St. Louis
who has not been associated in some way with some of the events in the long
history of St. John's."[17]

Archbishop John J. Kain celebrated the fortieth anniversary Mass. In his sermon, Bishop John J. Glennon of Kansas City paid glowing tribute to Father
Bannon, "who had built St. John's and buried his heart there."[18] The Kansas City
prelate commented on the amazing fact that one-eighth of all the Catholics in
the United States enjoyed the leadership of bishops who formerly served at St.
John Church.

Archbishop Ryan of Philadelphia, one of the former pastors, spoke in even
more warm and personal tones. He said:

> One of my dear friends in life has been Father Bannon, the noble
> priest, who built this church and having completed it, gave it up because
> he heard there were many St. Louis men in the Confederate Army who
> had no chaplain. . . . At the risk of his life he crossed the lines of both
> armies and has left an imperishable record of personal bravery because of
> his devotion to duty afterward. Twice did General Price order Father

Left: Archbishop Patrick Ryan, one of six
priests who served at St. John the Apostle
and Evangelist and later became bishops,
praised Father Bannon on the fiftieth anniversary of the church.
Above: Bishop John J. Glennon, auxiliary of
Kansas City, praised Father Bannon in his
speech at the fiftieth jubilee of St. John's
Church in St. Louis.

Bannon off the field and back to his quarters, but he insisted on staying with his men. His heart is with us in this celebration.[19]

The new century provided another jubilee, the fiftieth year since Father Bannon's ordination to the priesthood in 1853. On June 18, 1903, "a very large group of edified spectators," the *House Diary* records, "attended the monthly meeting of the Young Men's Commercial Sodality, for many years one of the most flourishing and important sodalities. . . . Father Bannon had been its spiritual director since its inception."[20]

At the conclusion of the devotional part of the program, John Belden, one of the officers, opened the jubilee memorial with the remark that few individuals could look back upon a life of so much good work as their spiritual director. "Before many of those present were born," Belden remarked, "Father Bannon worked in varied spheres in the slums of great cities, in the camps, on land and sea, doing his Master's work, and doing it well!" He then presented to Father Bannon a handsomely illuminated tribute and a gold chalice set with precious stones as "a token of their deep hearty gratitude . . . and their esteem for him."[21]

A front-page feature in the *Irish Catholic* described the program and called the chalice "a splendid specimen of the silversmith's art, . . . with hand-chased Celtic interlacing, such as on the Book of Kells, one of the few, indeed, of the arts preserved in Ireland through its changed history."[22]

The secretary of the sodality discussed specifically the priest's influence in the business world of the Irish metropolis through the men he guided. "To Father Bannon's exertion was due also much that was best in the commercial life of Dublin; whilst in other countries were to be found many whose strong Catholic principles were formed under his influence."[23]

Father Bannon thanked the members for their gifts and kind words and recalled, as the secretary had done, the absent ones who had gone to other climes. He was thankful for the good work all had done in Dublin and elsewhere, and praised their punctuality, propriety, spirit of poverty, and devotion. They had set an example for others. He knew they would carry on.

The sodalists then called upon two prominent members of the Irish Province to add their comments. The able and formal Father Nicholas Walsh, a former provincial, author of books and a preacher of renown, credited the sodality's success to Father Bannon's devotion to its interests. The father provincial at the time, the less formal Father John Conmee, spoke more at length. "There are few men in the Catholic Church," he stated, "who could point to such a wonderful work in the priesthood extending over the same period as had been accomplished by Father Bannon." Then, turning to the sodalists, he went on:

"There was nothing that could give a better lesson to their Christian people than the example given by the members of the Sodality."[24]

A few years later, a tribute to Father Bannon in the Dublin paper, the *Evening Telegraph*, reflected the views of these distinguished Jesuits at his Jubilee celebration. "His work of predilection was the formation and direction of his great Sodality for Commercial Young Men," the writer stated. "In this work he devoted a zeal and energy which were only equalled by the devotedness and affection of those for whom he so unselfishly laboured."[25]

While Father Bannon continued to preach regularly at the church, he spoke at only one major occasion recorded in the *House Diary*. He gave "an eloquent and instructive sermon" to a large congregation at a solemn religious festival on November 6, 1904, in commemoration of the Saints of the Jesuit Order.[26] The addition of one word to the diarist's comments on Father Bannon's sermon was novel. All other Jesuit preachers the diarist called eloquent. To Father Bannon's eloquent efforts he added another adjective, "instructive" in this instance, and "informative," "persuasive," or "telling" on other occasions.[27]

Besides the bimonthly gift of twenty pounds from the sodality, Father Bannon received many other gifts during the early years of the new century. At a time when the Sunday collection at the church averaged thirty-five pounds, a Miss Cantwell gave ten pounds as a gift to Father Bannon in September 1901. At Christmas time she gave another four pounds in his name. After that, she regularly gave four pounds every other month for a period of time.[28]

The community records for 1907 and the years immediately following show the income from an extensive list of stocks, gifts made in Father Bannon's name for companies such as Guiness, S. Clare Rails, West Telegraph, and Loughrea and Allymon Rails. Behind only one of these appears the name of the donor of the stock. No doubt many of these shares were gifts of members of the sodality. Be that as it may, these revenues formed a large part of the community income.[29]

Father Bannon lived frugally. In 1892, he purchased new trousers and a cassock, and had his boots and umbrella mended. His only extraordinary expenditure was twenty pounds for the already-mentioned trip to France. He requested slightly over eighteen pounds for his trip to Brixton in the early 1890s. After that year, fees to his physician, Dr. Cruise, formed the substantial part of his annual expenditures of seven pounds. All the while, he was bringing in more gifts than most of the rest of the community together.[30]

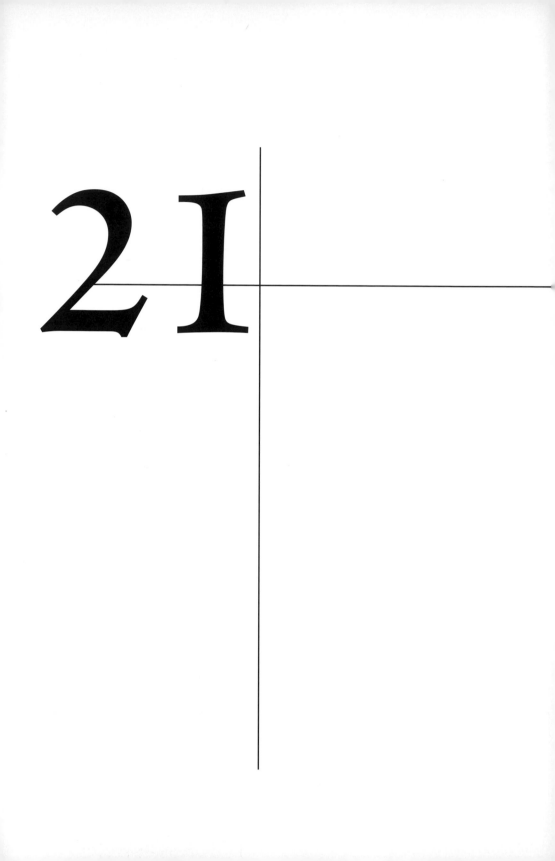

"Furl the Banner"

Early in the new century, a young South Carolinian, Yates Snowden, entered the life of the veteran Jesuit. An aspiring historian, Snowden would gain a place in the department of history at the University of South Carolina and eventually become the unofficial historian of his state. Although a Huguenot, young Snowden had long been a friend of the Catholic bishop of Charleston, Henry Pickney Northrop.

On one occasion, Snowden was a guest of the Carolina bishop when Bishop Benjamin J. Keiley of Savannah, a Virginian by birth, was also present. Snowden called the attention of the assembled guests to an article in the *North American Review* by journalist John Bigelow. The journalist, who had been U.S. consul in Paris during the Civil War, referred contemptuously to Bishop Lynch, the Confederate commissioner to the Papal States and, incidentally, a predecessor of Bishop Northrop in Charleston.[1]

"There are some references, too," Snowden went on, "to a certain Father Bannon, who appears to have given eminent service in Ireland.[2] In this article, Bigelow, who presumed that the priest was a pastor in Richmond, had made this statement: "What Father Bannon accomplished, if anything, by his mission, beyond getting out of Richmond, which had already become anything but a cheerful residence, and having his expenses paid during his absence, the records of the Confederacy have left no trace."[3] Bigelow concluded that the Confederate government was soon "aware that he [Father Bannon] was not accomplishing or likely to accomplish much."[4]

When he heard the name of the famous chaplain, Bishop Keiley broke in: "I know him well. He is now a Jesuit and lives with that community in Gardiner Street, Dublin."[5]

In a letter to Bishop Keiley the following school year (1904–5), Snowden, a graduate student at Columbia University, asked information about Bishop Lynch's mission to Rome.

In his answer, Bishop Keiley claimed little knowledge of that venture but had much to say about Father Bannon that he thought would interest Snowden. "Father Bannon was a secular priest," the bishop wrote, "and chaplain of a Missouri Regiment during the War between the States. After the fall of Vicksburg, Father Bannon made his way from Mobile to Richmond. I met him then in Petersburg, my native city, as he was going to Richmond."[6]

The St. Louis priest, Bishop Keiley went on, told Bishop McGill of Richmond that he was willing to perform any duty the bishop had in mind until the Missouri troops regrouped. When Father Bannon preached at Mass the following Sunday, the secretary of the navy, Stephen Mallory, attended the service. The secretary invited Father Bannon and the bishop to his home. But before they reached Mallory's residence, President Davis sent a message inviting them all to the White House of the Confederacy.[7]

President Davis asked Father Bannon to go to Ireland and use his influence to prevent young Irishmen from coming to the States for the purpose of entering the Yankee army. The bishop went on, "Representations had been made and bounties offered which had induced a large number of them to leave home and enlist in the Yankee service."[8]

Accepting President Davis's challenge, Father Bannon obtained $1,500 in gold, went to Wilmington, North Carolina, ran the blockade, landed in Halifax, and then embarked for Ireland. The bishop described at length the work of the priest as a special agent in Ireland and went on to assure Snowden that Father Bannon's work disrupted the program of federal enlistments in Ireland.[9]

Stirred by this letter of Bishop Keiley, Snowden wrote directly to Father Bannon in Dublin. He enclosed a copy of the message from the Savannah prelate and asked the Jesuit for a sketch of his career, with special emphasis on his work as a Confederate agent in Ireland. He also asked about the views of John Bigelow on Bishop Lynch's Roman mission, as expressed in the article in the *North American Review*.[10]

Father Bannon began his reply by assuring Snowden that Bishop Keiley's statement was, in most part, correct. Father Bannon changed a few items in the text. He said that he had little data and that his memory was not sharp. Nonetheless, he wrote a few remembrances. He began:

> After the fall of Vicksburg, I went to Mobile and thence to Richmond, with the intention of returning to Demopolis for the muster

Left: Yates Snowden, a young historian from South Carolina, visited Father Bannon and presumably intended to write an account of his chaplaincy. Snowden wrote much on South Carolina's history and nothing on Father Bannon, but he did preserve Bannon's papers at the university library in Columbia.

of the Missouri troops at the end of the two months furlough, stipulated at Vicksburg. Until then, I was content to remain and do duty in Richmond. The Irish mission was altogether unexpected, and acceptable only after Doctor McGill's approval and advice. . . . Of the success or failure of my efforts, the enclosed excerpts may are [*sic*] indirect evidences."

These excerpts, incidentally, were a few notes from Henry Hotze, a Confederate agent in London. "But yet more," the Jesuit went on, "in the fall of '67, Bishop McGill called on me in our college at Louvain, Belgium and told me that the Confederate Congress had passed a vote of thanks for my success in stopping the recruiting in Ireland, and voted me $3,000 as a bonus."[11]

On the matter of John Bigelow's insinuations about Bishop Lynch's trip to Rome, Father Bannon could direct little light. He had not seen the bishop's instructions or heard anything of their nature beyond the fact that the Charleston prelate would visit London, Paris, and Rome. At the bishop's request, Father Bannon had gone with him but did not attend any of the interviews.[12]

Gratified that he had received an answer from the priest, the enthusiastic historian wrote again on August 5, asking for a record of personal experiences. Father Bannon wrote eleven days later:

> To a younger man, the suggestion would be inspiring, invigorating, an opportunity of giving entertainment to many, and not a little pleasure to myself. For me, at seventy-six years of age, it appears to be formidable, an impossible project. I write slowly and stiffly. It would require two or three hours a day for a couple of days in the week, for some months, perhaps years to come, on which I cannot count, and on the whole it would prove a task and a burden too heavy and exacting for Yours Sincerely, John Bannon.[13]

The length of time the old Jesuit presumed he would have to spend putting down all his recollections suggests that the memoirs would have gone into as many volumes as those of General Grant.

Gradually, Snowden made up his mind to prepare a sketch of Father Bannon's life for either the *American Historical Magazine* or one of the reviews, preferably an illustrated one that would carry a picture of the Confederate chaplain.[14] On his way home from Columbia University at the end of the term the following year, June 1906, Snowden stopped at the Congressional Library in Washington and copied from the originals, then in possession of the U.S. government, all of Father Bannon's dispatches from Ireland to Judah Benjamin, the Confederate secretary of state.[15]

In 1907, Snowden and his wife accompanied Bishop Northrop and his secretary, Father Joseph Budds, to Europe. Early in July, he reached Dublin and, with the bishop and the priest, visited Father Bannon. The Carolina historian called Father Bannon's attention to their earlier correspondence and repeated his request for data on the ex-chaplain's work as a Confederate agent. Again, Father Bannon expressed regret that he could help so little.

After a pleasant visit and a tour of the impressive church, Snowden prepared to leave. But before he did, he handed Father Bannon the copies he had made of the priest's own reports to Secretary Benjamin. Father Bannon would find on the back something probably new to him, an enthusiastic endorsement of his work by President Jefferson Davis. Snowden would return the next day to pick up his papers after Father Bannon had read them.[16]

On Snowden's return the next afternoon, Father Bannon greeted him warmly:

> You have opened, sir, what I thought was a closed page of my life. As I wrote you in New York, and told you yesterday, I have few letters and documents bearing on my work for the Confederacy, and, if I had the inclination, I could not trust to my memory to record reminiscences. But you appear to be more interested in my career than anyone I know, and I am, therefore, going to give you all such papers in my possession, for I shall not be here much longer.[17]

Father Bannon then reached into the pocket of his black cassock and took from it a pile of memoranda, papers, and letters. Much of the material consisted of snippets relating to such trivial matters as minor expenditures. But two items were of great importance: Father Bannon's secret instructions in the handwriting of Secretary Benjamin, and the original notebooks and diary of Father Bannon as a chaplain with the Missouri Confederates. While all the diary was in pencil and some of it undecipherable,[18] it proved to be a treasure, a fitting ending to a rich trip for Snowden.

Snowden made an effort to find out more about Bannon's family and early years. He corresponded with Father J. J. Head, a priest of the Archdiocese of St. Louis who came from Strokestown, Bannon's place of origin. Father Head gave the historian the address of John O'Farrell of Strokestown, a relative of the chaplain on his mother's side. Snowden wrote O'Farrell, telling him that he planned to write a life of the versatile priest. No answer came.

Eventually, teaching and writing the history of South Carolina absorbed Snowden's time and interest. He published nothing on Father Bannon's career, but he saved his papers and placed them in the South Caroliniana Library at the University of South Carolina.

Four years after Snowden's visit to the Jesuit in Dublin, another Southerner, Albert C. Danner, quartermaster of the First Missouri Brigade during the Civil War, visited the aging priest. In the summer of 1911, Danner and some friends were touring Scotland and Ireland by motorcar. They spent Sunday, August 13, in Dublin. Since the quartermaster had gotten Father Bannon's address from a friend in Mobile, he went to see the priest at St. Francis Xavier Church. The doorkeeper at the adjoining Jesuit residence seemed surprised that the American wanted to see Father Bannon. He presumed that the visitor wished to make his confession and escorted him to a small parlor reserved for private conferences. He then went to find the Irish Jesuit.

The doorkeeper returned and told Danner that he would have to go to Father Bannon's room, since the octogenarian could no longer walk up and down steps. Danner found that the veteran looked "old and broken."

Father Bannon could not place his guest at first. But when the quartermaster talked of old times and places where the Missouri brigade had served, he began to recall their association. Danner brought a gift for the priest, a new book by author Mary Johnson that gave a thrilling account of Stonewall Jackson's campaigns in the valley of Virginia. Father Bannon had heard of the book and wanted to read it but had never had the opportunity.

At the conclusion of the visit, as Danner was saying good-bye, Father Bannon insisted on giving the visitor his blessing. He said that "even if Danner and he were not of the same church, his prayer and blessing could do no harm—if it did no good."

"I was agreeable," Danner wrote, "thinking just as he did, and going home shortly after that, on the ocean, when a big storm struck us, I was not sorry that I had received the blessing bestowed upon me and that the prayer had been said for me by this good, faithful Catholic priest."[19]

Eight years later, six years after Father Bannon's death, Danner read an article in the *Confederate Veteran* that told of Pope Pius IX's letter to President Jefferson Davis of December 3, 1863. In this letter the Holy Father thanked the Southern president for his appreciation of the papal efforts for peace. Danner responded with an article titled "Father Bannon's Secret Mission."[20] Danner suggested that the man who delivered Davis's letter to the Pope may well have been Father John B. Bannon, chaplain of the First Missouri Brigade, C.S.A. He was wrong in this statement, but in other tributes to the Missouri chaplain, he reflected a common appreciation. "Father Bannon was brave, courageous, energetic," Danner wrote, "and liked by all in the Missouri Army, Protestants as well as Catholics."[21]

Father Bannon's once oak-tough frame continued to weaken in the early fall of 1911. He took leave of his faithful sodalists after the Benediction that closed their retreat in November of that year. By that time, he had endured twelve months of pain and suffering. The once splendid and robust figure that had graced most of the pulpits in the land, now stooped and enfeebled, trudged slowly down the center of the sanctuary toward the communion rail. As he walked, there occurred "an incident of such . . . touching character, that," in the words of the storyteller, "seldom or never has had its parallel been recorded in the history of the Catholic metropolis."[22] Like a wind sweeping across the country from the Atlantic, an outburst of applause filled the church. The spontaneous and continued acclaim unnerved the old priest for some time. Gradually, he straightened to his full six feet in height, and calling on the ancient power of his eloquence, he recalled the success of the sodality through its many years. He urged the members to give to his successor the same loyalty they had shown him and to battle the evil forces that would destroy Ireland's faith and fair fame. All then knelt for his blessing. The sodalists gathered to shake his hand, perhaps for the last time.[23]

During that summer of 1911, John Naughton, Father Bannon's fellow novice in 1865 and an outstanding missionary, passed on.[24] Three other noted Jesuits would die in Dublin the following year: Father Nicholas Walsh, the former provincial biographer and spiritual writer who had spoken at Father Bannon's jubilee;[25] another missionary, Father John Hughes, a popular community man, successful superior in Galway, and eventually spiritual director of the Dublin Metropolitan Police;[26] and the poet and prose stylist Father Matthew Russell, brother of the eminent Lord Russell of Killowen, chief justice of England who added to his own writing over forty years the mission of nurturing young authors and acting as publisher for the earliest poems of Oscar Wilde, a friend of W. B. Yeats.[27]

It should surprise no one that Father Bannon's name does not appear among the numerous clergy at these funerals. Likewise, after October 31, 1910, his name does not appear on the Mass list. He suffered a slight stroke in early November, and his hand was paralyzed. He did not try to write until mid-March of 1911 when he attempted a letter to Captain Joseph Boyce, thanking him for sending a group of papers that included the current *Bulletin* of Saint Louis University. Father Bannon wrote that this material had particular interest for the Jesuits who were professors at the New "Royal" Irish University.

"I have not been down stairs for five months," he wrote. "But for the month past I have been able to get daily Mass at 11 o'clock in the organ loft of the church which is on the same level as my room and accessible to me."[28] He closed with a blessing for all the Boyces.[29]

This was the last of his letters to have come down in any collection. He lived on slightly more than two years until the summer of 1913. "His calm endurance and powerful vitality," a contemporary newspaper stated, "sustained him. He bore his sufferings patiently and retained consciousness and interest in life until a few hours before he passed away."[30] The day was Monday, July 14, 1913, less than a month after his sixtieth anniversary in the priesthood.

That very afternoon the *Evening Telegraph* carried this statement:

> The Community of Jesuit Fathers in Upper Gardiner Street have lost within a comparatively short time some of their best known and distinguished members. They had to deplore the deaths of Father Nicholas Walsh, Father John Naughton, Father John Hughes and Father Matthew Russell, four men of great eminence and distinction, each in his own sphere, who added luster to their Order, and whose services to the Church

and their country in the varied lines of apostolic activity cannot soon be forgotten. And now another name as illustrious is added to the list. The Rev. John Bannon . . . passed away in the early hours of this morning.[31]

The headline in the *Evening Telegraph* ran as follows: "A Famous Irish Jesuit Chaplain in the American War." The writer summarized the main activities and events of Father Bannon's long life—facts and dates that have already appeared in this account of his life—and then penned a remarkable tribute:

Father Bannon was a man of no ordinary gifts . . . a personality of massive character, with ardour and energy characteristic of his powerful will and kindly heart, a keen intellect and a mind filled from his vast experience of life, and extensive reading in theology and literature of the day . . . a commanding appearance, a voice of peculiar sweetness and power . . . a pulpit orator of the very first rank, with a force and charm rarely equalled . . . a wise and comforting adviser . . . a generous benefactor . . . a true friend . . . a man of deep religious feeling, of profound humility and simplicity of character . . . great strength of will and heart tender as a mother's.[32]

A tribute in the *Irish Catholic* stated:

In his passing away, the city is deprived of a great personality, the poor of a generous friend, his friends of a wise adviser, his order of a distinguished member, whose name and work have added lustre to the Irish Church. To his brother and relatives, to whom he was so tenderly attached, his death will be more than a personal loss, and to his brothers in religion much sympathy will be offered.[33]

The *Irish Catholic Directory* offered, under the date of July 14, a few additional words of praise: "After a long suffering, patiently borne, the Rev. John Bannon, S.J., died today. By his death the Society of Jesus has been deprived of a brilliant and illustrious member. A man of great learning and vast experience, it will be hard to fill his place."[34]

The *Evening Telegraph* carried Father Bannon's photograph on page two the day after his death. It showed the priest in full vigor of young manhood, presumably shortly after he had returned to the Green Isle and shaved off the black beard of the Southern battlefields.[35]

Seventy-nine priests from all over Ireland—diocesans, Dominicans, Carmelites, Franciscans, and Passionists, as well as Jesuits—attended the funeral Mass on Thursday, July 17. The chief mourner was Patrick Nooney of

Top: The Jesuit plot at Glasnevin Cemetery in Dublin.
Bottom: Detail of the Jesuit plot.

Mullingar,[36] a nephew whose marriage he had witnessed almost thirty years before. A magazine in far-off Maryland had this to say at the time:

> Those who were present at the farewell to his famous sodality of fifteen hundred men, founded and directed by Father Bannon for close to thirty years, will not easily forget the scene of genuine emotion and deep love shown in the crowded church at Gardiner Street, for the venerable old director of eighty-two, who for so many years had been not only a wise and comforting adviser but a sincere and true friend.[37]

The sodalists came in equal numbers for his funeral. They marched eight abreast from the church to Glasnevin Cemetery more than a mile away. As they left the mortuary just west of the tall monolith that marks the final resting place of Daniel O'Connell, the Liberator, a photographer took a picture of the funeral procession for the *Evening Telegraph*.[38]

A walkway leads from the mortuary to the Jesuit plot one hundred yards to the west. The influential Jesuits mentioned in the article in the *Telegraph* the day of Father Bannon's death already had their places there, as did a priest, little known then, but who today is the most world famous of them all, the poet Gerard Manley Hopkins. Father Bannon took his place under the Celtic cross that surmounts the Jesuit resting place, the first of a forest of Celtic crosses that stretches to the north and the west. Late that evening, the July sun still stood high and bright in the summer sky.

Above: A Union re-enactor stands guard at the grave of the Confederate chaplain.

Abbreviations

BCN: GS Brief Chronological Notes, Gardiner Street
BD Bannon's Diary
BRE Book of Receipts and Expenditures
BS Boyce Scrapbook
CIP *Catalogues* of the Irish Province
Cons IP *Consultors*, Irish Province
DEP *Dublin Evening Post*
ET *Evening Telegraph*
F: GS Files, Gardiner Street
HD: SFX House Diary, St. Francis Xavier
HRS *Historical Records and Studies*
IC *Irish Catholic*
ICD *Irish Catholic Directory*
IJH *Irish Jesuit History to 1914*
IPA Irish Province Archives
LD *Diary of General Henry Little*
MEN: IP *Menology*, Irish Province
MHS Missouri Historical Society
MJA Midwest Jesuit Archives
NDS *Notre Dame Scholastic*
PP Pickett Papers
RHMM *Robert Haly's Mission Memoirs*
SLAA St. Louis Archdiocesan Archives
WB *Western Banner*
WL *Woodstock Letters*
YSP Yates Snowden Papers

Endnotes

1. Early Years

1. Dublin, Registry of Deeds, 568221, July 9, 1829.
2. Peter Kenrick, St. Louis, to Milne, Vienna, Austria, August 29, 1844, in John Rothensteiner, History of the Archdiocese of St. Louis (St. Louis: Blackwell and Wielandy, 1928).
3. Letter of Archbishop Paul Cullen, Dublin, August 15, 1855, copy in the files of the author.

2. St. Louis: Church and Community

No notes. For further information about St. Louis in the 1850s, see chapter 8 of William Faherty, *St. Louis: A Concise History* (St. Louis: St. Louis Convention and Visitors Bureau, 1990); or William Faherty, *The St. Louis Irish: An Unmatched Celtic Community* (St. Louis: Missouri Historical Society Press, 2001), chapters 6–9. For further information on the Catholic community of St. Louis at the time, see William Faherty, *Dream by the River: Two Centuries of St. Louis Catholicism* (St. Charles, Mo.: Piraeus, 1968), chapters 15–18.

3. First Years in St. Louis

1. *The Western Banner* (hereafter WB), November 28, 1858.
2. Parish Diary, December 7, 1858, St. John the Apostle and Evangelist Church.
3. Ibid., October 1859.
4. "List of Mayors," in *Heritage St. Louis* (St. Louis: n.p., 1964), 178; see also *St. Louis Globe-Democrat*, November 13, 1898.
5. WB, November 3, 1860.
6. Ibid.

7. Parish Diary, November 4, 1860.

8. *St. Louis Republican*, March 14, 1861.

9. Kenrick's Account Book, St. Louis Archdiocesan Archives (hereafter SLAA), 71.

10. Rothensteiner, *History of the Archdiocese of St. Louis*, 2.

4. The Nation Walks to the Brink

1. WB, December 1, 1860.

2. Ibid., December 15, 1860.

3. Walter B. Stevens, *Centennial History of Missouri*, vol. 1 (St. Louis: S. J. Clarke Publishing Company, 1921), 706.

4. Ibid., 712.

5. Lillie Knapp Bloomfield to Mrs. Charles K. O'Connell, May 24, 1937, in John Knapp Collection, Missouri Historical Society (hereafter MHS).

6. Testimony of an unnamed volunteer, ibid.

7. "Camp Jackson Papers," MHS. Two other Bannons, a James and a John, appear in the St. Louis Directory for 1861. Neither is listed on militia rolls.

8. Louis C. Gerteis, *Civil War St. Louis* (Lawrence: University Press of Kansas, 2001).

9. M. J. Murphy to Father Sesnon, St. Louis, October 24, 1919, in SLAA.

10. Boyce to Snowden, St. Louis, September 5, 1918, in Yates Snowden Papers (hereafter YSP), South Caroliniana Library, University of South Carolina, Columbia, S.C.

11. Undated clipping in Billon Scrapbook, vol. 2, MHS.

5. Father Bannon Goes "South"

1. Bannon's Diary (hereafter BD), January 16, 1862, in YSP.

2. Ibid., July 23, 1862.

3. Ibid., February 14, 1862.

4. Ibid., January 25, 1862.

5. Bannon to Benjamin, Dublin, April 19, 1864, in Pickett Papers (hereafter PP), no. 4, in Library of Congress, Division of Manuscripts.

6. Dabney Maury, "Recollections of the Elkhorn Campaign," *Southern Historical Papers* 2 (January–December, 1876), 180–82.

7. BD, January 27, 1862.

8. Ibid., January 16, 1862.

9. Ibid., January 22, 1862.

10. Ibid.

11. Ibid., May 11, 1862.

12. Ibid., July 8, 1862.

13. Ibid., January 25, 1862; January 29, 1862; February 20, 1862.

14. Ibid.

15. Ibid., March 7–8, 1862.

16. Ibid., July 31, 1862.

17. Ibid., February 2, 1862.

18. Ibid., February 3, 1862.

19. Ibid., February 5, 1862.

20. Ibid., February 9, 1862.

21. Ibid., March 1, 1862.

22. Ibid., March 2, 1862.

23. Ibid., January 31, 1862.

24. Ibid.

25. Ibid.

26. Charles Pitts, *Chaplains in Gray* (Nashville, Tenn.: Broadman Press, 1957), 39.

27. *Memphis Appeal*, September 4, 1861, quoted in Pitts.

28. Pitts, *Chaplains in Gray*, 111.

29. Blanchard to Benjamin, December 2, 1862, quoted in Dom Aidan Henry Germain, *Catholic Military and Naval Chaplains, 1776–1917* (Washington, D.C.: Catholic University of America, 1929), 118.

30. Dabney Maury, *Recollections of a Virginian in the Mexican, Indian, and Civil Wars* (New York: Charles Scribner's Sons, 1894). An unpublished copy is in the possession of Dr. Philip Tucker, 173.

31. M. M. Quaife, ed., *Absalom Grimes: Confederate Mail Runner* (New Haven, Conn.: Yale University Press, 1926), 66.

6. Curtis Moves into Arkansas

1. BD, February 14, 1862.

2. Bannon, Priceville, Mo., to a friend in St. Louis, July 16, 1862. Printed copy in Billon Scrapbook, vol. 2, MHS.

3. BD, February 16, 1862.

4. Ibid., February 17, 1862.

5. Ibid., February 18, 1862.

6. Ibid., February 20, 1862.

7. *Catholic Almanac*, 1861, 119.

8. BD, February 28, 1862.

9. William Faherty, *Henry Shaw: His Life and Legacies* (Columbia: University of Missouri Press, 1987), 122.

10. John Gould Fletcher, *Arkansas* (Chapel Hill: University of North Carolina Press, 1947), 151.

11. Ibid.

12. Shelby Foote, *The Civil War: A Narrative*, 3 vols. (New York: Random House, 1958–74), 721.

13. Fletcher, *Arkansas*, 152.

14. BD, March 2, 1862.

15. Ibid.

16. Ibid., March 3, 1862.

17. Ibid., March 4, 1862.

18. Ibid., March 5, 1862.

19. Ibid., March 6, 1862.

7. The Greatest Battle of the Trans-Mississippi

1. BD, March 8, 1862.

2. John W. Bond, "The Pea Ridge Campaign," in *The Battle of Pea Ridge, 1862* (Rogers, Ark.: The Park, 1963?).

3. Foote, *The Civil War*, vol. 1, 290–91.

4. BD, March 8, 1862.

8. Reminiscing About Pea Ridge

1. Wilson Hunt, *Battle of Elkhorn Tavern*, painting in museum adjacent to the White House of the Confederacy, Richmond, Virginia.

2. *Missouri Republican*, November 14, 1885.

3. Ibid.

4. "Experiences of a Confederate Chaplain," in *Letters and Notices of the English Jesuit Province*, October 1867, 202–6.

5. "Champ Clark Scrapbook," MHS.

6. Southern bivouac, an undated excerpt.

7. William Hyde and Howard Conard, eds., *Encyclopedia of the History of St. Louis: A Compendium of History and Biography*, vol. 4 (New York: Southern History Co., 1899), 2,440.

9. Changing Fronts

1. BD, March 17, 1862.

2. Ibid., March 23, 1862.

3. Ibid., March 28, 1862.

4. Ibid., April 3, 1862.

5. Ibid., April 4–5, 1862.

6. Sister Mary Eulalia Herron, *The Sisters of Mercy in the United States, 1843–1928* (New York: Macmillan, 1929), 82.

7. BD, April 4–5, 1862.

8. Ibid., April 9, 1862.

9. Ibid., April 11, 1862.

10. Ibid., April 12, 1862.

11. Ibid., April 13, 1862.

12. Foote, *The Civil War*, vol. 1, 724.

13. Ibid., vol. 2, 3.

14. BD, April 13, 1862.

15. Foote, *The Civil War*, vol. 1, 381.

16. Daniel Hannefin, *Daughters of the Church: A Popular History of the Daughters of Charity in the United States, 1809–1987* (Brooklyn, N.Y.: New City Press, 1989), 131.

17. *Letters and Notices*, 202–6.

18. Ibid.

19. Ibid.

20. Foote, *The Civil War*, vol. 1, 376.

21. Ibid.

22. BD, April 13, 1862.

23. *Diary of General Henry Little* (hereafter LD), U.S. Army Military History Institute, April 13, 1862.

24. Germain, *Catholic Chaplains*, 108–9.

25. LD, April 13–16, 1862.

26. BD, April 13–16, 1862.

27. Ibid.

28. Ibid., April 17, 1862.

29. Ibid.

30. Ibid., April 18, 1862.

31. Ibid., April 22, 1862.

32. Ibid., April 27, 1862.

33. Ibid., April 28, 1862.

34. Ibid., May 9, 1862.

35. Ibid., June 2, 1862.

36. Ibid., Apr. 26, 1862.

37. Ibid., April 30, 1862.

38. Ibid., April 28, 1862.

39. Ibid., April 29, 1862.

40. Ibid., April 29, 1862.

41. Ibid., April 30, 1862.

42. Ibid., May 1, 1862.

43. Ibid., May 2, 1862.

44. Ibid., May 4, 1862.

45. Ibid., May 9, 1862.

46. Ibid.

47. Ibid., May 8, 1862.

48. Ibid., July 27, 1862.

49. Ibid., May 9, 1862.

50. Ibid.

51. Ibid., May 26–27, 1862.

52. Ibid., May 8, 1862.

53. Maury, *Recollections of a Virginian*.

54. *Letters and Notices*, 201–2.

55. *St. Louis Republic*, August 1, 1913, quoted in *Confederate Veterans* 21, no. 9, 451.

56. Ibid.

57. Ibid.

58. Peter Tissot, "A Year with the Army of the Potomac," *Historical Records and Studies* (hereafter HRS) 3, no. 1 (January 1903): 78–79.

10. Iuka and Second Corinth

1. Foote, *The Civil War*, vol. 1, 389.

2. BD, July 1862.

3. Ibid., July 13, 1862.

4. Foote, *The Civil War*, vol. 1, 716–17.

5. BD, September 13, 1862.

6. Ibid., September 14, 1862.

7. Foote, *The Civil War*, vol. 1, 718–19.

8. Ibid., 719–20.

9. BD, September 19, 1862.

10. Ibid.

11. Ibid.

12. Hyde and Conard, *Encyclopedia*, 2, 440.

13. Ibid.

14. BD, September 28, 1862.

15. Ibid., October 4, 1862.

16. Ibid.

17. Hyde and Conard, *Encyclopedia*, 2, 441.

18. Foote, *The Civil War*, vol. 1, 725.

19. BD, October 10, 1862.

20. Ibid., October 3, 1862.
21. Ibid., October 12, 1862.
22. Ibid., December 13, 1862.
23. Ibid., December 15, 1862.
24. Ibid., April 15, 1862.
25. Adjutant General's Office Confederate Archives, ch.1, file no. 86, p. 378, quoted in Germain, *Catholic Chaplains*, 108–9.
26. BD, January 1, 1863.
27. Ibid., January 2, 1863.
28. Ibid., January 4, 1863.
29. Ibid., January 5, 1863.
30. Ibid., January 10, 1863.
31. Ibid., January 10, 1863.
32. Ibid.
33. Ibid., January 31, 1863.
34. Commission of Reverend John B. Bannon, in YSP.
35. Ibid.
36. Ibid.
37. BD, March 5, 1863.
38. Ibid., March 12, 1863.
39. Ibid., March 19, 1863.

11. Vicksburg: Citadel above the River

1. BD, March 29, 1863.
2. Ibid.
3. Ibid.
4. Ibid., April 1, 1863.
5. Ibid.
6. Ibid., April 3–7, 1863.
7. Ibid., April 19–20, 1863.
8. Ibid., April 29, 1863.
9. William Henry Elder, *Civil War Diary* (privately printed, n.d.), 29. A copy is in the possession of the author.
10. Ibid., 30.
11. BD, April 30, 1863.

12. Lt. Col. Alden McClellan, New Orleans, to Capt. A. C. Danner, May 18, 1919, in Boyce Scrapbook, MHS.
13. Bannon, Fort Gibson, to friend, April 1863, in Boyce Scrapbook (hereafter BS), MHS.
14. BD, May 1, 1863.
15. Ibid., May 1, 1863.
16. HRS 26 (1936), 94.
17. BD, May 2, 1863.
18. Ibid.
19. Ibid., May 14–18, 1863.
20. Ibid., May 19, 1863.
21. Ibid., May 25, 1863.
22. Ibid., May 27, 1863.
23. John Leavy Journal, Salt Lake City, Utah, 23–24.
24. BD, June 23, 1863.
25. Ibid., June 25, 1863.
26. Herron, *Sisters of Mercy*, 245 46.
27. Ibid.
28. *Letters and Notices*, 206–8.
29. BD, June 25, 1863.
30. Sgt. James Hogan to his father, July 27, 1863, MHS.
31. BD, June 3, 1863.
32. Sgt. James Hogan to his father, July 27, 1863, MHS.
33. BD, July 3, 1863.
34. Ibid., July 4, 1863.

12. How Great a Chaplain?

1. Germain, *Catholic Chaplains*.
2. Ibid., 112.
3. *Notre Dame Scholastic*, bound copies in the archives of the University of Notre Dame.
4. Woodstock Letters (hereafter WL), bound copies in Midwest Jesuit Archives, St. Louis.

5. Philip Thomas Tucker, *The Confederacy's Fighting Chaplain: Father John B. Bannon* (Tuscaloosa: University of Alabama Press, 1992).

6. Cornelius Buckley, ed., *A Frenchman, a Chaplain, a Rebel: The War Letters of Père Louis-Hippolyte Gache, S.J.* (Chicago: Loyola University Press, 1981).

7. Joseph T. Durkin, S.J., ed., *Confederate Chaplain: A War Journal of Rev. James B. Sheeran, C.S.S.R.* (Milwaukee: Bruce Publishing Co., 1960), 57–58, 74–75.

8. T. S. King, "Letters of Civil War Chaplains," WL 42, no. 1 (1914), 170.

9. Ibid.; also Germain, *Catholic Chaplains*, 102–4.

10. Catalogue, New Orleans Province, Jesuit Order, 1865.

11. Durkin, ed., *Confederate Chaplain*.

12. Ibid., 32–33.

13. Ibid.

14. Ibid.

15. Ibid., 163.

16. Germain, *Catholic Chaplains*, 59–60.

17. Ibid., 63–64.

18. Obituary, Father Joseph B. O'Hagan, in WL 8, 173–83. Also *Voices of the Civil War: Fredericksburg* (Alexandria, Va.: Time Life Books, 1997), 78.

19. Ibid., 176.

20. Ibid., 180–81, quoted.

21. Tissot, "Year with the Army of the Potomac."

22. "Reminiscences of Gen. James O'Bierne," *Fordham Monthly* 5, no. 6 (March 1887), 89.

23. Ibid.

24. WL 14, no. 3 (1914), 375 ff.

25. Germain, *Catholic Chaplains*, 84.

26. James Smith, New York, to Adjutant GAR Post, Notre Dame, in *Notre Dame Scholastic* (hereafter NDS), January 15, 1898, 275.

27. Mulholland to Morrissey, Philadelphia, December 29, 1897, quoted in NDS, January 15, 1898, 275.

28. Ibid.

29. Robert S. Hall, *Knights Without Armor* (Danbury, Conn.: n.p., 1965).

30. Pitts, *Chaplains in Gray*.

31. "Some Recollections of Bishop Marvin and Others," in the Albert C. Danner Papers, in the private collection of Dorothy Danner Travits, of Mobile, Alabama.

32. Maury, *Recollections of a Virginian*.

33. Danner Papers.

34. Recollections of Capt. Joseph Boyce, in MHS.

13. Confederate Agent

1. Keiley, Savannah, to Snowden, June 15, 1905, in YSP.

2. Benjamin to Bannon, September 4, 1863, in YSP.

3. F. A. Litz, Father Tabb: *A Study of His Life and Works* (Baltimore: Johns Hopkins Press, 1923), 31–32.

4. Benjamin, Richmond, to Hotze, September 4, 1863, in *Messages and Papers of the Confederacy* vol. 2, 562.

5. Ibid.

6. Bannon, Dublin, to Benjamin, November 17, 1863, in PP, no. 1.

7. Bannon, Dublin, to Benjamin, November 22, 1863, in PP, no. 2.

8. Ibid.

9. Bannon, Dublin, to Benjamin, December 15, 1863, with enclosure, in PP, no. 3.

10. Bannon, Dublin, to Benjamin, January 19, 1864, in PP, no. 4.

11. "Some Civil War Documents: A. B. 1862–64, Pope Pius IX and President Davis," in *Records of the American Catholic Historical Society*, vol. 14 (Philadelphia: The Society, 1903), 264–74.

12. Bannon, Dublin, to Benjamin, January 19, 1864, in PP, no. 4.

13. Bannon, Dublin, to Benjamin, April 9, 1864, in PP, no. 7.

14. *Freeman's Journal*, February 15, 1864.

15. Bannon, Dublin, to Benjamin, February 17, 1864, in PP, no. 5.

16. Hotze to Benjamin, March 12, 1864, in PP, no. 38.

17. Bannon, Dublin, to Benjamin, March 9, 1864, in PP, no. 6.

18. Ibid.

19. Ibid.

20. Bannon, Dublin, to Benjamin, April 9, 1864, with enclosure, in PP, no. 7.

21. *Times* (London), March 8, 1864.

22. R. L. Lynch, "Recollections," in YSP.

23. Capston, Dublin, to Benjamin, August 24, 1864, in PP, no. 41.

24. Bannon, Dublin, to Benjamin, May 28, 1864, in PP, no. 8.

25. Lynch, "Recollections."

26. Ibid.

27. Ibid.

28. Ibid.

14. Whither the Call?

No notes.

15. Reorientation in Erin

1. Kelly, Melbourne, to Reynolds, n.d., quoted in Laurence Kenny, "Father John Bannon, S.J.," HRS 26, 93.

2. *Informationes* of the novices from the years 1860 to 1895, in the Irish Province Archives (hereafter IPA).

3. Ibid.

4. Ibid.

5. Registrar of Deeds in Ireland, January 17, 1865, Henrietta Street, Dublin.

6. Catalogue of the Irish Province (hereafter CIP), 5.

7. *Evening Telegraph* (hereafter ET), July 14, 1913.

8. CIP.

9. Ibid.

10. *Tullabeg House Journal*, September 25, 1865.

11. CIP, 1866.

12. Bannon, Dublin, to Snowden, February 20, 1905, in YSP.

13. Speech of Captain Joseph Boyce.

14. *Irish Catholic Directory* (hereafter ICD), 1869, 378.

15. Ibid., 379.

16. Rothensteiner, *History of the Archdiocese of St. Louis*, 296.

17. ICD, 1869, 379.

18. *Letters and Notices*, 202–6.

19. Ibid. See chapters 8 and 9.

16. Into the "Heart of the Irish Church"

1. Brief Chronological Notes, Gardiner Street (1860–1914) (hereafter BCN: GS), in *Missions of the Irish Province*, 49–50.

2. Emmet Larkin, "The Devotional Revolution in Ireland," *American Historical Review* 27 (1972): 625–27.

3. Patrick Corish, *The Irish Catholic Experience: A Historical Survey* (Dublin: Gill and Macmillan, 1985), 184.

4. ICD, 1914, 519–20.

5. Corish, *Irish Catholic Experience*, 192–93.

6. Ibid., 201.

7. Ibid., 199.

8. Ibid., 203.

9. Kevin Laheen, ed., *Robert Haly's Mission Memoirs, 1863–1876* (hereafter RHMM), in IPA.

10. Ibid., November 1867.

11. Ibid.

12. Ibid.

13. Ibid.

14 ICD, 1869, 296–97. See also the *House Diary of St. Francis Xavier* (hereafter HD: SFX), February 2, 1868, in IPA.

15. "Obituary of Father Robert Haly," in *Irish Jesuit History to 1914* (hereafter IJH), 153. See also Rev. Henry Browne, S.J., "Father Robert Haly, S.J.," in *A Roll of Honour: Irish Priests and Prelates of the Last Century* (Dublin: Catholic Truth Society, 1905), 277–94.

16. Kevin Laheen, "Mission in Clare: 1853 Style," *Pioneer*, April 1992, 12.

17. Corish, *Irish Catholic Experience*, 210.

18. HD: SFX, February 2, 1868. Quoted in ICD, 1869.

19. RHMM, 14.

20. IPA, 1870–80.

21. *Londonderry Journal*, February 27, 1869.

22. Ibid., March 3, 1869.

17. By Train or by "Bian"

1. RHMM, 20.

2. Ibid., July 6, 1869.

3. RHMM, July 1869.

4. Ibid., 14.

5. Ibid.

6. Ibid.

7. Ibid.

8. Ibid., 28.

9. Ibid., 30.

10. Ibid., 38.

11. Ibid., 41.

12. Ibid.

13. Ibid., 20.

14. Ibid., 91.

15. Ibid., 31.

16. Ibid., 36.

17. Ibid., 34.

18. Ibid.

19. Ibid.

20. Ibid., 35.

21. Ibid., 38.

22. *Cork Examiner*, December 27, 1869, 2.

23. Ibid.

24. Ibid.

25. Ibid.

26. Ibid.

27. RHMM, 41.

28. Ibid.

29. Ibid., 43.

30. Ibid., 53.

31. Ibid.

32. Ibid., 57.

33. Ibid., 59.

34. *Ballyshannon Herald*, July 9, 1870, 3.

35. Ibid., col. 6, p. 4.

36. Ibid., 3.

37. RHMM, 56.

38. Raymond Clancy, "American Prelates at the Vatican Council," HRS (New York: The United States Catholic Historical Society, 1937). The text of the *concio* is contained in Appendix V, 28: 93–131.

39. Peadar Mac Suibhne, *Paul Cullen and His Contemporaries: With Their Letters from 1820–1902*, vol. 5 (Naas, Ireland: Leinster Leader, 1961–77), 95.

40. Cullen, Rome, to Conroy, May 11, 1870, quoted Ibid., 105.

41. Ibid., 133.

42. Ibid., 133.

18. "A Pulpit Orator of the First Rank"

1. RHMM, 60.
2. Consultors, Irish Province (hereafter Cons IP) 1870.
3. Ibid., July 3, 1872.
4. Ibid., July 4, 1872.
5. Ibid., 1872.
6. Ibid., 1870–72.
7. Charles O'Connor, "The Sodality of Our Lady in Ireland in the Nineteenth Century," in *Jesuit Year Book*, 1945, 134.
8. Ibid.
9. Lambert McKenna, *Life and Work of James Aloysius Cullen, S.J.* (London: Longmans, Green and Co., 1924), 296.
10. CIP, 1878, 6.
11. O'Connor, "Sodality of Our Lady."
12. List of retreats given by Father John B. Bannon (1869–1913), compiled by Kevin Laheen, in IPA.
13. Cons IP, July 4, 1872.
14. E. A. D'Alton, *The History of Ireland* (London: Gresham, 1912), 254–55.
15. *Dublin Evening Post* (hereafter DEP), May 16, 1868.
16. D'Alton, *History of Ireland*, 255.
17. ICD, 1872, 267.
18. HD: SFX, May 4, 1871.
19. ICD, 1872, 282.
20. DEP, March 24, 1872.
21. BCN: IP, 31.
22. Bannon, Dublin, to De Smet, January 5, 1872, in the Midwest Jesuit Archives, St. Louis (hereafter MJA).
23. De Smet, St. Louis, to Bannon, August 5, 1872, in MJA.
24. Bannon, Dublin, to De Smet, August 21, 1872, in MJA.
25. Ibid.
26. Rothensteiner, *History of the Archdiocese of St. Louis*, vol. 2, 100.
27. Philip Donnelly, *A History of Castlederg* (Castlederg: n.p., n.d.), 128.
28. *Londonderry Journal*, August 30, September 27, October 4, 1876.
29. Donnelly, *History of Castlederg*, 130.
30. Ibid., 130–31.
31. Ibid., 131.
32. Ibid., 132.
33. Ibid.
34. HD: SFX, Jan 8, 1877; ICD, 1878, 218.
35. Ibid., February 8, 1877.
36. Ibid., February 4, 1877; ICD, 1878, 220.
37. Ibid., March 3, 1877.
38. Ibid., November 11, 1878.
39. Ibid., February 9, 1878.
40. ET, July 17, 1911.
41. HD: SFX, May 31, 1877; ICD, 1878, 229.
42. ICD, 1878, 237.
43. Ibid., 239.
44. Ibid., 1879, 222.
45. Ibid., 1879, 238; HD: SFX, May 28, 1878; *Freeman's Journal*, May 29, 1878.
46. HD: SFX, August 21, 1878.
47. *The Irish Catholic* (hereafter IC), July 19, 1913, 5.
48. Baptismal Records, Cathedral of Mullingar, July 10, 1853.
49. CIP, 1881, 16.
50. L. G. Moorhead, M.D., St. Stanislaus College, Tullabeg, July 31, 1881, in Files at Gardiner Street (hereafter F: GS).
51. Moorhead, Tullabeg, to Sturzo, undated, presumably the same day as the previous statement, in F: GS.
52. Fallon, Rathfarnham, to Tuite, October 17, 1881, in F: GS.

53. CIP, 1883, 8.

54. Porter to Delaney, October 11, 1882, in IPA.

55. Thomas Morrissey, *Towards a National University: William Delaney, S.J., 1835–1924* (Dublin: Wolfhound Press, 1983), 69.

56. John Bannon, *The Life of John Mitchell* (Liverpool: John Denver, 1882).

57. Bannon to Benjamin, December 15, 1863, with enclosure, in PP, no. 3.

58. Bannon to Benjamin, January 19, 1864.

59. Samuel Ossory Fitzpatrick, *Dublin* (Dublin: Mero Press, 1977), 283.

60. IJH, 1870, 45; Peter Costello, *Dublin Churches* (Dublin: Gill and Macmillan, 1989), 98.

61. ICD, 1836, 120.

62. Fitzpatrick, 281.

63. ICD, 1914, 520.

19. "The Only Possible Candidate"

1. Keller, Dublin, to Anderledy, in the Roman Archives of the Society of Jesus, Irish Province, 1,004.

2. Ibid.

3. Ibid.

4. Ibid.

5. CIP, 1885, 5.

6. IC, July 19, 1913.

7. McKenna, *James Aloysius Cullen*, 99, 297.

8. Ibid.

9. BCN: GS, 55.

10. Record of funerals at Gardiner Street, September 1, 1882, in IPA.

11. Ibid., December 24, 1885.

12. Ibid., May 24, 1888.

13. Ibid., July 3, 1872.

14. Ibid.

15. "Brief Memoir of Father Patrick Duffy, S.J.," in *Menology of the Irish Province* (hereafter MEN: IP).

16. Ibid.

17. Boyce, Donegal, to Leavy, July 13, 1887, quoted in *Missouri Republican*, August 15, 1887.

18. Ibid.

19. BCN: GS, 55.

20. Bannon, Dublin, to Guibor, August 2, 1887, quoted in *Missouri Republican*, August 17, 1887.

21. Ibid.

22. Ibid.

23. MEN: IP, 103.

24. IJH: 1914, 45.

25. Ibid.

26. HD: SFX, August 29, 1893.

27. IJH: 1914, 46.

28. HD: SFX, September 28, 1888.

29. Ibid., July 22, 1888.

30. Ibid., February 24, 1889.

31. Ibid., March 10, 1889.

32. Ibid., May 19, 1889.

33. Gerlach, Rome, to Faherty, May 6, 1985.

34. Kenny, Dublin, to Bannon, December 14, 1889, in IPA.

20. A Time of Jubilees

1. BCN: GS, 58.

2. Book of Receipts and Expenditures, HD: SFX (hereafter BRE), in F: GS.

3. Litz, *Father Tabb*, 31–32.

4. Ibid., 99.

5. BCN: GS, 62.

6. Bannon, Dublin, August 2, 1895, to J. M. Barlow, in MHS.

7. The author saw this chalice on a visit to Gardiner Street in June 1990.

8. Joseph Boyce, *Diary of a Trip to Ireland*, 1896, in the possession of a grandson, Edward Boyce of

St. Louis.

9. BS, undated, in MHS.

10. Schedules of sermons, HD: SFX, in IPA.

11. BCN: GS, 65.

12. Ibid., 68.

13. Monthly Council Meetings of the Sodality, F: GS.

14. Ibid.

15. James Joyce, "Grace," in *Dubliners* (London: G. Richards, 1914).

16. James R. Thrane, "Joyce's Sermon on Hell; Its Source and Backgrounds," in *A James Joyce Miscellany*, ed. Marvin Magalaner (Carbondale: Southern Illinois University Press, 1962), 37–78.

17. F: GS, November 13, 1898.

18. Ibid., November 28, 1898, 12.

19. Ibid.

20. HD: SFX, June 18, 1903.

21. Ibid.

22. IC, July 19, 1903.

23. Ibid.

24. Ibid.

25. ET, July 14, 1913.

26. HD: SFX, November 6, 1904.

27. Ibid.

28. Ibid.

29. BRE, 1901.

30. Ibid., 1907.

21. "Furl the Banner"

1. Snowden, Columbia, S.C., to O'Farrell, November 27, 1913, in YSP.

2. Ibid.

3. John Bigelow, "The Southern Confederacy and the Bishops," *North American Review* 158 (1893), 463.

4. Ibid.

5. Snowden, Columbia, S.C., to

O'Farrell, November 27, 1913, in YSP.

6. Keiley, Savannah, to Snowden, January 25, 1905, in YSP.

7. Ibid.

8. Ibid.

9. Ibid.

10. Snowden, New York, to Bannon, January 1905, in YSP.

11. Bannon, Dublin, to Snowden, February 2, 1905, in YSP.

12. Ibid.

13. Bannon, Dublin, to Snowden, August 16, 1905.

14. Snowden, Columbia, S.C., to O'Farrell, November 27, 1913.

15. Ibid.

16. Ibid.

17. Ibid.

18. Ibid.

19. Danner Papers.

20. *Confederate Veteran* 27 (March 1919), 116.

21. Ibid.

22. ET, July 17, 1911.

23. Ibid.

24. MEN: IP, 93.

25. Ibid., 103.

26. Ibid., 96.

27. Ibid., 97–103.

28. Bannon, Dublin, to Boyce, March 20, 1911, in BS.

29. Ibid.

30. ET, July 14, 1913.

31. Ibid.

32. Ibid.

33. IC, July 19, 1913.

34. ICD, 1914, 520.

35. ET, July 15, 1913.

36. IC, July 19, 1913.

37. WL 42, 395.

38. ET, July 17, 1913.

Photo Credits

Index

About the Author

I n investigating the life of Father John B. Bannon, author-historian William Barnaby Faherty, S.J., visited Strokestown on the Shannon, where Father Bannon was born, and Dublin, where Bannon died. He went to Castleknock, where youthful John Bannon attended prep school, and Maynooth, where he studied theology.

Father Faherty said Mass and preached often at St. John the Apostle and Evangelist Church in St. Louis, the church Pastor Bannon built. The author taught history classes on Saint Louis University's Frost campus, the site of the state militia encampment in 1861. He followed Chaplain Bannon's flight to northwest Arkansas and the First Missouri Infantry's trail around Pea Ridge. He passed through Corinth, Mississippi, on the way to Vicksburg. While he rejoices in the preservation of the Union, he could understand Father Bannon's emotional ties to the South.

In Ireland, he visited every town where Father Bannon preached and conducted retreats. The more he followed the career of the great chaplain, the more he saw Father Bannon grow in stature.

All the while, Father Faherty, a native of St.Louis and professor of history, taught at Saint Louis University and wrote thirty other books on subjects ranging from women's rights to the exploration of space. The majority dealt with St. Louis institutions and personalities. He chaired several regional history societies and was president of the Missouri Writers' Guild. The County Historical Society named its annual award in his honor.

Irish prime minister Bertie Ahern and Missouri governor Bob Holden praised his earlier work in Irish American history.

On September 1, 2001, he celebrated his seventieth year in the Jesuit order. He promises at least one more book.

Further Reading

Complementary Readings on Father Bannon's Life

Philip Thomas Tucker has written the best overall survey of Father Bannon's life, *The Confederacy's Fighting Chaplain: Father John B. Bannon* (Tuscaloosa: University of Alabama Press, 1992). While Tucker concentrates on the Civil War, he gives his readers a glimpse of the pre- and postwar years.

Dom Aloysius Plaisance, O.S.B., summarizes these early years in Ireland and the United States in the *New Catholic Encyclopedia*, vol. 2, 52–53. He devotes only one long sentence to Father Bannon's later years in Ireland (1865–1913). The *Menology* of the Irish Jesuit Province carries a splendid obituary—a reprint of a tribute in the *Dublin Evening Telegraph* published the night of Bannon's death, July 13, 1913.

Monsignor John Rothensteiner's *History of the Archdiocese of St. Louis* (St. Louis: Blackwell Wielandy, 1928) and the present author's *Dream by the River: Two Centuries of Saint Louis Catholicism, 1766–1997* (St. Louis: River City Press, 1997) describe Father Bannon's arrival in St. Louis, his building of St. John the Apostle and Evangelist Church, and his departure for the South.

The story of Father Bannon's secret mission to Ireland is related by Ignatius L. Ryan in "Confederate Agent in Ireland" in *Historical Records and Studies of the United States Catholic Historical Society* 26 (1936): 68–88. A communication from historian Laurence Kenny, S.J., to the editors of the *Historical Records and Studies* appears in the same issue (pages 92–98). It provides interesting stories of Father Bannon's early years in the Jesuit order, as fellow novices recall the incidents years later.

The present author includes a short sketch of Father Bannon in his *Rebels or Reformers? Dissident Priests in American Life* (Chicago: Loyola University Press, 1987). Louis McRedmond mentions Father Bannon on page 195, as a chaplain in the American War, in *To the Greater Glory: A History of the Irish Jesuits* (Dublin: Gill and Macmillan, 1991).